UNFINISHED BUSINESS

THE FIGHT FOR WOMEN'S RIGHTS

This publication accompanies the British Library exhibition
Unfinished Business: The Fight for Women's Rights

Lead Partner

Founded by Anne Boden OBE in 2014, Starling is the first British bank to be established by a woman, and is proud to be Lead Partner of *Unfinished Business: The Fight for Women's Rights*

The exhibition is generously supported by Joanna and Graham Barker

First published in 2020 by
The British Library, 96 Euston Road
London NW1 2DB

Text copyright © the authors 2020

Volume copyright © British Library Board 2020

Images copyright © British Library Board
and other named copyright holders 2020

British Library Cataloguing-in-Publication Data
A catalogue record for this publication is available
from the British Library

ISBN 978 0 7123 5395 3

Designed by Here Design Ltd
Printed and bound in Italy by Printer Trento

UNFINISHED BUSINESS

Edited by
Polly Russell and
Margaretta Jolly

THE FIGHT FOR WOMEN'S RIGHTS

PREFACE 6
Polly Russell and Margaretta Jolly

CONTRIBUTORS 8

INTRO 10
Polly Russell

BODY 16

20 IMAGE
FRAMING WOMEN
Anita Biressi

40 BIOLOGY
UNDER THE MALE MICROSCOPE
Angela Saini

ON THE MALLEABILITY OF THE BODY
Juliet Jacques

62 AUTONOMY
AUTONOMY IN AND THROUGH THE BODY
Debbie Challis

LIBERATING PLEASURE
Zoe Strimpel

MIND 86

90 EDUCATION
ACCESSING EQUAL EDUCATION
Laura Carter

REIMAGINING EDUCATION
Ann Phoenix

110 WORK
WORKING WOMEN
Pamela Cox

128 POLITICAL PRESENCE
RACE, PUBLICNESS AND IMPERIAL FEMINISM
Sumita Mukherjee

WOMEN IN PUBLIC LIFE
Caitríona Beaumont

VOICE 152

156 PROTEST & PARTNERSHIP

CREATIVITY AND INVENTION
Sasha Roseneil

MEN IN FEMINISM?
Nicholas Owen

180 RECOVER

RECOVERING TRADITIONS, INSPIRING ACTION
D-M Withers

RECOVERING WOMEN'S WRITING
Mercedes Aguirre

200 EXPRESS

SISTAHS DOING IT FOR THEMSELVES
Gabriele Griffin

DREAMING AND DEMANDING
Sheila Rowbotham

MAP 218

A snapshot of Feminism in the UK, 1972–93
Zoe Strimpel and The Business of Women's Words team

AFTERWORD 220

FINISHING THE BUSINESS?
Margaretta Jolly

ACKNOWL-EDGEMENTS 224

Polly Russell and Margaretta Jolly

INDEX 226

ILLUSTRATION SOURCES 233

Unfinished Business

Unfinished Business – the book and the exhibiton which inspired it – was born of a lengthy labour and even longer gestation. It had multiple mothers and many midwives. Of these it's clear that *Unfinished Business* owes much to those feminist activists and researchers who have for decades been creating feminist libraries, archives and classrooms, transforming what we understand to be historically significant. We feel deep gratitude to their tenacity, foresight and curiosity.

Curatorial colleagues at the British Library back in 1990, many now long retired, were clearly attuned to these new currents of understanding. They produced a Women's Studies guide to the collections, complete with chapters on oral histories of governesses and teachers, the life of Asian women as depicted in Eastern manuscripts, and nineteenth-century African-American women's writing. Their work drew attention to the women's lives and gender histories hidden in the collections. This work, and the broader context of feminist activism and enquiry, helped inspire new acquisitions. Sisterhood and After: The Women's Liberation Oral History Project and the archives of the feminist publisher Virago, for instance, were added to the Library's collections in the 2010s.

There has been an enthusiastic response to these histories from British Library audiences, be they teachers and students who attend learning workshops on site, the more than one million visitors to the Sisterhood & After and Votes for Women websites or the scholars who work away in the Library's reading rooms.

Then, in 2018, with the centenary of the Representation of the People Act, there was a wonderful groundswell of celebrations, commemorations and displays about women's history and suffrage across the UK. The energy created during this year was intoxicating, and it was in this context that the idea for a large exhibition at the British Library was mooted; after all, the fight for women's rights did not end in 2018. It remains unfinished business.

From the outset the ambition for the exhibition was to connect the contemporary moment of debate and discussion with the long and rich history of women's campaigning. We wanted to put vistors in touch with its material culture, intellectual impetus, and sights and sounds to convey the urgent, visceral and often moving nature of women's struggles. We wanted to showcase priceless artefacts alongside the equally touching ephemera of activism. We also strongly wanted to set this in the context of other struggles, including for racial, sexual and transgender justice, and to showcase the changing nature of masculinity as well as femininity through artefacts and writings by antisexist men. In a dynamic and collective history, we therefore dedicate this book to all those who are fighting for women's rights and gender justice today.

CONTRIBUTORS

Dr Polly Russell is Lead Curator for Contemporary Politics and Public Life at the British Library. She is also a food historian and co-presenter of the BBC's *Back in Time for...* series. Polly has been the British Library lead in a number of research collaborations including the Leverhulme-funded 2012–2015 Sisterhood and After: The Women's Liberation Oral History Project with the University of Sussex. She also led the project to digitise the entire run of *Spare Rib* magazines in order to make them freely available on the internet.

Margaretta Jolly is Professor of Cultural Studies at the University of Sussex working with the British Library to support the collection of women's liberation history. Her books include *The Encyclopedia of Life Writing* (2001), *In Love and Struggle: Letters in Contemporary Feminism* (2008) and *Sisterhood and After: An Oral History of the UK Women's Liberation Movement* (2019). She is also Principal Investigator for The Business of Women's Words: Purpose and Profit in Feminist Publishing and of Sisterhood and After: The Women's Liberation Oral History Project, funded by the Leverhulme Trust and partnered with the British Library.

BODY

Anita Biressi is Professor of Media and Society at the University of Roehampton. She is an editor of the *Journal of Gender Studies* and former Chair of the MeCCSA Women's Media Studies Network. Her recent publications include investigations of the media representation of the 'good girl' in politics and activism, and women's voices in the news.

Angela Saini is an award-winning British science journalist and broadcaster. She presents science programmes on the BBC and her writing has appeared in *New Scientist*, *The Guardian*, *The Sunday Times* and *Wired*. Her latest book is *Superior: The Return of Race Science*. Her previous book, *Inferior: How Science Got Women Wrong*, was published in 2017 to widespread critical acclaim and has been translated into eleven languages. Angela has a Masters in Engineering from the University of Oxford and was a Fellow at the Massachusetts Institute of Technology.

Dr Juliet Jacques is a writer and filmmaker based in London. Her most recent book was *Trans: A Memoir* (Verso, 2015). Her short fiction, essays and journalism have appeared in *Granta*, *Frieze*, *Sight & Sound*, *The Guardian*, *London Review of Books*, *The New York Times* and many other publications. Her short films have screened in galleries and festivals worldwide.

Dr Debbie Challis is Education and Outreach officer at the Library of the London School of Economics, where she works in public engagement with the Women's Library and other collections. She has published widely on the history of archaeology in the context of modern political history and ideology, including *The Archaeology of Race: The Eugenic Ideas of Francis Galton and Flinders Petrie* (2013). She is currently working on a personal memoir drawing on the history of reproductive politics, infertility and maternal loss.

Dr Zoe Strimpel is a cultural and social historian of gender, intimacy and feminism in modern Britain. She writes a weekly column for the *Sunday Telegraph* and is a frequent contributor to BBC Radio and television, where she enjoys unpicking the riddles of modern romance. Her next book, *Seeking Love in Modern Britain: Gender, Dating and the Rise of the Single*, will be published by Bloomsbury in March.

MIND

Dr Laura Carter is a historian who works on education, popular culture and social identities in twentieth-century Britain. She is based at Murray Edwards College, University of Cambridge.

Ann Phoenix is Professor of Psychosocial studies at the Thomas Coram Research Unit, Department of Social Science, UCL Institute of Education, and a Fellow of the British Academy. Her research is mainly about social identities and the ways in which psychological experiences and social processes are linked and intersectional. It includes work on racialised and gendered identities and experiences: mixed-parentage, masculinities, consumption, young people and their parents, the transition to motherhood, families, migration and transnational families. Much of her research draws on mixed methods and includes narrative approaches.

Pamela Cox is Professor of Social History and Sociology at the University of Essex. She has been a presenter of, and contributor to, many television history series including *Servants* and *Shopgirls* for the BBC and *Edwardian Britain in Colour* and *The Thirties* *in Colour* for Channel 5. Her books include *Bad Girls in Britain* (2012) and *Shopgirls* (2014, with Annabel Hobley). The women within her family tree have worked as farm labourers, maids, shop assistants, clerks, munitions workers, nurses, housewives and public health leaders.

Dr Sumita Mukherjee is a historian at the University of Bristol who specialises in the history of women, migration and the British Empire in the nineteenth and twentieth centuries. She is the author and editor of a number of books, including *Indian Suffragettes: Female Identities and Transnational Networks* (2018).

Dr Caitríona Beaumont is Associate Professor in Social History at London South Bank University, UK, and Director of Research for the School of Law and Social Sciences. Her publications include numerous articles and chapters on twentieth-century Irish and British women's history, focusing particularly on the history of female activism and the contribution of voluntary women's organisations to the history of the women's movement. Her most recent publications include *Housewives and Citizens: Domesticity and the Women's Movement in England, 1928–64* (Manchester University Press, 2015); 'What Do Women Want?: Housewives' Associations, Activism and Changing Representations of Women in the 1950s' (*Women's History Review*, 2017); and 'Housewives and Citizens: Encouraging Active Citizenship in the Print Media of Housewives' Associations during the Interwar Years' (*Women's Periodicals and Print Culture in Britain 1918–1939: The Interwar Years*, Edinburgh University Press, 2018). She is currently working on the history of female activism in Britain, 1960 to 1980.

VOICE

Sasha Roseneil is Professor of Interdisciplinary Social Science and Dean of the Faculty of Social and Historical Sciences at UCL. She has written extensively about women's movements and feminist politics, as well as about sexuality, intimate life and social change. Her books include *Disarming Patriarchy: Feminism and Political Action at Greenham*; *Common Women, Uncommon Practices: The Queer Feminisms of Greenham*; *Remaking Citizenship in Multicultural Europe: Women's Movements, Gender and Diversity*; and *Beyond Citizenship: Feminism and the Transformation of Belonging*.

Dr Nicholas Owen is Praelector in Politics at The Queen's College, Oxford, and Associate Professor in the Department of Politics and International Relations at the University of Oxford. He is the author of *Other People's Struggles: Outsiders in Social Movements* (Oxford University Press, 2019), *The British Left and India: Metropolitan Anti-Imperialism, 1885–1947* (Oxford University Press, 2007) and articles in *Past & Present*, *Journal of Modern History*, *Historical Journal*, *The Journal of Imperial and Commonwealth History*, *Twentieth Century British History* and many edited collections.

Dr D-M Withers is currently Research Fellow at the University of Sussex, working on the Leverhulme-funded project The Business of Women's Words: Purpose and Profit in Feminist Publishing. Their research engages with the cultural heritage and memory of feminist social movements and the politics of the archive. D-M's book *Feminism, Digital Culture and the Politics of Transmission: Theory, Practice and Cultural Heritage* won the 2015 Feminist and Women's Studies Association book prize and they co-authored *The Feminist Revolution: The Struggle for Women's Liberation* (2018), an archival-illustrated study of transnational women-centred movements of the 1960s to the 1980s (published by Smithsonian/Virago).

Dr Mercedes Aguirre is Lead Curator of the Americas Collections at the British Library, and a co-curator of the exhibition *Unfinished Business: The Fight for Women's Rights*. Her research focus is on the relationship of literature and politics in the 1930s, and she has published on the work of women writers and the Spanish Civil War, including Sylvia Townsend Warner and Nancy Cunard.

Gabriele Griffin is Professor of Gender Research at Uppsala University, Sweden. She is coordinator of a Nordforsk-funded Excellence Centre on Women in Technology-Driven Professions (nordwit.com). She is also editor of the Research Methods for the Arts and Humanities series (Edinburgh University Press). Her most recent book is *Body and Intimate Labour: Understanding Bioprecarity* (co-ed., Manchester University press, 2020).

Sheila Rowbotham, who helped to start the women's liberation movement in Britain, has written widely on the history of feminism and radical social movements. Her most recent books are *Edward Carpenter: A Life of Liberty and Love* (2008), *Dreamers of a New Day* (2010) and *Rebel Crossings: New Women, Free Lovers and Radicals in Britain and the United States* (2016). Formerly a professor at The University of Manchester, she is now an Honorary Fellow at Manchester and has received an honorary doctorate from the University of Sheffield.

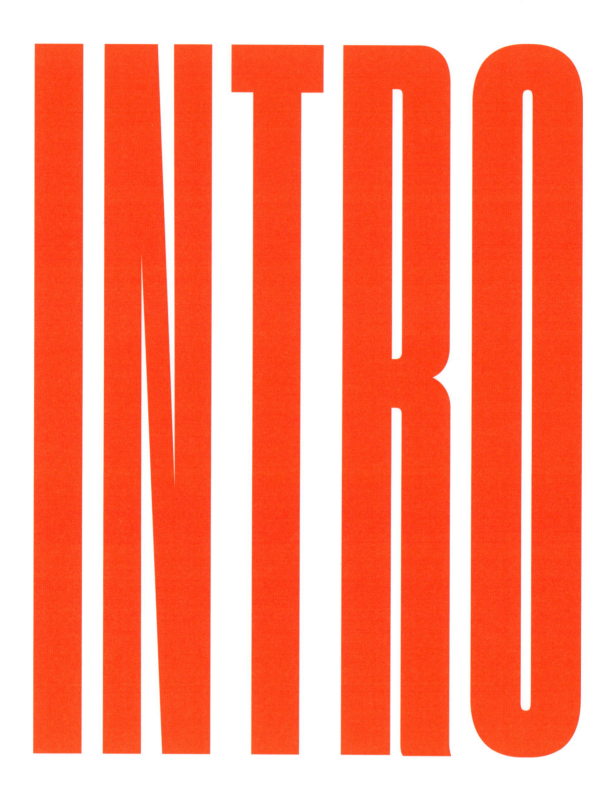

INTRO

— **DR POLLY RUSSELL**

When I was 10 my mum gave me a book called *Girls Are Powerful: Young Women's Writings from Spare Rib*.[1] This book changed my life. I distinctly remember sensing, how I don't know, that it was radical and risky, and that as a result it would raise eyebrows, invite sniggers and be derided. Intuiting this, and feeling neither courageous nor powerful, I kept the book a secret, hidden under my mattress. But I clung to it and the messages it conveyed like a life raft through my transition from child to teenager to young adult. It was affirming, reassuring and reframing, and it was from there that my passion for feminist ideas and politics sprang.

Today no one can doubt that girls are powerful, when the likes of environmentalist Greta Thunberg, education activist and Nobel Prize winner Malala Yousafzai, slam poet Suhaiymah Manzoor-Khan and gun control campaigner Emma González, among others, are challenging and changing the world. So much has been achieved since the writer and philosopher Mary Wollstonecraft dared argue in 1792, against all prevailing wisdom, that girls should be educated. Thanks in large part to the struggles of earlier generations, many women today are able to take centre stage in politics, science, the arts, law, the media and public life. And, unlike in 1984 when my mum gave me *Girls are Powerful*, feminist ideas and politics are finally mainstream in the UK and much of the world.

Nevertheless, for all these achievements, girls and women remain under a state of explicit or implicit siege. Across the globe women are still subject to cultural, legislative and economic forces which conspire to limit and control their lives. In many parts of the world girls are still unable to access basic education due to poverty and inequality. Twenty per cent of women around the world had an unmet need for contraception in 2017, abortion remains illegal in twenty-six countries, and 41 per cent of women globally experience restricted access to abortion services.[2] The epidemic of sexual violence and harassment which spawned the #MeToo movement is an ever-present threat, and while 90 per cent of the world's billionaires are men, women globally provide ten trillion dollars of unpaid care to support economies every year.[3]

In the UK period poverty, underfunding of women's refuges, low levels of rape convictions, a gender pay gap, sexual harassment and a lack of reproductive rights constitute the terrain of feminist activism. Day to day I see my 15-year-old daughter and her friends: audacious, bold and well able to hold their own in debates about gender and sex. They are sensitive to intersectional inequalities and comfortable with the complex and changing landscape of sexual and gender politics. But at the same time this generation is navigating an insidious landscape of commercialised sexualisation; they live with the image-obsessed tyranny of social media, and those who are people of colour, gay, non-binary or trans experience harassment and discrimination on a regular basis. Wherever you live, women's rights and the feminist dream of a fairer world are still very much unfinished business.

No wonder, then, that in 1966 the feminist psychoanalyst Juliet Mitchell coined the expression 'the longest revolution' to describe women's struggles for structural and cultural change. This revolution is relevant, fascinating and ongoing, and that is why we staged the exhibition *Unfinished Business: The Fight for Women's Rights*. For centuries women have had to fight to assert control over every aspect of their lives. As the 2018 centenary celebrations for some women gaining the vote in the UK demonstrated, it is a subject which millions of people are engaged with and fired up by. We wanted to build on the momentum of the centenary to facilitate further debate and discussion about this unfinished business.

We decided to organise the exhibition around the overarching themes of Body, Mind and Voice. Feminist philosophy has led the way in refusing Cartesian distinctions between mind and body. It has insisted on recognising the integral relation of the two as fundamental to an understanding of gender and women's struggles. Related to this, the concept of 'voice' – being allowed to speak and being heard – has been central to women's capacity to fully inhabit the private, public and political. The Body, Mind, Voice structure recognises that to live a fully realised life, people must be able to choose how to use, experience and express their bodies, minds and voices. This choice, for many women today and in the past, has been denied.

Overleaf is a self-portrait tintype by Khadija Saye, a British-Gambian artist. Saye's haunting work tackles issues of racial and gender identity and the politics and histories of immigration and post-colonialism in contemporary Britain. The tintype format is central to Saye's artistic intention. As she explained in the catalogue for her exhibition at the Venice Biennale in 2017: 'The journey of making wet plate collodion tintypes is unique; no image can be replicated and the final outcome is beyond the creator's control … Each tintype has its own unique story to tell, a metaphor for our individual human spiritual journey.' Saye's tintype is a stunning expression of body, mind and voice, drawing together ideas of history and culture to insist on an intersectional understanding of identity. Tragically,

Below: Sisters Uncut are a new generation of feminists who deploy direct action to resist austerity, pictured here protesting against evictions in Stratford, September 2015.

Opposite: Khadija Saye, *Peitaw*, 2017. Tintype from the series *Dwelling: in this space we breathe.*

Saye died in the Grenfell Tower fire in 2018, an avoidable disaster which took the lives of at least seventy-two people and has come to symbolise wealth and power inequalities in the UK. Prominently featuring Saye's work not only highlights our intention to be inclusive, intersectional and challenging, but quietly condemns the kind of Britain which allowed the Grenfell fire to take place and ended the lives of so many, including an artist with a bright future.

Women speaking for themselves is a strong feminist tradition. In each section we included a quotation from an influential woman thinker whose ideas have impacted on understandings of gender, sex and feminism. To select just nine women to represent the fertile terrain of women's intellectual tradition was near impossible, but we felt it important to make clear that activism and ideas cannot be separated: they co-exist. Women's cartoons, which you will enjoy in this book, also paid tribute to the long tradition of feminist satire and feminist comic artists.

Crucially, because women's rights, equality and feminist activism are unfinished business, we have highlighted the work of nine contemporary activist campaigns in the UK. These include Now for Northern Ireland, Women for Refugee Women and Bloody Good Period. The organisations were invited to describe the importance and scope of their work in their own words. Such live struggles reframe the long history behind each of these areas of women's resistance. In the section focused on education, for instance, the work of Stemettes, an organisation dedicated to inspiring young women to take up STEM careers, was put in conversation with the history of women demanding the right to be educated from the Enlightenment onwards.

Written by sixteen experts and activists, the chapters in this book follow the exhibition's thematic structure, illustrating more than 100 pictures of objects featured in the exhibition. Every chapter contains examples of women's ingenuity. From mass marches, to civil disobedience, to strikes, to international conferences, to Twitter storms, women have

found powerful ways to protest inequality. Sasha Roseneil details this in surveying protest methods, from suffrage campaigners' use of purple, white and green, to the women-only camps protesting against US nuclear weapons at Greenham Common in the 1980s, to the faux-funeral procession organised by the campaign group Sisters Uncut protesting against cuts to women's refuges.

Women's liberation is more than women's business, however, and men and boys can only benefit from a world which refutes gender stereotypes, binaries and punishing expectations for men as breadwinners and fighters too. It was crucial, therefore, that *Unfinished Business* acknowledged how boys and men have often been women's allies, campaigning on their behalf and supporting their activism. Writing about this in a chapter titled 'Men in Feminism?', Nicholas Owen traces men's solidarity with women's rights from the 1869 publication of *The Subjection of Women* by the MP John Stuart Mill to the men's movement of the 1970s, which focused on strategies to combat sexism at a personal and societal level.

Above: Suffragettes making banners and pennants for a procession to Hyde Park, London, 23 July 1910.

Opposite: International Women's Day on 8 March started in 1911 and continues as a global celebration of the social, economic, cultural and political achievements of women as well as a call to action for equality.

Women's history, and especially the history of feminism and women's rights, is not and never has been without controversy and disagreement. The women's movement has often been criticised for its white and Eurocentric focus. As Sumita Mukherjee explains, many women involved in campaigning for suffrage were explicitly pro-Empire and aligned with an imperial project which oppressed colonised women. While for some women, therefore, feminism has been a resource to draw from and a place of sanctuary, for others, particularly women of colour and working-class women, it has been experienced as excluding, hierarchical and patronising. The challenge of thinking about gender and sex through an intersectional lens is vital if feminism is to deliver its revolutionary promise.

Unfinished Business aims to inspire visitors and readers alike, whatever their gender or age, with the dazzling breadth and complexity of women's activism in the UK. To make decisions about what to include in a finite space, we worked with an external advisory board comprised of scholars and activists, scoured the British Library's extensive collections and took inspiration from a host of external sources. Of these, the feminist libraries and archives stand out. Denied a place in official history and absent from literature, art, music and print culture, women from the start of the twentieth century insisted on uncovering, recording and archiving herstories. Central to this was the establishment of feminist libraries

and archives which, as D-M Withers details in their chapter 'Recovering Traditions, Inspiring Action', not only collected history but created it.

Feminist archives and libraries – often run on a shoestring by committed, skilled volunteers – were at the vanguard of an activist and scholarly movement which drew attention to the importance of collecting women's history. In recent years, no longer consigned to the margins, women's history has proven itself to be a popular and expanding field. Never was this clearer than in 2018 during the nationwide centenary commemorations of women first gaining the vote in the UK.[4] The year was marked by extensive media coverage of suffrage, commemorative marches in cities across the country, the unveiling of suffragette statues such as Emmeline Pankhurst in Manchester and Millicent Fawcett in London, and landmark exhibitions like *Represent!* at the People's History Museum in Manchester and *A Woman's Place* at the Abbey House Museum in Leeds.

The British Library has not been immune from the energetic and urgent focus on women's history. In the last decade or so curators and colleagues have made efforts to ensure the Library's collecting policies and services account for women's history. Notable projects include Sisterhood and After: The Women's Liberation Oral History Project, the digitising of *Spare Rib* magazine, the acquisition of the Virago archive and the development of learning websites dedicated to suffrage and women's literature, as well as a regular programme of school workshops on feminist activism in the twentieth century.

Archives, libraries and museums are the repository of a community's, nation's or individual's history. Though they may appear to be places designed for study and reflection, libraries, archives and museums are quietly radical and dynamic. The evidence they store can be used to challenge, change or confirm our understanding of the past, its relation to the present and its implications for the future. This is why it is significant that the British Library, the national library of the UK, has decided to tell the story of women's fight for rights. It is an acknowledgement that this history is important and relevant. It mattered yesterday – and it still matters today.

---

1   Susan Hemmings, ed., *Girls Are Powerful: Young Women's Writings from Spare Rib* (London: Sheba Feminist Press, 1982).

2   Joni Seager, *The Woman's Atlas* (Brighton and Hove, Myriad Editions, 2018) p. 67, https://reproductiverights.org/worldabortionlaws.

3   Ibid, p. 180.

4   Around 8.4 million women gained the vote in the UK in 1918. These included women aged over 30 who were householders, the wives of householders, the occupiers of property with an annual rent of £5, and graduates of British universities. Women who did not meet these requirements were not eligible to vote. This meant that only approximately two-thirds of the total population of women in the UK could vote in 1918. It was not until the Equal Franchise Act of 1928 that women over 21 were able to vote, increasing the number of women voters to over 15 million.

BC

DY

Women's bodies have always been sites of contestation and resistance. Whether it is the freedom to decide what to wear, the ability to control reproduction or the right to express sexual preferences and pleasures, women have had to push against the limits of cultural and legal expectations. In the twenty-first century the malleability of gender is more evident than ever before. This raises complex and deeply felt debates on what the future of legal as well as social gender should be, even within feminist circles. In this section, Anita Biressi examines the politics of representation and explores the radical and inventive ways women have found to challenge image and express themselves. In large part, sexual inequalities are rooted in so-called scientific accounts of the body, which have configured men as physically more able and intelligent than women. As Angela Saini explains, however, science does not exist outside of culture and so has often reinforced prevailing norms about men and women. Moreover, as Juliet Jacques explores, the categories of 'man' and 'woman' are not stable and never have been. Outside of science, representation has played a crucial role in perpetuating cultural stereotypes and distorting how women are perceived. Focusing on bodily autonomy, Debbie Challis notes how women have fought for equal rights within marriage, campaigned against sexual and physical violence and argued for access to contraception as ways of asserting control over their bodies and, therefore, lives. Bodies, however, have not only been experienced as sites of pain, oppression and control for women. Zoe Strimpel describes how, from the middle of the twentieth century onwards, women also asserted the right to sexual pleasure, freedom and expression.

— **DR POLLY RUSSELL**

BODY: IMAGE

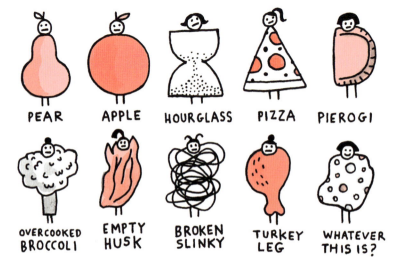

© Gemma Correll

'...in a world ordered by **SEXUAL IMBALANCE**, pleasure in looking has been split between active/male and passive/female. The determining male gaze projects its **PHANTASY** on to the female form which is styled accordingly.'

LAURA MULVEY (B.1941)
From 'Visual Pleasure and Narrative Cinema' (1975)

British filmmaker and academic Laura Mulvey drew on her engagement with the Women's Liberation Movement to understand and challenge power relationships in cinema. Her work changed film studies and is relevant to contemporary social media such as Facebook and Snapchat that originated in a culture of objectifying women.

Framing Women

— **PROFESSOR ANITA BIRESSI**

'We're not beautiful, we're not ugly, we're angry!' These words emblazoned the placards of Women's Liberation Movement (WLM) activists protesting at the 1970 Miss World beauty contest in London. The protestors were not attacking the women taking part, but rather the organisers and the press who publicised it – including compere Bob Hope, who jauntily remarked 'it's quite a cattle market here tonight'.[1] Millions of television viewers watched activists throwing flour bombs, stink bombs and fruit, and the protest inspired the formation of hundreds of feminist groups all over the country.[2]

Such scenes suggest why questioning media and culture has been central to struggles for gender equality. Despite all attempts to misrepresent them, women have found inventive ways to control and transform their images and to express themselves. This has included celebrating beauty in new guises. A pertinent example comes from Britain's black beauty competition for the Caribbean Carnival Queen, launched by Claudia Jones as part of the inaugural Notting Hill Carnival in 1959: Jones reinvented a demeaning ritual as a public, inclusive affirmation of black femininity and pride.[3] Thinking through the politics of appearance, across gender binaries and in contexts of multiple inequality, is undeniably complex. A starting point, however, is to examine the long history of misrepresentation, and what underpins it.

Two aspects of image-making have particularly troubled feminists. The first is that producers have positioned women as adjuncts to men: lovers, wives and daughters, but not adventurers, inventors, leaders or artists. The novelist Virginia Woolf observed in her famous 1929 essay *A Room of One's Own* that women's friendships with other women were hardly ever the central plot.[4] Not much had changed by 1985, when cartoonist Alison Bechdel and her friend Liz Wallace developed the cheekily intended 'Bechdel–Wallace test' to measure whether women were represented fairly in films. Passing the test required only three things: (i) It must have at least two female characters; (ii) They must both have names; (iii) They must talk to each other about something other than a man.[5] Seemingly simple, yet audiences, scholars and even some film industry bodies have applied this test to films and plays, only to discover how few storylines present women characters independently of their relationship to men. Many adverts would also fail this test. Though audiences are now offered a wider diversity of characters than perhaps ever before, we still have a long way to go before women are regularly represented in a fully rounded and individual manner.

A second concern is the depiction of women for the imagined enjoyment of a male viewer. The art historian John Berger, in *Ways of Seeing* (1972), showed how this tradition infused Western art from the fifteenth century onwards with its endless female nudes, whether the subjects were religious, erotic, mythical or domestic. Berger also pointed out the significance of the fragmentation of women's bodies, so the focus was on parts of the body rather than the whole person. Such objectification continued in the codes and conventions of advertising, music videos and magazines – sexism thus encompassed 'high' and 'low'. Berger summarised: 'One might simplify this by saying: men act and women appear. Men look at women. Women watch themselves being looked at.'[6]

An equally influential analysis was provided by the film scholar Laura Mulvey, who coined the concept of 'the male gaze' to understand the underlying structure of much Hollywood cinema. Mulvey drew on psychoanalytic psychology to explore the unconscious ways these viewing positions work, and, as she developed her ideas, explained that the 'male

Opposite: The Women's Liberation Movement fought against the objectification and sexualisation of women and, in 1970, took their protest to the Miss World beauty pageant at the Royal Albert Hall. Protestors gathered outside, holding banners reading 'Women are People too' and distributing leaflets which read 'We're not beautiful, we're not ugly, we're angry'.

Body: Image

23

In response to the racist violence and riots that swept through Britain in the summer of 1958 – in particular in Notting Hill and Nottingham – the Trinidadian-born activist and *West Indian Gazette* founder Claudia Jones started an annual indoor Caribbean carnival. The celebrations brought together artists, activists, writers and community leaders. The programme for the 1960 carnival included a beauty pageant. These pageants challenged racist beauty politics that marginalised black women.

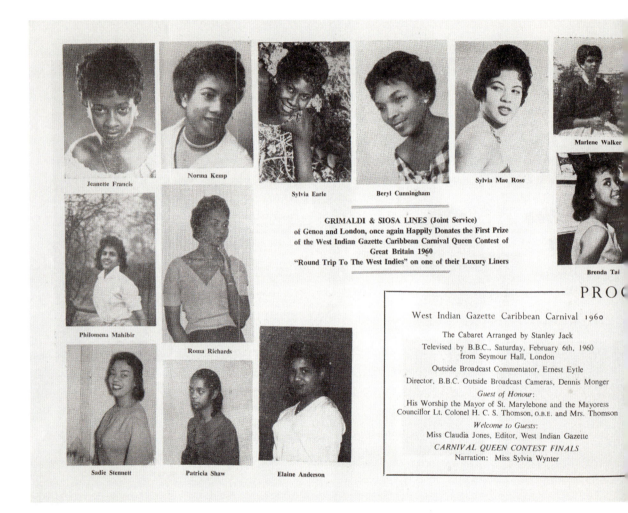

George Lamming   Jan Carew   Elma Y. Clarke   Dr. Victor Page   L. D. Weekes   Athena Crosse   Edwin McKenzie

Caribbean Carnival Queen Contest Judges

Nadia Cattouse Lindop   Anthony Irving   Samuel Selvon

Pearl Connor   Ken Ablack

Garnet Gordon, Q.C., C.B.E.

The 1960 Carnival Patrons: Mrs. Eslanda Goode Robeson; Dr. David Pitt; Mrs. Amy Ashwood Garvey; Mr. Nigel Fisher, M.P.; Mr. Charles Royle, M.P.; Mr. Fenner Brockway, M.P.; Mr. Marcus Lipton, M.P.; Capt. John Baird, M.P.; Dr. Eleanor Ettlinger; Mrs. Lena Jeger; Dr. John McFie; Dr. K. D. Kumria; Mr. Aalo Bashorun; Mr. Edward Scobie.

MME

CABARET

Maria Kamara—Fire Dancer
Rupert Nurse & His Orchestra
    King Sailors: Vernon Jack and Mike Goddard
Russ Henderson Steel Band
Tropicana Steel Band
Carnival Fiesta: Allistair Bain and his Caribbean Dance Troupe
    Corrinne Skinner, Jeff Henry, Joan Gray, Vida Veghanar and Shirley Neptune.
The New World Singers: under the direction of Parry Jones
Cy Grant
    Chorus: Accompanying Cy Grant: Katherine Pyne, Maureen Usden, and Sally Lubeck.   Bongo Player: Ivan Chinn.
Elaine Delmar
Lord Kitchener
Limbo Dancers Featuring Patsy Fleming
Crowning of Carnival Queen by Mr. Garnet Gordon, Q.C., C.B.E.
    Commissioner in the United Kingdom for The West Indies, British Guiana and British Honduras.
    Musical Score by Rupert Nurse

Carmen England, Chairman, Queen's Committee

Souvenir Cover Design: Pat Betaudier

Sylvia Wynter-Carew, Narrator, Queen's Contest

Rupert Nurse, Lord Kitchener, Russ Henderson

Below: The suffragette and women's rights activist Rosa May Billinghurst (1875–1953) became secretary of the Greenwich brand of the Women's Social and Political Union in 1910. That same year she was one of 159 women arrested at a demonstration outside the House of Commons. Billinghurst was disabled as a result of childhood polio, and campaigned in a tricycle, sometimes using it as a battering ram against the police.

Above: On 25 May 1914 the *Daily Mirror* featured photographs of suffragettes campaigning at a rally in Hyde Park. Suffragettes were frequently characterised as 'unwomanly'. The pictures here were accompanied by captions such as 'Dishevelled after fighting' and 'Screaming with impotent rage'.

gaze' is not restricted to men, any more than only women are gazed at.[7] However, too often, women and girls are culturally educated to watch obsessively over their appearance, particularly as they enter a potential heterosexual marriage market. This may go some way to explaining why women have often engaged enthusiastically with advertising, marketing, magazines and other cultural forms which objectify them.

Underlying these various visual 'regimes' is the assumption that men are active, women passive: masculinity equates to action, initiative, resourcefulness and movement in the public realm (such as politics or business) and femininity to reproduction, stability and the private realm (such as home-making, care-work and consumption). But this visual politics also entwines with a different set of structures born from histories of empire, slavery and racism, in which white viewers are positioned as those with the power to look, objectify and control. This can rearrange gender stereotypes and relations, for example in the demasculinising of black men through a 'white gaze', as the French-

Unfinished Business

Martinican psychiatrist and philosopher Frantz Fanon theorised as early as 1952.[8] Edward Said also coined the term 'Orientalism' in his 1978 exposition on the belittling depictions of Middle Eastern people and cultures by Westerners, including how the 'East' was often 'feminised'. His historical account, beginning from the late eighteenth century onwards, stressed how myths and images of the 'East' always conveniently reinforced Western superiority and, by implication, Western masculinity. Feminist scholars such as Reina Lewis explored this argument further by asking to what extent white women, specifically, had contributed to and complicated Said's model of imperial culture and its representations of 'others'. Chandra Mohanty effectively re-directed this discussion when she asked how Western feminists themselves might be implicated in positioning non-Western women as inferior or lacking. She made the pressing political argument that Western women's implicit self-representation as modern, educated and largely self-governing strongly depended on positioning other women as somehow 'less than' themselves.[9] Understanding how these historical and current structures entwine is vital to challenge media stereotypes and alienations.

Women who have challenged their role have often been condemned as ugly, undesirable and unfeminine, or dangerously over-feminine. For example, militant suffragettes from the Women's Social and Political Union (WSPU) insisted on their right to enter the public, male world and to participate as equal citizens. Consequently, they were often abused, mocked, stigmatised and misrepresented. Women campaigning for the vote came in for vicious media portrayals, for example, including this montage of photographs in the *Daily Mirror* of 25 May 1914, which focuses on faces seemingly contorted with rage. Press cartoons, picture postcards and music hall entertainment portrayed campaigners as aged harridans who were badly dressed and ill-tempered. They were also jokingly caricatured as desperate spinsters keen to be arrested so that they might secure the sexual attention of male police officers. One campaigner who sold the WSPU newspaper on the London streets found 'the sex filth which elderly men in particular seemed determined to inflict' the worst part of her job.[10] This propaganda presented protestors in contrast to the benign, charming and amiable 'Angel in the House' of the white Victorian middle-class ideal (see Cox in this volume). It suggested they were a threat to long-established and cherished family values.

Women campaigners were acutely aware of the importance of image in this context, and how to position themselves to gain maximum public support. Working-class activists, for example, were mindful of their precarious position in the public realm, risking being stereotyped as 'savage' socialists and labour activists who had strayed beyond their usual haunts, such as London's East End.[11] They often struggled, on tiny incomes, to dress well to make the right impression. In contrast, Rosa May Billinghurst, known as 'the cripple suffragette' to her peers, defied the prejudiced gazes of the able-bodied, spectacularly using her tricycle-wheelchair in militant protests. But such use of spectacle could play into the 'divide and rule' approach towards activists. Consider this sympathetic newspaper pen portrait of suffragette Teresa Billington, written by a female journalist, stressing the campaigner's femininity: 'Miss Billington is not at all the type of platform woman beloved of the comic papers. She is young, charming, soft voiced, and not devoid of a sense of humour. Her head is crowned with braids of nut-brown hair, and she gives the impression of a very attractive personality.'[12]

Women's Liberation Movement and Civil Rights activists, with Berger, Mulvey and Mohanty, were part of a feminist upsurge which understood that fifty years after women winning the vote there was a cultural revolution still to be won.[13] One way to fight, Mulvey suggested, would be to deliberately disrupt the viewing pleasures offered by conventional movie scenarios through experimental filmmaking, such as the Berwick Street Collective's avant-garde documentary on women working as night-cleaners (1974–8), and the Senegalese director Djibril Diop Mambéty in his 1973 film *Touki Bouki*.[14] A more accessible enterprise was the launch of *Spare Rib* by Marsha Rowe and Rosie Boycott in 1972. This was a regular monthly women's magazine, but it offered a dramatic alternative to the usual diet of beauty, romance and home. The first edition included a page of letters responding to the question 'What is a liberated woman?' News stories included making vasectomies free on the NHS, and women cleaners' pay. Detailed features on feminist history sat alongside articles about haircare and how to put up a shelf while, in a strand called 'Man's World', the footballer George Best shared his thoughts on women and the Liberation Movement. *Spare Rib* also drew attention to sexism in advertising, and encouraged readers to send in examples which were printed in its 'Tooth and Nail' section, or on its news pages.[15]

The women's movements were also inventive in responding to offensive advertising on the streets, defacing posters with some very eye-catching and witty graffiti. One promotion of a new range of small Fiat Panda cars ran with the slogan, 'If it were a lady, it would get its bottom pinched'. WLM photographer Jill Posener photographed the wonderful spray-painted response: 'If this lady was a car, she'd run you down.' Fiat didn't seem to learn its lesson, putting out another 1984 ad featuring a white, power-dressed woman sprawled across its roof saying 'It's so practical, darling'. The graffitied response? 'When I am not lying on cars I am a brain surgeon.' Another 1980s advert, for Pretty Polly tights, typified the ways in which women's bodies were both incapacitated and fragmented into parts. It showed a pair of long, shapely white legs breaking out of a giant egg with the strapline 'legs as soft and smooth as the day you were born'. A protester had added, in spray paint, the words 'born kicking' together with the twin symbols for lesbian love.

Right: 'Tooth & Nail' was a regular feature in *Spare Rib* magazine. It printed examples of sexist advertising and media copy, sent in by its readers. Often the examples dehumanised and sexualised women's bodies. It also included advice about how to complain and hold those responsible to account.

Below: Feminists and women's rights activists have always harnessed humour, satire and irony as a tool for change. This graffitied car advert, photographed by Jill Posener in 1979, is a good example.

Opposite: First edition of *Spare Rib* magazine, July 1972.

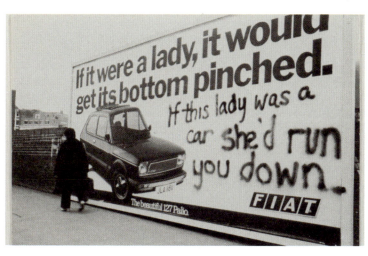

Body: Image

Activist photographers provided another response through groundbreaking self-portraiture. Jo Spence's aim was clear from her book title *Putting Myself in the Picture: A Political, Personal and Photographic Autobiography* (1986). She tells of her working-class upbringing and identity, early work as a high street photographer and failed attempts to inhabit various desirable feminine poses. These shaped her decision to move out from behind the camera to pose as her own model and take control of her own image. Particularly effective was her restaging of the clichés of children's, family and wedding photography to reveal the hidden pressures in everybody's 'family album'. Many of her works, including *Remodelling Photo History* (1981–2) and her self-portraits with breast cancer, were staged with her collaborator Terry Dennett to complicate the long photographic history of the male gaze. She also ran community photography workshops with Dennett, in which they demystified and democratised photography, especially to children, including building pinhole cameras from cardboard boxes and using milk bottles for lenses.

Joy Gregory was another photographer to have significantly pushed the boundaries of self-representation in this period, here as part of a Black arts movement countering racialisation and racism, which was intense in the 1980s. Gregory's *Autoportraits* (1990) engages with the black female presence or absence in Europeanised and colonial narratives of femininity. On one level, she puts the black self and body centre stage, reclaiming identity and subjectivity in beautiful images developed using a fine developing technique to give clear and velvet photographic tones.[16] Yet Gregory also cleverly plays with angles and frames, often allowing us to see only the back of a neck, or part of her face, or hands over eyes. In this way she refuses the viewer any easy grasp or visual exchange, offering clues to emotions and identities but – particularly perhaps for white viewers – nothing to appropriate or assume. Stuart Hall, who introduced the group exhibition by black British photographers at which *Autoportraits* was first exhibited in 1990, commented that 'the black figure' has historically been a site of 'intolerable splitting and projection'.[17] Gregory's images seem precisely to adopt the 'deconstructive' strategy that Hall describes as black photographers' response, deliberately disturbing and subverting 'the settled relations of identification and recognition across which the power relations of spectatorship constantly plays'.[18]

A final example of extraordinary self-portraiture comes from Khadija Saye, known for her series *Dwelling: in this space we breathe*. Exhibited in the Diaspora Pavilion during the 2017 Venice Bienniale Exhibition, each photograph shows her undertaking a Gambian spiritual ritual, holding different sacred objects such as a cow horn or prayer sticks. These explore Muslim and Christian as well as British-Gambian heritage: the artist referred to the series as charting 'the deep-rooted urge to find solace in a higher power'.[19] Her use of nineteenth-century tintype technology, with its layered, chiaroscuro effects, gives the impression of much older portraits, which inevitably suggest colonial contexts – yet also where identity and culture persist. Shockingly, Saye died aged only 24 in the 2017 Grenfell Tower fire in London. However, her haunting images will remain as breathtaking reminders of the reinvention and hope of resistant identities.

Despite such courageous reinventions of self, it is difficult to translate image into social power. This can be seen especially when women attempt to seek high-status or leadership roles. Women have often taken advice or direction on how to present themselves professionally to blend in. For example, from the mid-1970s onwards

Opposite: Remodelling Photo History: Colonization by Jo Spence, 1981–2. This self-portrait was part of a series in which Jo Spence used the medium of photography to document her own history. Her images often laid bare the female body, opening up a discourse of identity politics and challenging notions of sexuality, body politics and gender.

Unfinished Business

Body: Image

Joy Gregory's *Autoportrait* (1989) comprises a limited edition set of nine archival giclée prints. Gregory's work has often used self-portraiture and questioned ideals of feminine beauty. This series of photographs mimics the commercial shots of women in magazines. They question the absence of the black female in European narratives of women and beauty standards.

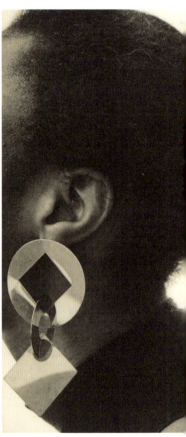

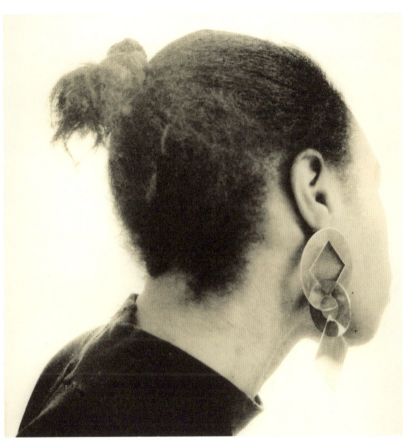

Body: Image

women workers employed power dressing strategies to help them convey their authority and gravitas. The dress code included a conservative style of tailored suits, exaggerated shoulders, subdued colours, scarves and discreet jewellery. As a uniform for working women this look has changed relatively little over the past decades.

Even when women do choose to dress conservatively their image *as women* can be hijacked in ways which challenge their authority. For example, when Prime Minister Theresa May and Scotland's First Minister Nicola Sturgeon met to discuss Britain's exit from the European Union and the potential break-up of the British Union – key issues of our time – the *Daily Mail* featured a front-page photograph of the pair with the headline 'Never mind Brexit, who won Legs it!' The article devoted close attention to the politicians' make-up, manicures and even to their legs – with a header declaring: 'Finest weapons at their command? Those pins!' This referred to Sturgeon's legs as 'altogether more flirty [than May], tantalisingly crossed … a direct attempt at seduction'. The women's posture and clothes were treated to detailed scrutiny: 'The First Minister's natty blue suit with white piping and matching light-coloured stilettos were unmistakably reminiscent of the Scottish flag … May, for her part, was stateswoman-like in a stylish navy jacket, a patterned dress and her trademark leopard-print heels.'[20]

Below: 'Legs-it' *Daily Mail* front cover, 28 March 2017, featuring the Prime Minister Theresa May and Scotland's First Minister, Nicola Sturgeon.

Opposite: Three Young Ladies sheet music, written and composed by E. W. Rogers in 1892 for Miss Vesta Tilley. Music hall theatre, with its pantomime dames and principal boys, allowed entertainers to subvert dress and gender stereotypes. Of the male impersonators performing at the turn of the twentieth century, Matilda Alice Powles – known as Vesta Tilley – was arguably the most popular.

Public criticism that the article was sexist and humiliating led the paper to amend its second edition by adding the lead-in 'Sarah Vine's light-hearted verdict on the big showdown'. Uniquely among the British daily papers, the *Daily Mail* has a majority female readership, and the paper tried to ward off public outrage by stressing that the article was, in fact, penned by a woman to amuse and entertain. It employed the common strategy of suggesting that feminist complainers have no sense of humour.

However the *Daily Mail*'s invocation of a woman behind 'legs-it' raises a conundrum: it is women who sustain much lifestyle journalism and the entertainment, fashion and beauty business. One explanation, as we have seen, is that women as producers and consumers of the image have internalised the 'male' or 'white' gaze. But there are other reasons why women, seemingly paradoxically, are so often drawn to such imagery. An obvious point is that it glamorises the domestic role and acknowledges the security it can offer. *Good Housekeeping*, launched in 1922, *Woman and Home* (1926), *My Home* (1928) and *Wife and Home* (1929) portrayed an independent, proactive, adaptable woman doing her bit by housekeeping after the war. The mid-century 'cult of femininity', which often stifled women in service to their husbands and families,[21] presented the new consumer culture as gorgeously fashionable and aspirational. As women of all classes began to enter paid work in the 1970s, and in response to the Women's Liberation Movement, Shirley Conran's 1975 self-help guide *Superwoman* was a bestseller despite its extreme contradictions. It included entries on topics such as 'How to be a Laundrymaid', house maintenance and 'The Working Girl's Toolbox', 'Sex (Maniacs) and the Single Girl' and 'How to Run a Home and a Job'. By 1990 her revised edition included sections on 'Bodywork', 'Your Public Image' and 'How to Get Help in the Home', which included the question: 'So what can a man do to help you?' Conran's *Superwoman* anticipated the advice that has continued ever since, as women are expected to be perfectly groomed (personal image, body and well-being), run a home, win at work and meet aspirations. Yet the fact is that fantasies of being able to do and have it all, in heels, has deep appeal.

A second explanation for the appeal of idealised women in the media is its lesbian or bisexual visual interest. Reina Lewis argues that reading mainstream women's fashion magazines 'against the grain' was historically a clandestine pleasure.[22] The lesbian gaze came into the mainstream during the 1980s and 1990s when lipstick lesbian chic and androgynous clothing moved over from the margins of gay culture

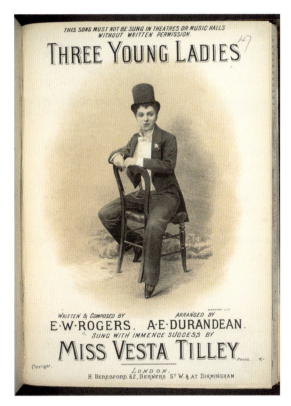

to the mainstream. Historically, women's playful performances with gender codes had also offered viewing pleasures for the lesbian and polysexual gaze. Theatre, film and popular culture offered platforms for entertainers to transgress codes of dress, manner and attitude. Vesta Tilley was a hugely popular music hall male impersonator, notable for her dapper dress. Hetty King, who had a similarly well-loved act, played across the class spectrum, appearing as toffs, cowboys and labourers.

While some might argue that this is a minority interest, it raises a general question about women's visual pleasure. The British-Chinese photographer Grace Lau, for example, has combined feminist campaigning to reverse both the male and Orientalist gaze with a career in the alternative erotica business.[23] Other women find work as models, as in the sex trade, because they have fewer means and therefore have to trade on bodily 'capital'. Both these arguments are faultlines for feminists wanting to protest the politics of image-making. The livelihoods of 'Page 3' glamour models was one argument used to combat attempts to stop the tabloid newspaper the *Sun* from publishing topless 'glamour' photographs of young women in its daily edition. In 1986 Clare Short MP brought The Indecent Displays (Newspapers) Bill before the House of Commons to enact legislation to ban the use of pictures in news and magazine print publications of naked or partially naked women in sexually provocative poses. Short received thousands of letters from many women across the United Kingdom expressing concern about the depiction of women in pornographic materials. It was this widespread concern that led to the formation in 1987 of the Campaign Against Pornography. When Short renewed her efforts in 2004 the paper retaliated by branding her a 'fat and ugly', 'jealous' 'killjoy'. In 2013 the campaigning baton was taken up by Caroline Lucas MP who was reprimanded for breaking the Westminster dress code by wearing a T-shirt bearing the slogan 'No More Page Three' to protest against the glamour model feature during a Commons debate. When challenged for trying to stymie a working-class career path, protestors have argued that the campaign is not against glamour models but against the obtrusive public visibility of sexualised images. Yet there remain real complexities in how to manage the politics of pornography, without undermining those who work in the business or resorting to censorship by the wrong hands or to the wrong degree.

The final reason why it is so difficult to challenge the damaging relationship of women to the media is that women remain the primary purchasers of goods and services – though people of all genders are increasingly being recognised as business opportunities. Today's world is ever more focused on consumption, while the fundamentals of advertising – stirring up a sense of lack and insufficiency – have not changed. Social media influencers and bloggers, often sponsored by global lifestyle brands, continue the magazine and public relations tradition of demonstrating how goods and services allow us to present our 'best selves' to the world. They illustrate and test 'before and after' methods of contouring the face, dressing for success, losing weight or toning bodies. Young people of all genders today spend great amounts of time, money and labour on managing appearance in a world where image counts so heavily.[24] Women who fail or refuse to live up to these ideals have had to work hard to be visible, to challenge the ways in which they themselves have been stereotyped and to overturn the expectations which have historically limited them.

However, just as activists in the 1960s and 1970s took up the challenge of changing such cultural offences, today a new round of media-savvy protestors are doing the same. *The Vagenda*, for example, lobbies as a feminist media watchdog with a zero-tolerance policy on sexist representation and *Everyday Sexism* provides a platform for women to speak out about their day-to-day experiences of sexism and harassment (both launched in 2012).[25] New generations across genders are retaliating against outmoded and alienating representations. They do so by claiming the right to be different, and to be themselves publicly and without shame. A recent example was the public backlash against the 2015 Beach Body advert for protein-based weight loss products, which featured a conventionally attractive, young, ultra-thin, fair-haired white woman in a yellow bikini looking directly into the camera. Next to her image was the question: 'Are you beach body ready?' The defacement of posters by members of the public, a petition and numerous individual complaints led the Advertising Standards Authority to investigate concerns.[26] The complaints were not upheld, but in 2018 a fashion brand reused the original Beach Body campaign design to acclaim, instead featuring three plus-size social media influencers.[27]

Body-positive campaigners like the British Sikh activist Harnaam Kaur are another step forward. Kaur came out on social media in 2014 as a bearded woman and built a career as a model, body-positive activist and motivational speaker. In interview she declared: 'I decided to keep my beard and step forward against society's expectations of what a woman should look like ... Today I am happy living as a young beautiful bearded woman.'[28] Kaur has become a media personality and influencer by virtue of her counter-cultural image. Bishamber Das, Grace Victory and Jameela Jamil have also been active via social media channels to claim public space and to break down barriers to personal confidence for women from every background. These campaigners argue that everyone should be free to enjoy a positive body image no matter what size, shape or ethnicity they are. No body-related topic is taboo, as they tackle subjects

Right: The actor and activist Jameela Jamil is a high-profile campaigner against the diet industry and dieting. In 2018 Jamil started I Weigh, a radical inclusivity campaign and a 'revolution against shame'. This picture, from a 2019 edition of *Stylist* magazine, shows Jamil standing triumphant by a smashed set of scales.

Below: Beach Body Ready push-back by plus-size fashion label Navabi, 2018.

Opposite: MP Caroline Lucas wearing a T-shirt in support of Lucy-Anne Holmes' No More Page Three campaign, House of Commons, 2013.

Body: Image

37

such as scarring, surgery, menstruation and the post-baby body. Body-positive activists such as any-body.org also collaborate with racial justice, LGBTQ+ and disability movements to promote self-confidence and self-respect for everyone.[29]

However, as we began, the politics of appearance is complex. Yes, we can and must celebrate these creative, beautiful, interesting interventions into image and self-image as great steps forward. Yet we must also acknowledge that today's celebrations of difference are entangled with an online marketplace ruthlessly pursuing new consumers, especially in the resurgent beauty business. Too often, new generations are forced to compete in a game of promotional self-branding where, even if there are more tools in a diversifying beauty box, image rather than action remains the point of femininity. The challenges must be to feminists here too, in finding a cultural politics adequate to a consumer-capitalist, still patriarchal, image-oriented world.

1. BBC News, 'Miss World: My Protest at 1970 Beauty Pageant', 5 March 2014, [https://www.bbc.co.uk/news/av/magazine-26437815/miss-world-my-protest-at-1970-beauty-pageant, accessed 22 September 2019].

2. Beatrix Campbell, 'Another World', *The Guardian,* 19 November 2010, [https://www.theguardian.com/lifeandstyle/2010/nov/19/feminists-disrupted-miss-world-tv, accessed 22 September 2019].

3. Rochelle Rowe, *Imagining Caribbean Womanhood: Race, Nation and Beauty Competitions,* 1929–70, pp. 167–76.

4. Virginia Woolf, *A Room of One's Own* (London: Hogarth Press, 1929).

5. http://bechdeltestfest.com/about/

6. John Berger, *Ways of Seeing* (London: BBC/Penguin Books, 1972) p. 46.

7. Laura Mulvey, 'Visual Pleasure and Narrative Cinema', *Screen*, vol. 16, no. 3 (1975), pp. 16–13; Laura Mulvey, 'Afterthoughts on "Visual Pleasure and Narrative Cinema" Inspired by *Duel in the Sun*', in *Feminism and Film Theory*, edited by Constance Penley (New York: Routledge, 1988), pp. 57–68.

8. Frantz Fanon, *Black Skin, White Masks* (New York: Grove Press, 2008). p. 89.

9. Chandra Mohanty, 'Under Western Eyes: Feminist Scholarship and Colonial Discourses', *Boundary 2, vol. 12, no. 3, On Humanism and the University I: The Discourse of Humanism* (Spring – Autumn, 1984), pp. 337.

10. June Purvis, '"DEEDS, NOT WORDS" The Daily Lives of Militant Suffragettes in Edwardian Britain', *Women's Studies International Forum*, vol. 18, no. 2, p. 93.

11. See Katherine Kelley, 'Seeing Through Spectacles: The Woman Suffrage Movement and London Newspapers, 1906–13', *European Journal of Women's Studies*, Sage, 2004, vol. 11, no. 3, pp. 327–53.

12. Sarah Pedersen, *The Scottish Suffragettes and the Press* (London: Palgrave Macmillan 2017), pp. 67–8.

13. British Library, Sisterhood and After: The Women's Liberation Oral History Project, [http://www.bl.uk/learning/histcitizen/sisterhood/clips/bodies-minds-and-spirits/body-experience/143246.html, accessed 22 September 2019].

14. http://www.bl.uk/learning/histcitizen/sisterhood/clips/activism/campaigns-and-protests/143934.html; https://www.criterion.com/current/top-10-lists/250-laura-mulvey-s-top-10

15. British Library, 'Body Image, Advertising and the Media', [https://www.bl.uk/spare-rib/articles/body-image-advertising-and-the-media, accessed 22 September 2019].

16. https://www.joygregory.co.uk/artists-editions/boxed-edition of autoportrait/

17. Sander Gilman, 'The Hottentot and the Prostitute: Toward an Iconography of Female Sexuality', *Black Venus 2010: They Called Her "Hottentot"*, ed. Deborah Willis (Philadelphia: Temple University Press, 2010); Cheryl Finley, 'Cinderella Tours Europe', ibid.

18. Stuart Hall, 'Black Narcissus', *Autograph: The Association of Black Photographers Newsletter*, June 1991, [https://shop.autograph-abp.co.uk/free/newspaper-june-1991?sort=p.price&order=ASC, accessed 22 September 2019].

19. Christie's, 'Heartwarming and Haunting: Two Works by Khadija Saye', [https://www.christies.com/features/Heartwarming-and-haunting-works-by-Khadija-Saye-9410-1.aspx, access 22 September 2019].

20. Sarah Vine, 'One was relaxed, every inch a stateswoman while her opposite number was tense and uncomfortable: SARAH VINE says May v Sturgeon was a knockout victory for the PM', *Daily Mail*, 28 March 2017, [https://www.dailymail.co.uk/debate/article-4354996/SARAH-VINE-says-v-Sturgeon-victory-PM.html, accessed 22 September 2019].

21. Marjorie Ferguson, *Forever Feminine: Women's Magazines and the Cult of Femininity* (London: Heinemann, 1983).

22. Peter Horne and Reina Lewis, *Outlooks: Lesbian and Gay Sexualities and Visual Cultures* (London: Routledge, 1996).

23. https://www.bl.uk/people/grace-lau

24. Ana Sofia Elias and Rosalind Gill, 'Beauty Surveillance: The Digital Self-Monitoring Cultures of Neoliberalism', *European Journal of Cultural Studies*, vol. 21, no. 1, 2018, pp. 59–77.

25. https://london.endangeredbodies.org/

26. BBC News, '"Beach Body Ready" Advert Not Offensive, Rules Watchdog', 1 July 2015, [https://www.bbc.co.uk/news/uk-33340301, accessed 22 September 2019].

27. Sabrina Barr, 'Plus-Size Fashion Brand Transforms Protein World's "Beach Body Ready" Advert into Body Positivity Campaign', *Independent*, 3 May 2018, [https://www.independent.co.uk/life-style/fashion/beach-body-ready-plus-size-campaign-body-positivity-protein-world-navabi-a8334516.html, accessed 22 September 2019].

28. Rock n Roll Bride, 'Flower Beard Bridals with Harnaam Kaur', [https://www.rocknrollbride.com/2015/06/flower-beard-bridals-with-harnaam-kaur/, accessed 22 September 2019].

29. http://www.any-body.org/body_activism/

GAL-DEM

gal-dem is an award-winning media company, committed to telling the stories of women and non-binary people of colour. We're addressing inequality and misrepresentation in the industry through platforming the creative and editorial work of our community across essays, opinion, news, arts, music, politics and lifestyle content.

BODY: BIOLOGY

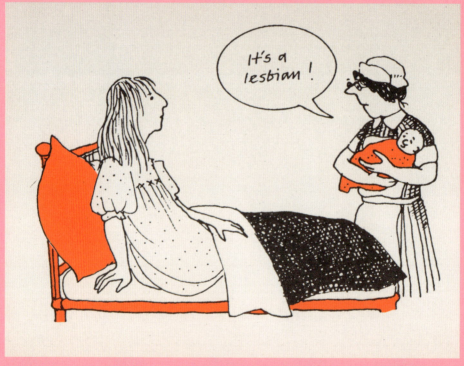

© Jo Nesbitt

40

'No matter whether one feels one's **GENDERED** and **SEXED REALITY** to be firmly fixed or less so, every person should have **THE RIGHT TO DETERMINE** the legal and linguistic terms of **THEIR EMBODIED LIVES**.'

JUDITH BUTLER (B.1956)
From interview in *The TransAdvocate* (online), 2014

Judith Butler's *Gender Trouble* (1990) challenged the conventional notion of fixed binary genders. It was foundational for queer theory as a discipline and opened new pathways for feminism. Her work showed how gender was formed in language and everyday interactions, and suggested possibilities of gender fluidity.

Under the Male Microscope

— ANGELA SAINI

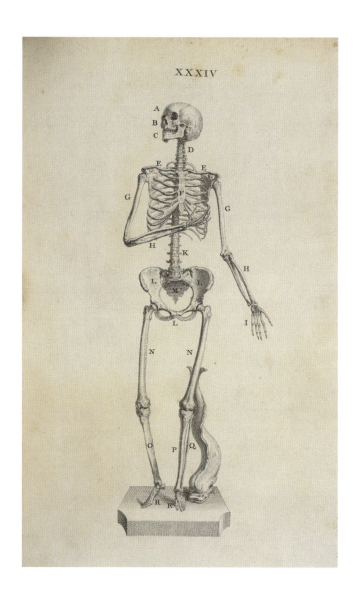

42   Unfinished Business

Women's bodies have always been misunderstood – sometimes deliberately, at other times for more prosaic reasons. These misunderstandings have often been driven by the sexual politics of the age. Whether it was the centuries-old male domination of scientific research, leading to bias, or an overt belief in the inferiority of women's minds and bodies, what science has told us has long been shaped by male subjectivity. Biology as a discipline bears the scars of women's struggles to be treated fairly and with empathy.

We imagine science to be uniquely impartial, cut away from the messiness of everyday life. But in truth, it never could be. Research is a human endeavour. And humans are fallible. Even something as innocent as an anatomical drawing can be loaded with political meaning. Surgeon William Cheselden's drawing of a woman's skeleton, published in 1733, for instance, doesn't reflect the proportions of a real person, but one imagined, taking as its inspiration a first-century Hellenistic sculpture of the goddess Aphrodite. Her skull is smaller, her hips wider. What masquerades as science is actually caricature, painting women as less mature versions of men, often as sexual or reproductive objects and without the same physical or mental strength.

Efforts to understand how the body works and why our species evolved the way it did are shaped by prior assumptions about the natural roles of women and men. If a woman's place was in the home as a nurturer, and a man's domain lay outside the home as a hunter and builder, it was assumed that our evolutionary story would begin with strong, powerful masculinity and softer, child-rearing femininity. Biologists should have been working beyond these myths, objectively shining a light on who we truly are. Instead, many laboured to argue that our bodies proved society's ideas about the innate gulf between women's and men's minds and bodies, that we are like separate breeds.

A case in point is the noted British embryologist and reproductive expert, Walter Heape, who in 1913 argued in his book *Sex Antagonism* that suffragists were wasting their reproductive energies when they went out to campaign for the right to vote.[1] There was the flavour of a threat to his writing, a warning that stepping outside their 'natural' role as wives, mothers and homemakers would have dangerous repercussions. He deliberately ignored the fact that working-class or enslaved women had always had to bear and raise children while working in fields and factories. It was the act of marching for greater rights to which Heape took exception.

This habit of justifying social structures using biology is the source of many more strange, often degrading, claims about female nature. Even the famously careful evolutionary biologist Charles Darwin couldn't help falling into this trap. When on Boxing Day in 1881, not long before Darwin's death in April 1882, a women's rights campaigner in Boston, Massachusetts, Caroline Kennard, wrote to ask him his views on women, his reply was remarkable.[2] He told her that women, though possessing morally superior qualities, had evolved to be the intellectual inferiors of men. In his opinion, the only way to breach this biological intelligence gap would be for women to carry out the same work as men, to be equal 'bread winners' – a step he then advised against, for fear of what it might do to the harmony of family life.

Darwin's error was to assume that the culture around him (that sliver of white, upper-class Victorian society to which he belonged) reflected the universal laws of nature rather than a long history of female oppression, where patriarchal family structures organised sexuality, childbirth and

Opposite: The first published illustration of a female skeleton in an English anatomy book, *Osteographia, or the Anatomy of the Bones*, by William Cheselden, 1733.

Body: Biology

43

Opposite: Caroline Kennard's reply to Charles Darwin, 28 January 1882.

Below: Charles Darwin's response to Caroline Kennard's question about female versus male intelligence, 9 January 1882.

care work. That women didn't have the right to vote, freedom to study or access to the professions, in this scheme of thought, was not a political injustice but the inevitable cultural product of biological differences. In challenging him, women like Kennard exemplified efforts throughout history, including Mary Wollstonecraft in the eighteenth century, Alice Lee in the nineteenth, and modern-day scholars such as evolutionary biologist Joan Roughgarden and biologist of sexuality Anne Fausto-Sterling, to rewrite skewed scientific narratives.[3]

Their efforts did little to change the opinions of male scientists in their time. But we can now recognise the bravery and wisdom in their words, and in the legacies they left behind. In 1907 after her death, Caroline Kennard's sister established a scholarship for a science student at all-women Radcliffe College in Cambridge, Massachusetts. Through the course of that century, more women would finally gain some of the same opportunities as men and prove themselves capable scientists. Their achievements did more than change perceptions; they also changed the direction of ideas.

Unfinished Business

Brookline Mass. U.S.A
Jan. 28 - 1882 -

Mr. Darwin
 Dear Sir -
    I thank you for your very kind reply to my letter of inquiry as to your opinion of the comparative intellectual abilities of the sexes. — I believe you are supported in your ideas of the greater moral qualities of the woman. — Before quite deciding as to her condition intellectually, will you excuse me if I remind you that recent results from efforts for her higher education, in your own country and in this, are very flattering and encouraging: and are opening for women avenues for individual improvement and for the general enlightenment of her sex. — and therefore, of necessity (according to the laws of heredity) for the advancement of the human race intellectually. Her enlightened intellect, united with her wholesome moral nature, can then with the aid of man (for in nature the male & female must work in sympathy together, you have taught us) — ordain, in a manner hitherto unthought of or practised upon, for the propagation of the best and the survival of the fittest in the human species.

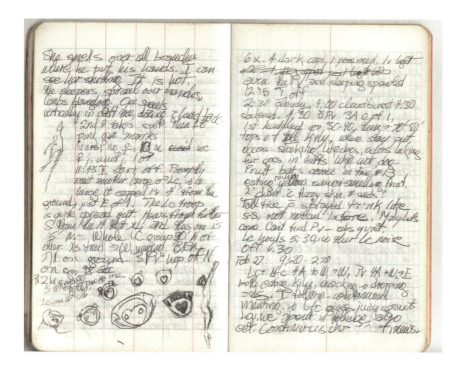

The late primatologist Alison Jolly is one such example of someone who worked within the framework of Darwinian evolutionary biology yet challenged its sexist assumptions. As her beautifully detailed field notebook documents, while working as a young graduate student in Madagascar in 1962, she observed that ring-tailed lemurs were female-dominant.[4] This ran counter to the received wisdom that all primates (including our own species) were male-dominant. As she later joked, the 'king' lemur of the DreamWorks animation movie *Madagascar* ought to have been a queen. She was also fascinated by the clever relationships lemurs pursued. In contrast to the orthodoxy that intelligence had evolved to master tools, she speculated that more likely it evolved through the challenge of maintaining complex societies. She was among those, including her Malagasy colleague Hanta Rasamimanana and Sarah Blaffer Hrdy, who argued that species' survival was as much the result of social cooperation as competition.[5]

Yet the struggle is not over. It remains important to understand the context and methods of scientific sexism. Darwin's cousin, Francis Galton, the person who defined eugenics – a belief that through selective breeding, it might be possible to create a superior race of people – married a love of statistics with a passion for studying human difference.[6] One time, he used a sextant to measure the proportions of a Khoikhoi woman's body in Namibia from a distance

without her permission or knowledge.[7] The woman is unnamed, but she is likely to have been the wife of one of the Nama interpreters. Galton's use of the sextant to measure her body was reductive and an imposition of both gendered and colonial power. Using a hidden counter in his pocket, he also furtively rated women across Britain to draw a beauty map of the country. In Galton's vision of a eugenic state in his supposedly Utopian novel *Kantsaywhere*, the ideal women had sex appeal and were clever incubators for perfect babies.

For men like Galton, science was not just a means of uncovering fundamental truths, but also a tool to gauge the inferiority and superiority of others. Comparison, measurement and the hierarchical

Opposite, above: Field notebook of primatologist Alison Jolly, c. 1962, documenting her discovery that ring-tailed lemurs were female dominant as a species.

Opposite, below: Alison Jolly's colleague Hanta Rasamimanana teaching in the Mandena Conservation Area, Madagascar.

Below: The sextant used by eugenicist Sir Francis Galton in 1850 to measure, without permission or knowledge, a Khoikhoi woman's body in Namibia.

grading of humans marks the bloodiest chapters of scientific history. Women, in this process of 'scientific' measurement, found themselves ranked firmly below men. Women of colour and people with disabilities have been ranked even lower. It might be assumed that the days of eugenics are over. Yet supposed scientific studies in gender-based 'IQ' and racially inflected population control measures continue. The data harvested by algorithms for 'objective' AI programmes themselves can cement social and racial privilege within society. There have been examples in application screenings of discrimination against female and non-European names.

Ultimately, of course, to rank oneself above another is to exercise power, and it is to this point that this story always returns. In her terrifying 1985 novel *The Handmaid's Tale*, Margaret Atwood illustrates how patriarchal control of female reproduction might look in a near-future totalitarian dystopia.[8] In her tale, women are divided into fertile slaves and infertile mistresses, both ultimately the losers in a violent regime where motherhood is their primary role, and fertility and sexual modesty their greatest virtues. In the hooded red cape worn like a veil by the handmaid – the cape reflecting male dominance over her body, and its red symbolising fecundity – we see these virtues elevated in cruel and perverse ways.

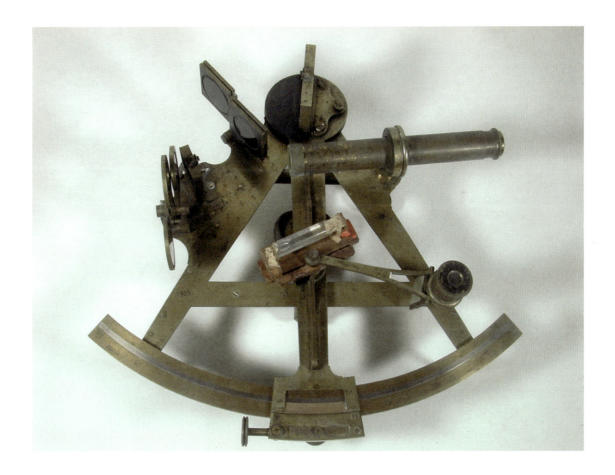

Body: Biology

Recently, the red cape has been taken up as a protest symbol to challenge modern-day misogyny. The horror of *The Handmaid's Tale* is that it's not so far removed from the historical and contemporary experiences of real women. In the United States, we see efforts to take away the right to abortion – though, as in Atwood's vision, a brisk 'trade' in the babies of poor or minority women operates for the childless whites who can afford them. In Iran and Saudi Arabia, veiling is mandatory. Female genital mutilation, a vicious ancient practice most commonly found in the Middle East, Africa and Asia, sees young girls cut and sewn up to physically stop them from having sex before marriage. It often leaves them in pain and discomfort for life, as well as inflicting psychological scars.

This practice echoes the Victorian practice of clitoridectomy in the UK. Dr Isaac Baker Brown was infamously expelled from the Obstetrical Society of London for using this surgery to treat epilepsy and hysteria. Although fellow professionals criticised his work, it was only because he performed these procedures on women without consent. *On the Curability of Certain Forms of Insanity, Epilepsy, Catalepsy and Hysteria in Females*, published in 1866, defends his treatment, dismissing complaints that he 'unsexed' women.

Reclaiming female sexual freedom and agency remains one of the greatest challenges for feminism. In the 1970s, leading male scientists, including evolutionary biologist Robert Trivers and anthropologist Donald Symons, believed that women were naturally more chaste than men, that they had far less interest in sex, even that the female orgasm hadn't evolved for women's pleasure but was an evolutionary vestige of the male orgasm, like nipples on a man.[9] Already, these outdated and sexist notions have been debunked.

In the process of rewriting narratives, womanhood is being redefined. To display our bodies as they are in all their diversity without shame is progress. To enjoy sex with partners of our choice, and to have access to contraception and abortion, is progress. Even to be unembarrassed by our vaginas, as artist Soofiya's *Vaginal Discharge* zine (overleaf) and the huge Vulva Quilt so gloriously celebrate, is progress. The quilt has been displayed by Daughters of Eve, an organisation founded by the British anti-FGM campaigners Nimco Ali and Leyla Hussein.

Yet to be who we are, without changing ourselves in the service of society's expectation of what the ideal woman should be – pubescent, freshly fertile, modest and servile – is an uphill battle, always fighting against biological versions of the stereotypes more commonly associated with beauty industries. Women continue to face judgement, some more than others, and what it means to be female remains bounded by myth. To accept women as diverse feels like the biggest difficulty of all. As we see in the intersection of class, religion and race with physique and gender, each woman is different, has her own desires, and faces her own challenges.

To identify as a woman is not necessarily to share in identical biological features with all other women, but to share in a set of experiences based on society's treatment of different classes and groups of women. If biology tells us anything – because as we know, it doesn't yet tell us everything – it is that the greatest source of difference in the human species is individual difference. While fighting for rights collectively as women, it's important to recognise that each woman will have different needs and pressures, just as we must remember that the gender category 'woman' is itself subject to debate.

Left: Women taking inspiration from novelist Margaret Atwood's *The Handmaid's Tale* to protest US President Donald Trump's visit to the UK, 4 June 2019.

Opposite: The Vulva Quilt, a work conceived by Tara Scott and made possible with the sisterhood of many contributors – including the Shoreditch Sisters of 2009/13, Equality Now, Daughters of Eve, Nimco Ali, Leyla Hussein and Birdy Imoke – to raise awareness of genital mutilation.

Artist Soofiya's *Vaginal Discharge* zine tackles the stigma associated with vaginas and women's bodies.

The work of neuroscientists Gina Rippon, author of *The Gendered Brain*, and Daphna Joel, co-author of *Gender Mosaic*, reveals that gendered behaviour is more likely the product of nurture than present at birth.[10] Who we are and what we become is heavily shaped by the societies we live in. Rippon and Joel argue that all brains include a mix of what we call typically male and typically female characteristics. There are no such things as female brains distinct from male brains. Even physically, although there are obvious average sex differences in height and upper body strength, these differences sit on a spectrum that makes it possible for some women to be stronger and taller than many men.

It was eugenicist Francis Galton who tried to get to the heart of what he described as nature and nurture, in an effort to distil what makes groups of people innately different from others. He saw people as having certain immutable qualities deep down, which couldn't be changed. But as researchers are beginning to understand, the scientific struggle to understand human nature is necessarily shaped by the fact that we are social beings, with cultural and technological means to reshape both our own and other species' biologies and futures. We do not exist in a vacuum, and neither can we survive in one. Who we are, deep down, is nothing at all without social and cultural input. It is up to us, then, to decide what that input should be in the service of a fairer society.

As scientific research moves forward, and especially as more women become scientists, intellectuals and leaders, the story of who we are is slowly shifting. Women are not a breed apart, with one defined natural role. While biology remains a crucial and wonderful resource for understanding how sex evolves and works, it has itself been rightly reshaped and held to account by those whom it previously overlooked or underestimated.

---

1 Walter Heape, *Sex Antagonism* (New York: Putnam, 1913).

2 Darwin Correspondence Project, 'Letter no. 13579', accessed on 25 August 2019, http://www.darwinproject.ac.uk/DCP-LETT-13579; Darwin Correspondence Project, 'Letter no. 13650', accessed on 25 August 2019, http://www.darwinproject.ac.uk/DCP-LETT-13650; Darwin Correspondence Project, 'Letter no. 13607', accessed on 25 August 2019, http://www.darwinproject.ac.uk/DCP-LETT-13607.

3 Joan Roughgarden, *Evolution's Rainbow: Diversity, Gender, and Sexuality in Nature and People* (Berkeley: University of California Press, 2009); Anne Fausto-Sterling, *Myths of Gender: Biological Theories about Women and Men* (New York: Basic Books, 1985).

4 Alison Jolly, 'Lemur Social Behavior and Primate Intelligence', *Science*, vol. 153, no. 3735, 1966, pp. 501–6; Alison Jolly, *Thank You, Madagascar: The Conservation Diaries of Alison Jolly* (London and Chicago: Zed Books, 2015).

5 Sarah Blaffer Hrdy, *Mother Nature: A History of Mothers, Infants, and Natural Selection* (New York: Pantheon Books, 1999).

6 Francis Galton, 'Hereditary Talent and Character', *Macmillan's Magazine*, no. 12, 1865, pp. 157–66, 318–27.

7 Francis Galton, *Narrative of an Explorer in Tropical South Africa* (London, New York and Melbourne: Ward, Lock and Co., 1891).

8 Margaret Atwood, *The Handmaid's Tale* (Toronto: McClelland and Stewart, 1985).

9 Donald Symons, *The Evolution of Human Sexuality* (New York: Oxford University Press, 1979).

10 Gina Rippon, *The Gendered Brain: The New Neuroscience That Shatters the Myth of the Female Brain* (London: The Bodley Head 2019); Daphna Joel & Luba Vikhanski, *Gender Mosaic: Beyond the Myth of the Male and Female Brain* (New York: Little, Brown Spark 2019).

BLOODY GOOD PERIOD

Menstruation is a normal, healthy biological function, but people who menstruate (women, girls, non-binary people and trans men) have long been shamed for bleeding. Bloody Good Period is a charity providing period supplies and menstrual education to refugees, asylum seekers and others who are unlikely to access these essentials. They also campaign for period equality – most definitely unfinished business.

On the Malleability of the Body

— DR JULIET JACQUES

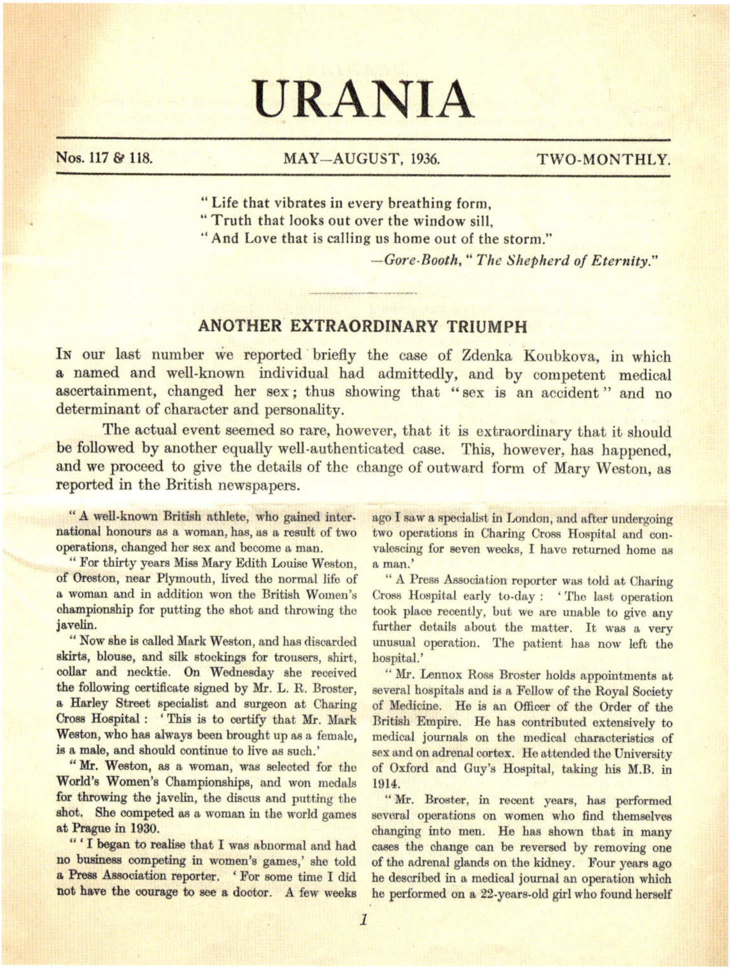

URANIA

Nos. 117 & 118. MAY—AUGUST, 1936. TWO-MONTHLY.

" Life that vibrates in every breathing form,
" Truth that looks out over the window sill,
" And Love that is calling us home out of the storm."
—*Gore-Booth, " The Shepherd of Eternity."*

ANOTHER EXTRAORDINARY TRIUMPH

In our last number we reported briefly the case of Zdenka Koubkova, in which a named and well-known individual had admittedly, and by competent medical ascertainment, changed her sex; thus showing that "sex is an accident" and no determinant of character and personality.

The actual event seemed so rare, however, that it is extraordinary that it should be followed by another equally well-authenticated case. This, however, has happened, and we proceed to give the details of the change of outward form of Mary Weston, as reported in the British newspapers.

" A well-known British athlete, who gained international honours as a woman, has, as a result of two operations, changed her sex and become a man.

" For thirty years Miss Mary Edith Louise Weston, of Oreston, near Plymouth, lived the normal life of a woman and in addition won the British Women's championship for putting the shot and throwing the javelin.

" Now she is called Mark Weston, and has discarded skirts, blouse, and silk stockings for trousers, shirt, collar and necktie. On Wednesday she received the following certificate signed by Mr. L. R. Broster, a Harley Street specialist and surgeon at Charing Cross Hospital: 'This is to certify that Mr. Mark Weston, who has always been brought up as a female, is a male, and should continue to live as such.'

" Mr. Weston, as a woman, was selected for the World's Women's Championships, and won medals for throwing the javelin, the discus and putting the shot. She competed as a woman in the world games at Prague in 1930.

" 'I began to realise that I was abnormal and had no business competing in women's games,' she told a Press Association reporter. 'For some time I did not have the courage to see a doctor. A few weeks ago I saw a specialist in London, and after undergoing two operations in Charing Cross Hospital and convalescing for seven weeks, I have returned home as a man.'

" A Press Association reporter was told at Charing Cross Hospital early to-day: 'The last operation took place recently, but we are unable to give any further details about the matter. It was a very unusual operation. The patient has now left the hospital.'

" Mr. Lennox Ross Broster holds appointments at several hospitals and is a Fellow of the Royal Society of Medicine. He is an Officer of the Order of the British Empire. He has contributed extensively to medical journals on the medical characteristics of sex and on adrenal cortex. He attended the University of Oxford and Guy's Hospital, taking his M.B. in 1914.

" Mr. Broster, in recent years, has performed several operations on women who find themselves changing into men. He has shown that in many cases the change can be reversed by removing one of the adrenal glands on the kidney. Four years ago he described in a medical journal an operation which he performed on a 22-years-old girl who found herself

1

In its issue of May–August 1936, the bimonthly journal *Urania* announced 'Another Extraordinary Triumph'. A little-known publication that ran from 1916 to 1940, it said in its mission statement that 'there are no men or women in *Urania*'; it dedicated itself to debunking the notion of 'sex', engaging with a vibrant sexological movement that had grown out of campaigns against legal suppression of sexual diversity and gender variance in nineteenth-century Britain and Germany.[1] This movement had not just questioned traditional ideas of 'male' and 'female': it had also successfully pioneered sex reassignment surgeries, and it was one of the first widely reported instances in the United Kingdom, on an athlete called Mark Weston, that *Urania* was celebrating.[2]

Weston had been a national champion in the women's javelin and discus throwing during the 1920s, and had represented Great Britain at the 1928 Olympic Games. Weston was not the first athlete to transition from female to male: *Urania* had previously reported on Zdeněk Koubek, who had recently had surgery and retired from athletics, having won two medals at the 1934 Women's World Games. One thing that is interesting for the contemporary reader, who may be weary of sensationalist or spiteful coverage of trans/non-binary people, is that *Urania* was not alone in covering Weston's story in a spirit of gentle curiosity. In January 1937, American bodybuilding magazine *Physical Culture* ran the headline 'Can Sex in Humans Be Changed?' In the article, Donald Furthman Wickets wrote that 'The old landmarks are going, nothing is static, everything flows … Life is created in the laboratory [and] sex is no longer immutable.'[3] There was no alarm about this potentially seismic change, however: reassignment was purely a matter for the individuals concerned and the scientists, with little detail given on the surgical techniques and no moral judgement offered on Weston marrying a woman.

During the Victorian era, there had been plenty of panic about 'vice' and 'unnatural offences', some of which concerned men who wore 'female attire' in public[4] – most famously in the case of Ernest 'Stella' Boulton and Frederick 'Fanny' Park, who were arrested in London in 1870. When the authorities grudgingly conceded that they could not be charged with sodomy, Boulton and Park were tried for 'conspiring to incite others to commit unnatural offences' by dressing as women, presumably to con unsuspecting heterosexual men into sleeping with them. The case collapsed, but after the judge lamented the lack of any law by which the defendants could be imprisoned, broader legislation was almost inevitable. In 1885, the UK's Conservative government passed the Criminal Law Amendment Act, which notoriously made any public or private act of 'gross indecency' between two men illegal, and punishable by two years' imprisonment with hard labour – it effectively criminalised anyone who deviated from social norms of sexuality and gender.

This, and the Oscar Wilde trials ten years later, galvanised British sexologists, who began research into homosexuality and bisexuality, as well as phenomena such as cross-dressing and gender dysphoria – termed 'transvestism' in a study published by German sexologist Magnus Hirschfeld in 1910, who separated gender identity from sexuality for the first time. Fighting a society that remained deeply conservative, Hirschfeld's British counterparts insisted that there had *always* been people who did not conform to standard ideas of 'male' and 'female': Havelock Ellis (1859–1939) termed men who dressed as, or wanted to be, women as 'Eonists' after the Chevalier d'Éon, an aristocratic French immigrant who lived as a woman in London from 1777 until her death in 1810. However, Ellis and others were

Opposite: Urania was a radical journal that reported on the lives of sex rebels and gender outlaws in the early twentieth century.

Body: Biology

55

SENTENCE ON MAN-WOMAN

Alteration of Law Urged in Petition

Special to "Reynolds's"

What action will the Home Secretary take in the amazing case of Hull, the 21-years-old St. Helens man now serving 18 months' imprisonment for masquerading as a woman?

AS "Reynolds's" announced they would, the British Sexological Society have now taken definite steps to present a petition asking for reconsideration of this sentence. Their action is being supported by penal reform societies and by many prominent doctors. The Home Secretary is believed to be sympathetic to the object of the petition.

WOMANISH WAYS

Reconsideration rather than reprieve is being asked for, "Reynolds's" understands, so that the whole question of the law in relation to "anti-types" may be revised.

Hull, according to the medical evidence led at his trial, is one of "Nature's mistakes." He experiences all the emotions of a woman, and, when dressed in ordinary male attire, is liable to come under suspicion by the police because of his womanish ways

"Reynolds's" learns that the experiments now being made in a London hospital on the subject of "Sexual inversion" are not directed towards finding a "cure" for the "anti-type." Their aim is merely to enable women to remove, say, hair growth from the face and to correct physical tendencies.

Above: Report from *Reynold's News*, October 1932, about Augustine Hull.

Opposite: The poet and author Radclyffe Hall with her lover and partner, the sculptor Una Trowbridge, photographed in 1927.

unable to persuade the British establishment that sexual diversity and gender variance should be accepted simply because they could be traced as far back as ancient Greece and Rome, and the law remained in place.

The 1885 Act did not mention lesbianism or what we would now call transgender or non-binary identification, but female-to-male people and gender-nonconforming women still found themselves facing unwanted legal attention during the interwar period. Radclyffe Hall endured an obscenity trial after publishing her novel *The Well of Loneliness* (1928), which featured an 'invert' protagonist called Stephen Gordon who was born a girl but yearned to be a man, and had relationships with women; in 1929, trans man Colonel Victor Barker was charged with making a false statement on a marriage certificate after having wed Elfrida Emma Haward in Brighton six years earlier, and was sentenced to nine months' imprisonment for perjury. However, the vast majority of prosecutions for cross-dressing and media stories about transsexual people involved trans women and anyone else whose birth certificate had originally recorded 'male'.

The intense public interest that began with Boulton and Park's trial was maintained well into the twentieth century, stoked by prurient media coverage that, along with the law, intended to intimidate nonconformists into silence. In November 1931, the news broke that 21-year-old Augustine Hull from St Helens had been sentenced to eighteen months in prison with hard labour for 'masquerading as a woman' after trying to marry a labourer. The British Sexological Society petitioned against the verdict, saying a practitioner had examined Hull and found 'a medical curiosity' – someone who was 'a male person with a feminine mind' whose condition, recognised in medical law and practice, was 'congenital' and had persisted since early childhood.[5] Despite protesting on scientific terms rather than on the moral ones preferred by their Victorian antecedents, the campaign was unsuccessful, and Hull remained in jail: the Home Secretary was not persuaded by the historical argument, and the authorities were not aware (or perhaps just not interested) in the sexologists' separation of sexuality and gender identity.

Nonetheless, those striving for greater acceptance of gender-variant people continued to argue on biological grounds, focusing less on individuals who wore the clothing of the 'opposite' sex and more on those whose bodies did not fit into medically accepted categories – whom we would now call 'intersex'. On 1 January 1932, the *News Chronicle* reported on the case of a 14-year-old who had been recorded at birth as female but had now 'been declared a male'. A medical expert at Charing Cross Hospital stated that: 'There have been a number of cases in which girls who have been normal females up to a certain age have suddenly developed into males. Their voices deepen and they grow a moustache or beard.'[6] Telling the *Chronicle* that there had been plenty of cases 'in which it is almost impossible to determine sex at birth', the medic talked about which glands became active at puberty and how they affected secondary sex characteristics, insisting that such changes were 'rare in the human race, but quite common' amongst animals such as hens and pigs.[7] At the time, medics at Charing Cross Hospital were working on techniques to 'correct physical tendencies' such as facial hair removal for trans women, but the *Chronicle* also noted, casually, that 'six women who have taken on male characteristics' had been treated at Charing Cross Hospital, which performed the operation on Weston in 1936 and became the main UK centre for gender reassignment, offering psychiatric care as well as hormones and surgery for transsexual people after the Second World War.

Unfinished Business

Body: Biology

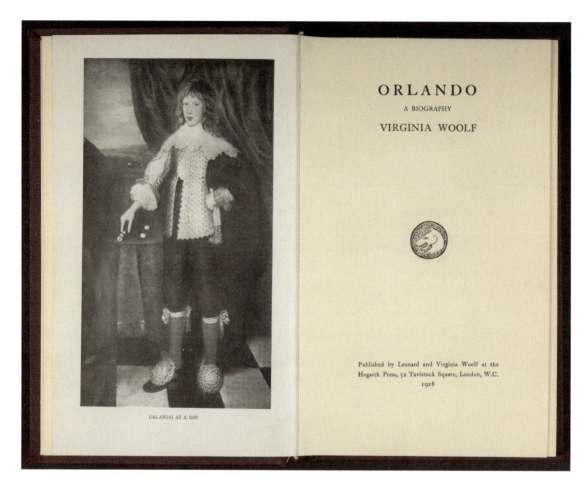

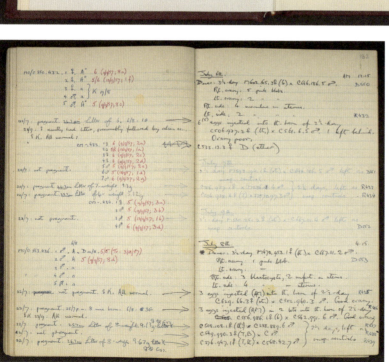

58

Unfinished Business

Right: Christine Jorgensen (1926–1989), after her sexual reassignment surgery and hormone therapy, April 1953. She was the first person to become famous for the controversial medical procedure.

Opposite, above: First edition of Virginia Woolf's *Orlando*, 1928.

Opposite, below: Anne McLaren's embryo transfer notebook, 1955–9.

In December 1952, transsexual woman Christine Jorgensen became a global media sensation. For the press, Jorgensen – a former GI who had just returned to the US after surgery in Denmark – became a symbol for postwar anxieties about changing gender roles, as well as those about the potential, and potential excesses, of scientific technology, which could not only split the atom but also turn men into women. Elsewhere, less immediate – and thus less spectacular – explorations were being made into the possibilities of the sexed body, such as those conducted by developmental biologist Anne McLaren between 1955 and 1959.

McLaren's embryo transfer notebook is barely comprehensible to the casual observer, with phrases such as '3 eggs injected' offering just the faintest clue as to her field of study. In 1958, working with John Biggers at the Royal Veterinary College, London, McLaren produced a litter of mice grown from embryos developed outside the uterus and then transferred to a surrogate mother – work that led to the advent of in vitro fertilisation (IVF) technologies and the birth of Louise Brown, the first 'test tube baby', two decades later. Surgical techniques did not (and still do not) enable transsexual women to give birth – an early attempt at uterus transplantation led to the death of one of the world's first transsexual people, Lili Elbe, in 1931. Coming so soon after the Jorgensen case, McLaren's experiments further undermined the idea that physical sex, and the social roles attached to the 'male' and 'female' body, were immutable: if reproduction could be taken outside of the uterus in this way, then perhaps the traditional role of women as the primary caregivers to children in heterosexual relationships, where the men earned an income, could also be changed.

Towards the end of the twentieth century and into the twenty-first, having secured a handful of legal rights and formed communities, Western trans and non-binary people grew more explicit in exploring their identities through art and literature. We had a heritage to draw on: not just *The Well of Loneliness* but also another, far more playful and innovative novel, also published in 1928 by a friend of Hall's – *Orlando* by Virginia Woolf. *Orlando*, a 'biography' of a poet who lives for centuries and changes sex at will, has long been an inspiration for those who see creative possibilities in gender expression; among those has been artist/photographer Diana Michener, who illustrated Woolf's text in 2005. (Indeed, *Orlando* still resonates: Andrea Lawlor's recent novel *Paul Takes the Form of a Mortal Girl* essentially transplants the story to the American queer underground of the 1990s, following a shape-shifting hero/ine through the era's gay bars, feminist festivals, gigs and film screenings.) Despite being over ninety years old, *Orlando* comes close to capturing the spirit of contemporary British trans and non-binary culture, moving away from an attempt to convince hostile outsiders of the biological basis for gender variance, towards a celebratory attitude that aims to give confidence to a community, and which posits that it is morally right for trans and non-binary people to be accepted on our own terms.

Body: Biology

Opposite: This poster by the contemporary trans/non-binary black artist Travis Alabanza celebrates hair that grows on gender non-conforming faces, destabilising the idea that stubble is the 'natural' property of men and masculinity.

Travis Alabanza's poster 'My Stubble Has No Gender' is a bold, positive expression of this attitude. One of a number of talented trans and non-binary people of colour to emerge in the UK in recent years, alongside artists Evan Ifekoya and Raju Rage, and poets Jay Bernard and Nat Raha, performance artist Alabanza detaches a classic indicator of maleness and masculinity from its gendered associations with striking simplicity. Alabanza's work is part of an approach where trans and non-binary people define the terms by which we see ourselves, and work to make outsiders understand the importance of those terms, expanding the possibilities of language and, as such, human conceptions of gender. First, this approach aims to make people realise that everyone has a gender, and a gender identity, in the same way that gay, lesbian and bisexual activists popularised the idea that everyone has a sexuality, and that heterosexuality is not neutral. It then works to suggest that (as the feminist slogan has it) biology is not destiny, separating both physical characteristics and traditional gender roles from the categories of 'male' and 'female', creating space into which new identities can grow. Like the early twentieth-century sexologists, we understand that the body is malleable, and that once this idea is accepted, new possibilities will continue to emerge.

1   Niamh Carey, 'The Politics of Urania', *The Glasgow Women's Library*, https://womenslibrary.org.uk/explore-the-library-and-archive/lgbtq-collections-online-resource/the-politics-of-urania/ (accessed 17 July 2019).
2   Clare Tebbutt, 'The Spectre of the "Man-Woman Athlete": Mark Weston, Zdeněk Koubek, the 1936 Olympics and the uncertainty of sex', *Women's History Review*, vol. 24, iss. 5, 2015, pp. 721–38.
3   Donald Furthman Wickets, 'Can Sex in Humans Be Changed?', *Physical Culture*, January 1937, http://blog.modernmechanix.com/can-sex-in-humans-be-changed/ (accessed 17 July 2019).
4   Such terms appeared frequently in newspapers and trials of the era.
5   Anon., 'Man Who Posed as Woman', *Birmingham Gazette*, 26 January 1932, p. 3.
6   Anon., 'Sex Determination', *News Chronicle*, 1 January 1932, p. 7.
7   Ibid.

BODY: AUTONOMY

© Kate Beaton

'The **PROGRESSION** or **EMANCIPATION** of any class ... takes place through the **EFFORTS** of individuals of that class. All women should **INFORM** themselves of the condition of **THEIR SEX**, and of **THEIR OWN POSITION**.'

HARRIET MARTINEAU (1802–1876)
From *Society in America* (1837)

British writer, abolitionist and feminist Harriet Martineau was a high-profile intellectual in her day but was almost forgotten until the last few decades. Seen now as a foremother of sociology, her work on research methods, self-writing and disability is still relevant and established a feminist tradition of independent work aiming for freedom and autonomy.

Autonomy In and Through the Body

— DR DEBBIE CHALLIS

Poverty-stricken couple with five children, photographed in London's East End. The man holds a bunch of pawn tickets in his hand. Without access to contraception, couples were unable to control the size of their families and, as a consequence, many were unable to escape poverty and even destitution.

Central to the history of women's rights is control over their bodies. One of the first modern women's rights campaigns was for the basic right to walk at night without fear of harassment or arrest. From 1869, Josephine Butler led the Ladies' National Association for the Repeal of the Contagious Diseases Acts. This was to campaign against legislation passed by Parliament between 1864 and 1869 that aimed to control the spread of venereal disease in the armed forces, by allowing the arrest of any woman suspected of being a prostitute in a port town. Doctors would then physically inspect these women for signs of sexually transmitted disease. Men were not similarly arrested or inspected, and the campaign focused on this inequality. In 1870, Butler told the Royal Commission on contagious diseases, 'Let your laws be put in force but let them be for male as well as female'. The debate laid bare how male representatives, elected only by men, legalised the medical 'rape' of women. The legislation was not repealed until 1886.

Women also had to fight for the right to safe childbirth and support through pregnancy. After gaining hard-won entrance to the medical profession, women challenged the medical neglect of the study of obstetrics and gynaecology in Britain. In 1898, Elizabeth Garrett Anderson – who in 1865 became the first female doctor to qualify in England – pointed out that the 'risk to a particular woman' is 'measured by the conditions immediately around her, and mainly by the skill and by the antiseptic zeal of those in attendance on her'.[1] She wrote this at a time when infant mortality was beginning to fall, but there was no correlating decrease in maternal mortality until the 1930s.[2]

There were pioneers such as Dr Annie McCall, who opened the Clapham Maternity Hospital in 1889, staffed by and to train women. Supported by leading figures in the female suffrage movement, McCall made it her life's work to put 'the absolute needs of the expectant woman first'.[3] Ann Oakley, herself a pioneer in the study of women's experience of childbirth in the 1970s, has pointed out that 'Annie McCall's achievements are completely absent from standard narratives of pregnancy care'.[4] McCall's charitable hospital provided quality maternity care along with, unusually for the period, antenatal guidance and postnatal care for some of the poorest women in South London.

The Co-operative Women's Guild was founded in 1883 (as the Women's League for the Spread of Co-operation, changing its name the following year).[5] It developed under the direction of Margaret Llewelyn Davies into a campaigning group with 52,000 members by the time it published *Maternity: Letters from Working Women* in 1915.[6] The 348 letters included in that book were written in response to a 1914 parliamentary report on the provision of a maternity benefit and antenatal care. The first edition sold out within three months. The letters are a vivid insight into the conditions in which working-class women gave birth, and the impact on them of almost constant pregnancy. The writer of Letter 100, for example, described herself as 'a wreck at 30' after seven children and one miscarriage over eleven years.

Llewelyn Davies and other social reformers used these letters as proof of the horrendous environment in which women laboured, bore and brought up children. In part, they were fighting the idea that inheritance, or 'nature', was solely to blame for the conditions in which they lived and so it would therefore make no difference to improve their environment, for example by maternity allowances. The Maternity and Child Welfare Act was finally passed in 1918, the same year that some women gained

Body: Autonomy

the vote in parliamentary elections. It expanded provision by local authorities for maternity clinics and district midwives. But provision was not mandatory and still relied on voluntary and charitable institutions.

The rights to not have children and to decide when and how many to have are related to medical and technological developments as well

as political freedom. There was some understanding of contraceptive methods in the nineteenth century: the first birth control clinic was opened in Holland in 1882, and a cervical (or 'Dutch') cap invented there soon after. Contraceptive devices, such as caps or condoms, improved with developments in the production of rubber products. Dr Marie Stopes published the bestselling *Married Love* about sexual pleasure in 1918, and the handbook to contraception *Wise Parenthood* soon after. Keen to ensure that her message reached women unlikely to afford or have access to such books, Stopes also wrote a pamphlet, *A Letter to Working Mothers,* in 1919.[7] In this she gave instructions on how to use a cervical cap (with a clear diagram) as well as warning against the perils (and criminality) of abortion.

The politics of reproduction have always been related to economics and the social constructions of class, disability and race. Stopes' promotion of birth control was linked to her desire to prevent what was seen by some as 'racial degeneration'. Here she was influenced by eugenics, which had been defined in 1883 by Francis Galton to describe the science of breeding human beings with intelligence or other assumed desirable characteristics. Many progressive thinkers of the period engaged with eugenic ideas, and Stopes' engagement with it underlines how feminism could be entangled with racism and classism at certain points. Eugenic ideas were used in reproductive politics to determine who should and who should not have children. Although the horrific use of eugenics by the Nazis to sterilise and then exterminate those they believed to be unfit is, rightly, the most known example, women deemed unfit were also sterilised in Sweden, America and elsewhere. The cervical cap that Stopes designed was even called the 'Racial Occlusive Cap', which she promoted at the birth control clinic she opened on Holloway Road in London, the first in England, in 1921. Both Stopes and Dr Norman Haire, who ran the Malthusian League's birth control clinic a few years later, recorded and shared information on what contraception worked best. It is clear from their ideological support of and by eugenicists and the Malthusian League, however, that their clinics were as much to do with population control as freedom for women.

In 1918, Lettice Fisher founded the National Council for the Unmarried Mother and her Child (NCUMC). Unmarried mothers suffered not only profound social stigma but also state discrimination, as they were not entitled to maternity benefits until 1930. In her polemic *Save the Mothers*, Sylvia Pankhurst, herself an unmarried mother after having a baby at the age of 45 in 1927, pointed out that infant and maternal mortality could be five times higher among unmarried mothers.[8] Pankhurst supplied examples of mothers she knew who had been turned

Below: Marie Stopes' birth control clinic, in a caravan.

Opposite: 'Prorace' brand of cervical cap designed and promoted by Dr Marie Stopes. The name of this trademarked cap was connected to Stopes' belief in eugenics.

away from charitable, particularly religious, hospitals because they were unmarried. Dr Annie McCall was rare in prioritising the care of unmarried mothers, and caused controversy by placing them in the same wards as married women at her Clapham hospital.

The creation of the National Health Service (NHS) in 1948 meant equal provision of maternity care to mothers. Yet 'backstreet' abortion remained common due to the continuing 'shame' of being a single mother. If a husband left, single married mothers were also stigmatised and suffered financially. Women were also assumed to still need the support of a husband, so in the 1966 TV drama *Cathy Come Home* Cathy needs to be single to enter a shelter for herself and her children. Single mothers were often socially isolated. In 1970, Tessa Fothergill set up the support group Gingerbread for single parents, an action in line with the broader objectives of the Women's Liberation Movement.[9] Social attitudes have improved since, but single-parent families are still more likely to be in poverty and lack robust support networks.

Contraception was available only to married women through the NHS until the Family Planning Act 1967. Although the contraceptive pill made birth control easier, its side effects on women were not taken seriously – a point that magazine *Spare Rib* made in its parody article 'Breakthrough in Male Contraception' with a sub-heading 'Scrotal infection, only 2 died'.[10] Barrier methods, such as the cap, were advocated by many feminists as allowing women greater control and knowledge of their body.

Body: Autonomy

Above: How to Run a Self-Help Group, 2006. Pamphlet produced by the Single Parent Action Network.

Below: Oral contraceptive pills became available in the UK on the NHS in 1961, for married women only. This changed in 1967, when family planning clinics were permitted to prescribe single women with the pill.

Opposite: Sylvia Pankhurst with her son Richard, 1928.

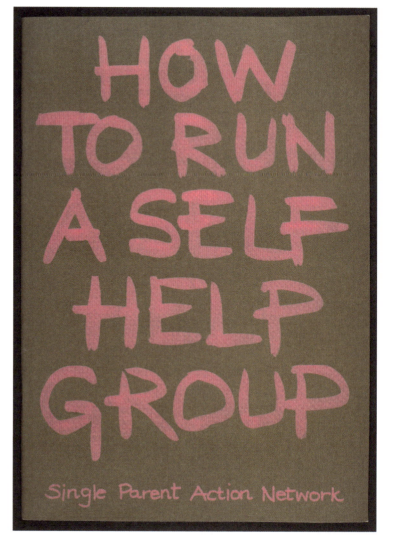

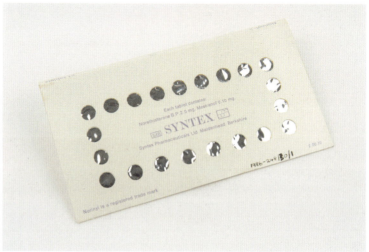

Unfinished Business

Body: Autonomy

NOW FOR NORTHERN IRELAND

Now for Northern Ireland is a campaign lead by bpas which brought together a coalition of organisations to successfully secure the decriminalisation of abortion in Northern Ireland. Bpas, a charity which sees more than 80,000 women a year for healthcare services at clinics across the UK, launched the campaign in October 2018 following decades of work by activists, charities and medical professionals in Northern Ireland and Great Britain. Bpas supports and advocates for reproductive choice – from contraception to infant feeding – and has led successful campaigns to reduce the cost of emergency contraception and allow the home use of abortion medication.

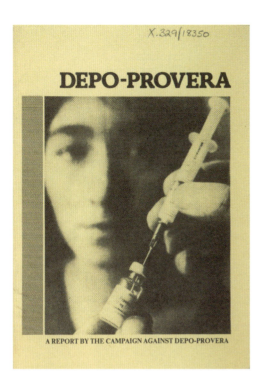

'Ban the Jab' leaflet from 1983 campaigning against the contraceptive Depo-Provera, which was disproportionately given to black and working-class women, sometimes without their consent.

Reproductive justice is not just about giving women the choice not to conceive, but also supporting the right to have children. Many women, especially those from lower socio-economic backgrounds, ethnic minorities and with disabilities, have their choices restricted, including by being coerced into longer-term contraceptive injections such as Depo-Provera. The politics of population control, as discussed in relation to Marie Stopes earlier, is fraught with such histories. It has only been as women's movements have joined across race, region, class and disability that a more complex understanding of reproductive justice has been forged. Rowena Arshad's discovery, while working for Scottish Education Action for Development in the 1980s, that Depo-Provera was being administered to women in a poor area in Scotland is a case in point. Knowing that the drug was simultaneously being promoted to Indian women, she encouraged wonderful solidarity between two groups normally divided by class, race and geography.[11]

The Abortion Act 1967 – still largely in force today – allows women in England, Wales and Scotland to have a pregnancy termination at up to twenty-eight weeks' gestation (revised to twenty-four weeks in 1990) if two doctors agree that the pregnancy would harm the woman's physical and/or mental health. Access to safe and legal abortion was a central issue of the British Women's Liberation Movement. Almost immediately, the 1967 Act was threatened by amendments and alterations. The National Abortion Campaign was formed from various women's groups in 1975 and ran the 'A woman's right to choose' campaign by grassroots groups on a local and national level.

The 1967 Act did not include Northern Ireland, where, until 2019, abortion remained illegal with a threat of life imprisonment, even for pregnancies as a result of rape and incest. The positive referendum vote to allow abortion at up to twelve weeks' gestation (and longer when the mother's life is at risk) in the Republic of Ireland in May 2018 exposed reproductive inequality in Northern Ireland. A few months before this public vote in Ireland, the United Nations human rights body found that the UK violated women's rights by restricting access to abortion in Northern Ireland.

The birth of a live baby by in vitro fertilisation (IVF) in 1978 radically changed how children could be conceived, and placed medical technology at the heart of reproductive politics. As well as giving hope to heterosexual couples struggling with infertility, IVF meant that women in same-sex couples or single women wanting to have a baby would eventually have an easier and more reliable method of using donor sperm. Some trans men have made the decision to become pregnant and have a child before or instead of fully transitioning.[12] As Donna Haraway has pointed out, feminist technoscience needs to consider freedom and justice across race and indeed species, in an age of environmental catastrophe; Ruha Benjamin brings together the politics of Black Lives Matter in thinking through how to 'cultivate kinfulness as reproductive justice'.[13] IVF comes at a huge financial (and emotional) cost, and across the country there is different access to fertility treatment due to differing guidelines laid down by regional healthcare trusts in the UK. This in turn reflects the disparities in reproductive health, particularly for the poorest. In 2017 infant mortality

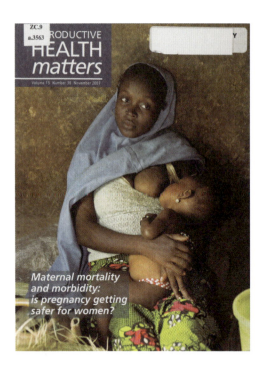

Marge Berer founded the journal *Reproductive Health Matters* with TK Sundari Ravindran in 1993 to publish research that centred around women's needs, experiences and voices. Importantly the journal used in-country peer reviewers and mentored authors so that regional contexts were included.

in the UK was 3.9 deaths per 1,000 live births, but with 5.2 per 1,000 live births in the most deprived areas compared to 2.7 in the least deprived.[14]

For women, asserting bodily autonomy has not been limited to reproductive choice. Women have often been subject to physical and sexual violence from men, and this has also been a focus of feminist campaigning from the nineteenth century onwards. In the 1800s women's rights in marriage were extremely limited, and legal and social change was slow. Anne Brontë's *The Tenant of Wildfell Hall* (1848) is a vivid account of the extreme cruelty and abuse that a woman could legally suffer at the hands of her husband. Brontë was influenced by the plight of fellow writer Caroline Norton a decade earlier, whose husband beat her so badly that she miscarried and then did not allow her to see their children. Norton campaigned for the Custody of Infants Act 1839, which gave mothers custody rights to children under 7 years old and access rights to older children. The abused wife in *Tenant* changed her name and lived in secrecy with her child, using her work as an artist to support them both. Artist Emily Mary Osborn drew on the precariousness of art as a profession for women in her painting *Nameless and Friendless*, which depicts a female artist avoiding the 'sexualised stares' of the 'predatory vision of men about town' as a dealer inspects her work.[15] It was exhibited at the Royal Academy in 1857, the same year that women first received the legal ability to seek a divorce or nullification of marriage.

Despite such early initiatives, domestic abuse over the nineteenth and early twentieth centuries was rarely spoken of, and there was little provision for women subjected to sexual, physical and emotional violence in the home. The Women's Liberation Movement in the early 1970s saw this as a key element of patriarchal control. The right to a life free from violence thus became a major demand. In 1971, Erin Pizzey established Chiswick Women's Aid (now Refuge) as a safe haven for women, and Women's Aid networks were soon established across the four nations of the UK.

Alongside this vital network, Southall Black Sisters (SBS) was established in 1979 to meet the needs of Asian and African-Caribbean women and to highlight and challenge all forms of gender-related violence. With their inclusive, imaginative campaigning, SBS embraced the notion of intersectionality long before the concept was popular. Their first major campaign in 1984 was motivated by the suicide of Krishna Sharma after years of domestic abuse. SBS protested at the inquest and organised a march to the house of Sharma's abuser, reversing and challenging traditional notions of shame, dishonour and abuse. In 1989, in the light of increasing religious fundamentalism and the growth of ultra-conservative movements across the world, SBS worked across religious divides and set up Women Against Fundamentalism. In the 1990s, in a landmark case, SBS secured Kiranjit Ahluwalia's freedom after her conviction for murdering her husband was overturned on appeal on the basis of the years of domestic abuse she had endured. SBS continues to campaign for women's rights and has been the inspiration for generations of feminist campaigners and activists seeking to work across race, gender and class divides, and to put an end to gender violence. Organisations like SBS and Women's Aid are constantly pushing for

Right: The Lesbian Custody Charter, produced in the 1980s, outlined the prejudice lesbians faced and insisted on their parental rights. At the 1974 National Women's Liberation Movement Conference in Edinburgh, the 'Sixth Demand', arguing for 'The right to a self-defined sexuality – an end to discrimination against lesbians', was passed. From that point on, the national conferences were women-only. Social attitudes took a long time to change. Action for Lesbian Parents was founded in 1975 after three high-profile custody cases where lesbians were refused custody of their children.

Below: Nameless and Friendless by Emily Mary Osborn, 1857.

LESBIAN CUSTODY CHARTER

1. **An end to discrimination against lesbian mothers**

   Many lesbians are mothers and we all live with the threat of losing custody of our children solely on the grounds of our sexuality.

2. **An end to the additional discrimination faced by lesbian mothers as a result of racial discrimination**

   The racism of the legal system operates to discriminate against black and ethnic minority lesbian mothers. Also, some lesbian mothers are discriminated against by racist and sexist immigration and nationality laws and practices.

3. **An end to the additional discrimination faced by lesbian mothers who are working class**

   Working class lesbian mothers face extra discrimination because of the anti-working class attitudes of judges and lawyers. Also many do not have the middle class privileges of education, language, connections and finances.

4. **An end to the additional discrimination faced by lesbian mothers as a result of disability**

   At present, lesbian mothers are treated as though they are incompetent and unable to care for children because they have a disability.

5. **An end to lesbian mothers' enforced separation from their children**

   Courts frequently deny lesbian mothers custody and access rights and give custody to fathers wo may have had little or no involvement in the children's upbringing. Judges have threatened to put children into local authority care rather than leave them with their lesbian mothers.

6. **An end to the enforced separation of children from their lesbian mothers**

   The stated desire of children to live with their lesbian mothers is often discounted.

7. **No conditions on a lesbian mother's custody or access rights**

   Lesbian mothers who are awarded custody or access often have very restrictive conditions imposed on them. For example, lesbian mothers have been told that they must not let their children see their lover. Often supervision orders are placed on lesbian mothers whereby the Social Services keep watch over a mother's behaviour and lifestyle.

8. **Lesbians should have the same rights as heterosexuals to foster and adopt**

   Local authorities should welcome lesbians as adoptive or foster parents. They should make statements in support of lesbians caring for and having custody of children.
   Young lesbians should have the option of requesting a placement with a lesbian mother.

9. **Lesbian co-parents should not be denied custody or access rights on the grounds of their sexuality**

   At the moment lesbians bringing up children with their lovers or involved in shared childcare are denied custody by the courts, for example, should the biological mother die. Lesbian lovers and co-parents are also discriminated against by the courts refusing them any contact with children they have been living with/caring for.

10. **An end to the myth of the normal family**

    It is time that the courts and social services recognised that there are many varied forms of family structures and that the nuclear family (mother, father and 2.3 children living together) is no longer the 'norm', nor is it necessarily 'in the best interests of the child/ren'.

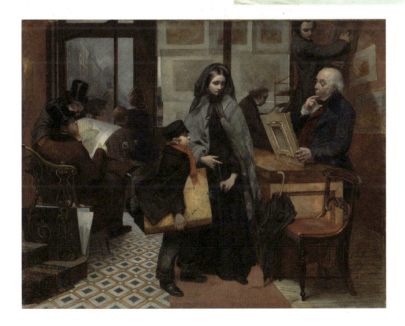

Body: Autonomy

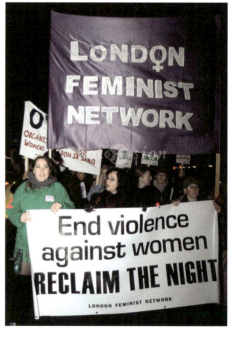

Opposite, below right: Women on a Reclaim the Night march, London, 2006.

Opposite, above and below left: Banners for Southall Black Sisters designed by Shakila Taranum Maan. The top banner was designed for the anti-Trump protest of 2018.

greater protection of women from different forms of abusive behaviour in domestic relationships, such as coercive control, which was criminalised in England and Wales in 2015.

Despite all these efforts, however, marital rape was not made illegal in the UK until 1991 and women are around twice as likely to experience domestic abuse than men.[16] Arguably this reflects the inequity over control, freedom and justice for women's bodies so vividly exposed in the Contagious Diseases Acts of the 1860s. These battles are not merely historical. In the tradition of feminist 'Reclaim the Night' marches, launched in 1977 in response to the so-called 'Yorkshire Ripper' murders, a 'Reclaim the Park' march took place on 28 June 2019 in London's South Norwood Country Park after several sex attacks there. The fight for women to have control over their own bodies continues.

---

1. Elizabeth Garrett Anderson, 'Letter: Deaths in Childbirth', *British Medical Journal*, 17 September 1898, pp. 839–40.
2. Irvine Loudon, *Death in Childbirth: An International Study of Maternal Care and Maternal Mortality 1800–1950* (Oxford: Oxford University Press, 1992) p. 15.
3. Patricia Barrass, *Fifty Years of Midwifery: The Story of Annie McCall M.D.* (London: Health For All Publishing Co., 1950).
4. Ann Oakley, *Women, Peace and Welfare: A Suppressed History of Social Reform, 1880–1920* (Bristol: Policy Press, 2018), p. 224.
5. The organisation was briefly known as the Women's Co-operative Guild before becoming the Co-operative Women's Guild.
6. M. Llewelyn Davies (ed.), *Maternity: Letters from Working Women* (London: Virago, 1915, repr. 1978).
7. Marie Carmichael Stopes, *A Letter to Working Mothers on How to Have Healthy Children and Avoid Weakening Pregnancies* (London: H. Fielding Science Library, 1919).
8. E. Sylvia Pankhurst, *Save the Mothers* (London: Alfred A. Knopff, 1930), p. 115.
9. This merged with the National Council for the Unmarried Mother and her Child to form Gingerbread in 2007.
10. 'Breakthrough in Male Contraception', *Spare Rib*, 93, April 1980.
11. Rowena Arshad interviewed by Rachel Cohen, Sisterhood and After: The Women's Liberation Oral History Project, 2010–13. British Library Sound & Moving Image Catalogue reference C1420/21, transcript p. 73/track 02. © The British Library and The University of Sussex.
12. The film *Seahorse* follows the journey of Freddy McConnell as he has a baby. *Seahorse*, 2019, directed by Jeane Finlay.
13. Donna J. Haraway, 'The Virtual Speculum in the New World Order', *Feminist Review*, 55, 1997, p.48; Ruha Benjamin, 'Black AfterLives Matter: Cultivating Kinfulness as Reproductive Justice', *Boston Review. A Political and Literary Forum*, 2018, http://bostonreview.net/race/ruha-benjamin-black-afterlives-matter [accessed 15 August 2019].
14. Office of National Statistics, *Child and Infant Mortality in England and Wales: 2017. Stillbirths, infant and childhood deaths occurring annually in England and Wales, and associated risk factors*. https://www.ons.gov.uk/peoplepopulationandcommunity/birthsdeathsandmarriages/deaths/bulletins/childhoodinfantandperinatalmortalityinenglandandwales/2017#increase-in-the-infant-mortality-rate-in-england-and-wales-in-2017 [accessed 30 June 2019].
15. Deborah Cherry, 'Going Places: Women Artists in Central London in the Mid-Nineteenth Century', *The London Journal*, 28(1), 2003, pp. 90–1.
16. According to a 2018 Office of National Statistics report, an estimated 1.3 million females reported being victims of domestic abuse as compared to 695,000 male victims (https://www.ons.gov.uk/peoplepopulationandcommunity/crimeandjustice/bulletins/domesticabuseinenglandandwales/yearendingmarch2018).

Body: Autonomy

Liberating Pleasure

— DR ZOE STRIMPEL

Handbill distributed ahead of a talk about repealing the Contagious Diseases Act by campaigner Josephine Butler, during the 1872 Pontefract by-election.

Throughout the modern period and in most cultures, women's sexuality has been subject to close regulation. Efforts to control or deny it greatly intensified in the nineteenth century, as the ideology of separate gendered spheres emerged, producing the 'Angel in the House' ideal of womanhood (see Cox in this volume). The assumption of virtuous disinterest that defined ideas of respectable Christian feminine sexuality during the reign of Queen Victoria had been substantially fractured by the end of the First World War. But the urge to corral women's sexual desire into the respectable pen of matrimony continued for decades. By the 1970s women had had enough, and retaking control over our own bodies and desires was one of the great motors of the Women's Liberation Movement.

Victorian anxieties about carnality stemmed from deeply held, Christian ideas about the gender order. Women were divided into wives and mother figures and 'fallen' women – prostitutes, the promiscuous, or unwed mothers. On one hand women were assumed to have low or non-existent libidos, an anatomy supplied for the purposes of dutiful wifehood only (although until the end of the nineteenth century female orgasm was thought necessary for conception to take place). On the other hand, female sexuality was seen as so powerful it could destroy society as well as 'ruin' women should it go rogue and escape the bounds of conjugality or chaste spinsterhood. Life was made as hard as possible for single mothers, the promiscuous and prostitutes, while men involved in illicit sexual activities could far more easily slip from censure.

Starkly visible around prostitution, this sexual double standard provoked a surge of feminist action in Britain. The Contagious Diseases Acts of the 1860s subjected prostitutes rather than their clients to humiliating physical interrogations and arrest. Campaigners led by Josephine Butler worked tirelessly for their repeal and won out in the 1880s. Butler and her allies had a sexually conservative agenda: their aim was to purify, not liberate, women's sexual relations with men. But they had succeeded in bringing, for the first time, an unflinchingly gendered vision of sexuality into the public domain.

From the 1880s, a set of bohemians, utopians, New Women and radical medics began to consider sex in new, psychologically inflected ways, working within the new field of sexology. Havelock Ellis, whose *Sexual Inversion* (1896) was the first English textbook about homosexuality, also explained women's desire as an agentic force in its own right in essays such as 'The Erotic Rights of Women, and the Objects of Marriage' (1918).[1] In 'The Play-Function of Sex' (1921), he lamented marital neglect of women's pleasure and described the profound psychological and spiritual potential of women's erotic awakening.[2]

Although the late nineteenth century saw a major upsurge in new ways of thinking about female sexuality, women were still expected to keep their desires firmly within the bounds of (heterosexual) class-appropriate marriage. The price for trying to do otherwise was steep and violent. Edith Lanchester, a middle-class, self-declared New Woman with an honours degree from London University, learned this the hard way. In 1895, she decided to live openly with her lover, a railway clerk and socialist comrade called James Sullivan. The decision so shocked her family that they forced her to be examined by a doctor who deemed her insane, as evidenced by choosing to commit social suicide with a free union. The cause of her insanity, her father said, was over-education. Meanwhile Sullivan's lower station in life added considerably to Edith's

Below: Edith Lanchester, committed to a lunatic asylum for living openly with her lover outside of marriage, 1895.

Opposite: Nineteenth-century ivory dildo purchased at auction in Paris by Samantha Roddick, founder of the sex-positive erotica shop Coco de Mer. It is unclear whether this object was designed to be used by women for their own gratification, or for the gratification of men, or both. Either way, it certainly raises the possibility of catering to women's sexual desire.

crime. As the doctor who deemed her insane described the case in the *British Medical Journal*, Edith had intended to 'live in illicit intercourse with a man in a station of life much below her own'.[3] Asked by her father if she would marry Sullivan, she replied she would not, and that marriage was immoral. He responded by pinioning her arms to her sides with a rope, dragging her into a carriage and shipping her off to a private lunatic asylum in Roehampton. But a successful publicity campaign waged by her supporters meant that three days later she was released and went to live with Sullivan, never seeing her father again.

The sometimes terrible pressures on women to suppress and conform disfigured the sexual landscape for many – especially those who fell outside the matrimonial norms. Nonetheless there could be astonishing pleasure for women, including self-pleasure, in marital sex. Evidence of sexual pleasure – and particularly female sexual pleasure – is harder for historians to recover than evidence of pain or pathology.[4] Yet objects such as an ivory nineteenth-century dildo demonstrate the existence of a market in luxury goods which may well have been for female sensual delight. In 2017 an ivory dildo surfaced in County Meath, Ireland, which had been carved in China from the tusk of an Indian elephant and was a gift from a husband to a wife in 1843.

Letters like that of Emma Roe to her husband Alfred, a Presbyterian minister on the American East Coast, show how openly and fully women's sexual desire could be expressed within marriage in the nineteenth century. A religious pair who chose to see their erotic co-fixation as godly, they exchanged erotic letters while Alfred was travelling for work. For Emma,

Unfinished Business

Below: Peg's Paper was published from 1919 to 1940, and contained fictional romance, news about film stars, letters and even fortune-telling. It was one of the first women's magazines aimed at working-class female readers.

Opposite: Throughout much of the nineteenth and twentieth centuries, boys and girls were subjected to a sexual double standard. In this 1979 edition of the *Mother's Union* magazine for teenagers, girls were warned that sexual encounters would lead to physical, social and psychological crisis. Boys, by contrast, were simply warned that sex with a girl under the age of 16 is illegal. The notion of mutual and informed consent, and the recognition that girls and boys should be equally informed about sex, are relatively recent.

reproduction, sexual pleasure and love all went together in a blaze of glory. Of nursing their baby, she wrote: 'As I lie awake with her at my breast I think of you. Sometimes if I remember the exciting letters you have lately written – or imagine what our pleasure shall be when side by side again I get so excited …'[5] The pair sustained a long, reproductive and sexually recreative marriage through the frequent exchange of erotic letters.

Economic upheaval in the early twentieth century saw the emergence of new outlets for women's desire. Young women were finding new sources of income through careers in offices and schools. A huge market in novels, magazines and penny papers written by women for women sprang up to serve them, exploring and extolling erotic and romantic fantasy in a range of exotic contexts. From the 1920s cinema offered a new array of heart-throbs, such as Rudolph Valentino in *The Sheik* (1921) and Douglas Fairbanks in *The Thief of Bagdad* (1924). Onlookers fretted about the corruption of young women and courtship in the early twentieth century at the hands of 'the shopgirl romance' but could do little. The new generation of young working women would 'pop a book into a bag to read on the way to work, by train or omnibus', helped along by the launch of new circulating libraries.[6] WH Smith had introduced bookstalls into railways stations in the late nineteenth century, Boots druggists launched a library service in 1898, and Mills & Boon was founded in 1908, although the specialisation in romantic novels did not come until the 1930s.

Interwar and mid-twentieth-century women's romance offered a piquant mixture of the erotic and the traditional. Mills & Boon novels promoted a traditional picture of marriage to a rich 'prince charming' who would relieve the hard-working, penny-pinched young woman of life's cares, but also demonstrated the cultural ascendancy of female desire. In contrast to the remarkably disembodied romantic heroes of Victorian leading gentlemen (Heathcliff notwithstanding), these were hunks with 'lean, muscular-looking arms'.[7] The romantic narratives that poured from novels, newspapers such as *Peg's Paper* and silent films with smouldering heroes deftly responded to and stoked genuine erotic yearning – clichéd and sometimes offensive in their treatment of Arabian or other imperialist 'fantasy' settings though they seem in retrospect. Lustiness was articulated by a widening range of literate young women. Shopgirl Eva Slawson, on reading H. G. Wells' *The New Machiavelli* (1911) wrote of 'my most rampant moods, when nature thunders in me and almost demands expression of love and completion of the act …'[8]

The first decades of the twentieth century saw a growing insistence on the value of marital sex in which women enjoyed an equal share of pleasure. One of the most strident advocates of this was birth control campaigner Marie Stopes. In her 1918 bestseller *Married Love*, Stopes helped countless husbands to better understand and prioritise their wives' sexual responses. Stopes felt that limiting children among the working classes was an urgent social necessity, and saw that couples who learned to harness and enjoy sensual pleasure would be more inclined to control their fertility.

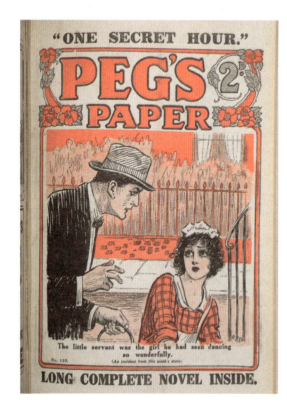

Unfinished Business

But while understandings of female pleasure in Britain were being revolutionised, the ideological framework remained steadfastly conservative. To Stopes, for instance, women's sexual desire was only to be gratified within marriage. Women who had sex outside of it were to be despised and discouraged and were addressed with hostility. Masturbation was permissible for 'women over 30, if they understand it is dangerous and control the use to not more than twice a month, it is sometimes beneficial'.[9] Stopes' partly progressive sexual vision was also very problematically entwined with eugenicist ideas of population purification, as Debbie Challis explains elsewhere in this volume. And despite having had female crushes herself when younger, lesbianism was a 'disease', and Stopes didn't reply to lesbians who wrote to her.[10]

In fact, lesbianism presented a double affront to late imperial British sensibilities. Not only was it a 'perversion' along with all homosexual love, but it took women's sexual economy outside of the reach and control of men. This rendered it politically explosive and psychologically vexing, manageable only when left in the shadows, or put down to close friendship at a time when female friends often shared beds, caressed and held hands. The publication in 1928 of Radclyffe Hall's *The Well of Loneliness* shattered any doubts about the intensity of woman-on-woman, and gender non-conforming desire. The thoughts of the public had suddenly come, in Virginia's Woolf's words, to 'centre on Sapphism', and the results were violent.[11] 'I would rather give a healthy boy or a healthy girl a phial of prussic acid than this novel', wrote James Douglas, editor of the *Sunday Express*. 'Poison kills the body but moral poison kills the soul.'[12] His view won out and the book was banned in Britain.

It would be decades before lesbianism would openly regain the centre ground through the feminist movement, which helped pave the way for a far more explicit, wide-ranging and this time critically acclaimed lesbian literary genre. Sarah Waters' award-winning bestseller *Tipping the Velvet* (1998), her first novel, is set in the Victorian period and describes – in the style of erotic memoirs of the late nineteenth century – the romps between a working-class ingénue and a cross-dressing woman in the streets of London.

The no-holds-barred, vibrant queer cultural landscape epitomised by Waters' novels flourished in part thanks to the work of the Women's Liberation Movement in the 1970s and 1980s. The WLM recognised the immense political importance and personal promise of same-sex female desire, and from the early 1970s lesbianism became a battleground in the movement's fight for bodily autonomy. Debates over the place and purpose of political lesbianism – a choice-led revolt against patriarchy and the phallus – coexisted with a wave of previously straight-acting women discovering, exploring and committing to newfound genuine attraction to other women.

Below: Front covers of *Our Bodies Ourselves*, from editions published all over the world.

Opposite: Tipping the Velvet was adapted into a BBC television series in 2002, starring Rachael Stirling as Nan and Keeley Hawes as Kitty.

The Women's Liberation Movement unleashed women's desire in other ways too, joining with a range of sexual rights movements to define protest around pleasure, fun and excitement as much as suffering, from kiss-ins to wheelchair discos. Sometimes the frisson of political rage produced unexpected erotic outcomes. Jo Robinson recalled waiting for hours outside Claridge's to protest against Richard Nixon and then missing him. 'I went home and I was so furious, I was so angry, that I masturbated with real anger and had a fantastic orgasm for the first time in my life.'[13]

The WLM's project of liberating women's desires by liberating their bodies required nothing short of a revolution in physiological self-knowledge. Key to this revolution was the publication of *Our Bodies Ourselves* (first edition 1971), which emerged from meetings of the Boston Women's Health Book Collective in the 1960s. The book evolved through a process of information-gathering, experience and discussion papers, and an ethos that 'validated women's embodied experiences as a resource for challenging medical dogmas ... and, consequently, as a strategy for personal and collective empowerment'.[14] Accessible and warm, OBOS was an immediate success, and would go on to sell millions of copies and local versions, including the UK's 1978 edition by Angela Phillips and Jill Rakusen.[15] OBOS offered not only granular detail about women's genitals, but instructions on how to explore them. Guided by the spirit of OBOS, self-examination groups flourished within the global women's health movement. Participants would use speculums to look closely at their own and each other's vaginas and cervixes. Self-examination was about improving both sexual as well as physical well-being and understanding, including helping those who had never or struggled to achieve orgasm. In Britain, the feminist magazine *Spare Rib* oversaw the first 'pre-orgasmic' group in Britain in 1976 to help women who had never orgasmed to explore their own sexual response in a feminist setting.

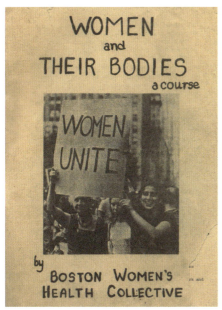

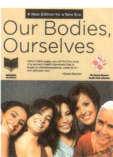

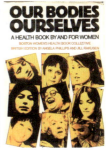

Body: Autonomy

83

Opposite: Towards a pro-consent revolution, 2014, explains in a clear and direct way how to ask for consent. It sees consent as fundamental to honest and respectful communication. Campaigners want to extend teaching about consent to equip young people with the skills to negotiate sexual relationships, to counter myths about rape and to aim for a world where no one has to experience sexual violence.

Since being granted the vote in 1918 and then 1928, women have been repeatedly asked what it is they still want. Today, the answer still pertains to women's right to enjoy and experience their bodies and sex without coercion, violence or disrespect. In particular, new and vibrant feminisms are demanding an end to widespread sexual harassment, assault and liberties taken in the bedroom. Consent has therefore become a major battleground. The #MeToo movement has sharpened contemporary feminist calls for enthusiastic consent, and highlighted, through harrowing stories, that not being able to say 'no' doesn't mean yes. Commitment to the right to safe sex and to bodily autonomy has coalesced into new crowdfunded initiatives to end sexism everywhere from the bedroom to the street to the classroom. Homemade, colourful zines like Carro Berry's *Towards a Pro-Consent Revolution*, funded by Patreon, creatively and frankly discuss 'rapes, rape culture, sexual abuse/assault/harassment, stalking and other unpleasant and violent situations'. Level Up, a feminist organisation, also used crowdfunding to raise £75,000 to launch in January 2018. It's one of many new digital campaigns against harassment, sexist representations of women in the media and more. Level Up's commitment to intersectionality reflects the new feminist paradigm: at its core is the conviction that women's experience of sexism and embodiment will be shaped by race, sexual identity, class and other vectors of oppression.

Women's sexuality in Britain is no longer governed by strict rules of family morality and compulsory heterosexuality. The untethering of sex from reproduction, marriage and love over the course of the twentieth century has been profoundly freeing. But as every generation of women has found, with new freedoms come new attempts to curtail. As #MeToo demonstrated, violence and coercion remain a threat to women's right to pleasure, while also showing just how forcefully a digitally enabled global army of women can fight back.

---

1   Havelock Ellis, *Studies in the Psychology of Sex (Vol 2): Sexual Inversion* (London: Wilson & MacMillan, 1897); Havelock Ellis, *The Erotic Rights of Women, and the Objects of Marriage* (London: 1918).

2   Havelock Ellis, *The Play-Function of Sex* (London: 1921).

3   *British Medical Journal*, 2 November 1895, p. 1,127.

4   Peter Gay, *The Bourgeois Experience: Victoria to Freud, Vol.2, The Tender Passion* (Oxford: OUP, 1986), p. 119.

5   Ibid. p. 130.

6   Carol Dyhouse, *Heartthrobs: A History of Women and Desire* (Oxford: OUP 2017) pp. 3 and 17; Selina Todd, *Young Women, Work, and Family in England 1918-1950* (Oxford: OUP, 2005).

7   *Little Brown Girl* (1949), cited in Joseph McAleer, *Passion's Fortune: The Story of Mills & Boon* (Oxford: OUP, 1999), p. 152.

8   *Dear Girl: The Diaries and Letters of Two Working Women, 1897–1917*, in Thomson, T. (ed) p. 175, cited in Dyhouse, p. 16

9   Ruth Hall, *Dear Dr Stopes: Sex in the 1920s* (London: Andre Deutsch, 1978), p. 175, cited in Katherine Holden (2002) '"Nature Takes No Notice of Morality": Singleness and Married Love in Interwar Britain', *Women's History Review*, vol. 11, no. 3, p. 491.

10   Ibid., p. 496.

11   Charlotte Knight, *Defending The Well of Loneliness*, [https://www.penguin.co.uk/articles/2016/defending-the-well-of-loneliness, accessed 22 September 2019].

12   'A Book That Must Be Suppressed', *Sunday Express*, 19 August 1928.

13   Jo Robinson interviewed by Polly Russell, Sisterhood and After: The Women's Liberation Oral History Project, 2010–2013. British Library Sound & Moving Image Catalogue reference C1420/43, transcript p. 90/track 6. © The British Library and The University of Sussex.

14   Kathy Davis, *The Making of Our Bodies Ourselves: How Feminism Travels Across Borders* (Raleigh: Duke University Press, 2006), p. 2.

15   Ibid., p. 2.

"hi there... would it be OK if i came & sat down next to you?"

"i would love you to!"

CONSENT?
☑ ASKED FOR
☑ GRANTED

I ♥ CONSENT

The best way to perfect asking for, as well as granting or refusing consent? PRACTICE... PRACTICE... PRACTICE... in time it will become second nature. It's also a good idea to learn to love & respect yourself. It is hard to know what consent means (let alone give & receive it) without first believing that we are worth being afforded the respect of consent.

So, if we can grasp how important it is to gain consent for even the smallest of actions, it should be blindingly obvious how essential it is during intimate & sexual encounters. Of course, while all consent is important, the consequences & ramifications of not obtaining it in such situations are multiplied; we're talking about people's bodies &, at times, their most intimate parts. We should be comfortable with what's happening at each moment & thus consent should be the basis for all such encounters.

REMEMBER: the only way to be sure anyone wants you to do anything is to ASK!

HOW CAN ANYONE BE EXPECTED TO KNOW ...WHAT YOU REALLY REALLY WANT... IF THEY DON'T ASK?

Throughout history women have been deemed to be intellectually inferior to men. This has impacted on the ways they have been educated and the extent to which they have been able to engage in public life, and has, in large part, determined what work they have done. Writing about the history of women and education, Laura Carter details how and why women's activism from the Enlightenment to the present day has often focused on access to education and the right to be educated equally with men. Ann Phoenix looks at education from a different perspective, considering how during the 1970s black feminist activists campaigned for better education for non-white children and established a powerful network of supplementary schools. These reflected the sometimes very different priorities that black and white women faced. Writing about the sphere of work, Pamela Cox reminds readers that contrary to myth, women have always worked – whether they have been paid or not – but have had to fight to gain entry to certain professions and have often been subject to discriminatory treatment. Struggles for women's emancipation, representation and expression, however, have often pitted the rights and freedoms of one group of women against another. Beyond work and education, Sumita Mukherjee details how suffragettes in the UK aligned themselves with imperial Britain, disregarding the oppression of their colonial sisters around the world, while Caitríona Beaumont examines women's struggles for political representation and the roles they have played in different aspects of public life.

— **DR POLLY RUSSELL**

MIND: EDUCATION

© Liz Mackie

'The **STRUGGLE TO SUCCEED** in **EDUCATION** and as **PROFESSIONALS** is set against well documented evidence of systemic institutional **GENDERED RACIST EXCLUSION.**'

HEIDI MIRZA (B.1958)
From '"Harvesting our collective intelligence": Black British feminism in post-race times' (2015)

Heidi Mirza is a British academic known for her pioneering research on race, gender and identity in education. She has an international reputation for championing equality and human rights for black and Muslim young people through educational reform.

Accessing Equal Education

— **DR LAURA CARTER**

Below: Photograph of crowds at Cambridge in 1897, protesting against women's petitions to get university degrees.

Opposite: Penny rocket firework thrown at women campaigning to be able to graduate from the University of Cambridge in 1897.

Women in Britain have long experienced a paradox in their relationship to education. Although greater access to education has underpinned almost every feminist claim, girls and women have always found education to be a simultaneously radical and conservative force in their lives. As much as acquiring new skills and knowledge has held the promise of advancement and equality, educational institutions have also worked to curtail and narrow women's ambitions, and to reproduce existing social orders of gender, class and race. The story of the place of education in women's lives in modern Britain is about the ongoing struggle to master and overcome this tension.

In the eighteenth century, arguments for women's education were associated with radical figures such as Mary Wollstonecraft (1759–97). In *A Vindication of the Rights of Woman* (1792), written in the aftermath of the French Revolution, Wollstonecraft criticised 'the custom of confining girls to their needle', thus 'narrowing their minds'. She argued for a national education system for girls and boys that would ultimately allow women to fulfil their roles as social and political citizens.[1] Her ideas were a product of Enlightenment thinking, which privileged reason acquired through education as a route to modernity.

Such radical thinking on female education was contradictory to the gender order of Victorian Britain, which strongly emphasised separate sex roles. But middle-class women's dominance of educational spheres at all levels by the mid-nineteenth century proved a decisive point of access to politics, especially as local government expanded across the late century. The 1870 Education Act created a national system of elementary education, administered by two thousand democratically elected local School Boards in England and Wales. Unusually, women were permitted to stand for these positions, and the period up to 1902 saw twenty-nine women elected to the London School Board alone.[2] The female presence on the School Boards injected women's experiences and perspectives into educational debates at the level of local politics.

The growing demand for schoolteachers from the 1870s, most of whom were women, expanded the provision and quality of professional training. From 1890 central government permitted the establishment of 'day training colleges' connected to higher education institutions. Trainee women teachers began populating the towns and campuses of universities

in greater numbers from the 1890s, stimulating broader campaigns for the opening up of higher education to women in Britain. This generated social and cultural tensions that pricked at the very heart of Victorian and Edwardian elite masculinities. The struggles at the ancient universities of Oxford and Cambridge epitomised these gender anxieties, where male students protested with unique pomp and hostility against women's petitions to become full, degree-taking members of the University.[3] Women were finally permitted to sit for degrees at the University of Oxford in 1920, but not until 1948 at the University of Cambridge.

Mind: Education

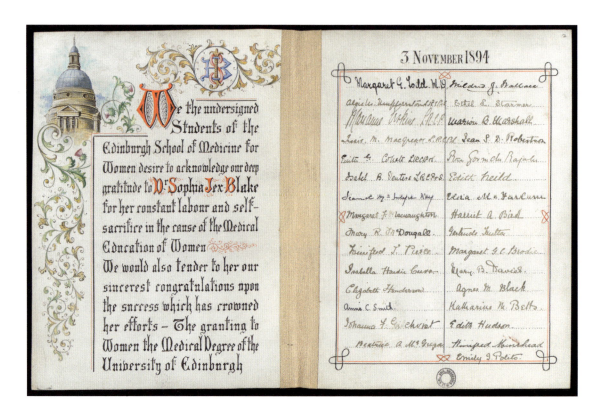

Other universities had allowed women to take degrees sooner, such as the University of London in 1878 and Owens College, Manchester in 1879. Yet these permissions, gradually granted, still contained exceptions when it came to giving women access to professional careers. Sophia Jex-Blake (1840–1912) led a campaign for women to be able to study medicine in Edinburgh. She recruited a group of women to sit the matriculation examination in 1869. Jex-Blake and her accomplices then fought throughout their degree to attend classes, clinical training and examinations, most of which were led by male lecturers who refused women students entry.[4]

Through such determined efforts, women became an unmistakable part of British university life, and by 1939 they accounted for 23 per cent of all students.[5] However, as the historian Carol Dyhouse has shown, their presence was still regarded as experimental by some in the interwar years.[6] Part of this precarity came down to the strategies women had used to circumvent the masculinised environment. They had carved out specific lectureships, scholarships and cultural spaces, such as halls of residence and women-only colleges, for themselves. These tactics left legacies that made the question of sex separation versus co-education an ongoing fault line in feminist educational thought.

University education was confined to a small proportion of middle-class women in the period before the Second World War. For most girls after 1880, when elementary education became compulsory up to the age of 10, formal schooling consisted of basic reading, writing and arithmetic. In addition, the period before the First World War saw an intensification in the teaching of domestic subjects to girls. As the apparatus of state education consolidated, working-class girls were more decisively instructed in practical subjects preparing them for work in domestic service, including cookery, needlework and laundry. Boys, meanwhile, were more likely to take algebra and mechanical subjects on top of basic literacy and numeracy.[7]

In fee-paying secondary schools, attended by middle-class girls, domestic subjects were re-conceptualised as 'domestic economy', which stressed the scientific aspects of cooking and cleaning. This positioned domesticity as a form of liberal, scientific education that also had a practical application, since even elite girls were deemed unlikely to have any use for physics or chemistry.[8] Underlying these efforts to extend and formalise domestic education for both working- and middle-class girls in the period up to the First World War were anxieties about national efficiency, racial purity and imperial power. Even as official estimations of the purpose of mass education widened into the twentieth century, the starkly gender-differentiated curricula that were established in this climate proved difficult to dislodge.

Although the 1918 Education Act established various routes to secondary education for the working classes, there was still a very poorly worked-out sense of what this might actually be for, beyond low-skilled work. Expert estimations of working-class intellectual capacities remained deeply gendered and raced on biological grounds, and were also informed by a growing reliance on educational psychology and cognitive testing.[9] Most girls therefore continued to receive a domestically inflected elementary education and to enter domestic service, agricultural or manufacturing jobs at the new minimum school-leaving age of 14 (or younger if they secured work earlier). Figures like the formidable Ellen Wilkinson (1891–1947), who was from an upper-working-class family, received a secondary education, and won a scholarship to study history at Manchester University in 1910, were very unusual.[10] Progressive reformers, including Fabian socialists and the Labour Party, instead endorsed adult education after 1918 as a way to overcome the limited provision of secondary education and to inculcate good citizenship values. For example, in 1920 Hillcroft Residential College for Working Women was established, offering female wage-earners 'the opportunity of spending a year in quiet study, free from economic pressure and family responsibilities'.[11]

Between the 1930s and the 1970s women's participation in higher education stagnated; the period saw no further improvement in the representation of women students in British universities. This was despite the fact that the 1944 Education Act ushered in compulsory, free secondary education. This mid-century malaise is sometimes attributed to a dearth of feminist activism, but it is better to see it as a result of a combination of labour market and societal factors, including the falling age of marriage.[12] For most of this period universities still seemed like a hostile, inaccessible place for young women, who would continue to face discrimination in professional workplaces, even if they did manage to obtain the degree that would open the doors to them. A 1962 *Guide to Careers in Medicine* published by the British Medical Association warned girls to expect to answer 'searching questions about the conflicting demands of marriage and a medical career' in their interviews for medical school.[13]

Primary education (age 5 to 11) after the Second World War underwent something of a gender revolution. In 1926, 52 per cent of 9-year-olds had been educated in co-educational schools; by 1965 the figure had risen to 97 per cent.[14] But co-education rarely meant gender parity in school culture; boys and girls often had separate playgrounds and separate craft lessons (needlework versus woodwork), and teaching materials were saturated with traditional gender roles.[15] Women teachers staffed the rank and file of primary teachers (although most headships still went to men). Perhaps because of this, girls tended to be more academically successful than boys at primary level, typically outperforming them in the 'eleven-plus' examination that determined which secondary school they would attend. But these gains didn't last long, as girls tended to fall behind over the course of secondary schooling.[16]

Most pupils still did not win a grammar school place via the 'eleven-plus', and so went to a secondary modern school, where structural and cultural factors combined to disadvantage young women. By 1962 there were over 810,000 girls at secondary modern schools in England and Wales, compared to just under 350,000 girls at grammar schools.[17] The same gender bias that had been established in late nineteenth-century mass education persisted in the secondary moderns. A close analysis in the early 1960s found that 31 per cent of the maths classes in girls' schools of this type were doing only arithmetic, compared to 12 per cent in co-educational schools and 10 per cent in single-sex boys' schools.[18] Girls were overall less likely to have access to school-leaving examinations, and more boys than girls stayed on beyond the compulsory school-leaving age of 15 before the 1970s. Yet, despite this short period of secondary education, most women born between the mid-1930s and the mid-1950s did achieve social mobility, by working their way up in the modern service sector, in clerical, retail and social work jobs.[19]

The postwar grammar schools were regarded as the best route to gender equality in education, since they offered more uniform curricula, the opportunity to take 'O' and 'A' levels, and maybe even access to higher education. Many of the women who became activists in the Women's Liberation Movement after 1968 followed this route, or a parallel one in girls' independent schools.[20] However, school culture could also incubate gender inequalities in the grammar schools. We especially see this in the case of the non-biological 'STEM' subjects. Boys were far more likely to study science than girls: in 1961 male leavers with 'A' levels had a total of 16,674 science passes, compared to 4,893 for girls.[21]

Opposite: Grateful students of the Edinburgh School of Medicine for Women presented Sophia Jex-Blake with this certificate in 1894 to honour her contribution to 'the cause of the Medical Education of Women [...and] the granting to Women the Medical Degree of the University of Edinburgh'.

PICTURE XXVIII.

BRIGHTENING.

UNNECESSARY—not needed.
BRIGHTENING—making bright.
PURCHASED—got for money.
RIDICULOUS—absurd.
PRESERVED—taken care of.
DIFFICULT—hard.
PRECEDING—going before.
VIGOROUS—energetic.

THIS is Thursday morning at Daisy Lawn, my dears—Ellen's brightening day. She is busy in her back kitchen, and you shall watch her. Her copper or furnace is filled with water, and a good fire burning under it, made up of small-coal and cinders. Jane had showed her how unnecessary it was to burn large coal in these furnaces after first lighting them, and Ellen was careful always to have a box full of small-coal near ready for consumption, to save all needless waste of the lumps.

Right: Photograph by Henry Grant of a 'Mothercraft' lesson held in Archway, 1964.

Below: Ladybird Keyword series book *Things We Do*, 1966. The series was launched in 1964 and taught generations of children how to read. It was criticised in the 1970s for the stereotyping gender roles. On this page, not only are gender stereotypes at play, but racial ones too – the little girl has a black doll which she will be using to act out her domestic duties. In updated editions women were shown going out to work, men sometimes helped in the home and the daughter wore jeans and was more active.

Opposite: Domestic Economy: Or, the Marshalfield Maidens and the Fairy Ordina by Mrs W. H. Wigley, 1874, is an example of the genre of domestic economy for girls in the late nineteenth century.

Mind: Education

Right: Front cover of *The Great Divide: The Sexual Division of Labour, or 'Is it Art?'*, prepared for the Open University Art & Environment Course by The Collective, including Michelene Wandor, 1976. This image of a woman cleaning a toilet, and the reference to art, is a feminist reminder of the connection between labour, inequality and cultural production. The image alludes to Marcel Duchamp's 1917 artwork *Fountain*, in which he displayed a men's urinal at an exhibition in New York.

Below, left: Spare Rib front cover, October 1987. In a feature article titled 'Not Victims, Not Superwomen', Ruth Chigwada explores why the academic achievements of black girls were unrecognised. Chigwada argues this was a result of academic studies either focusing on girls (but without attention to race) or on black children (but without attending to gender).

Below, right: Pamphlet produced by the Women's Research and Resources Centre, 1981.

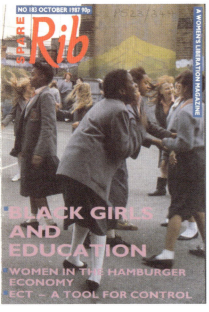

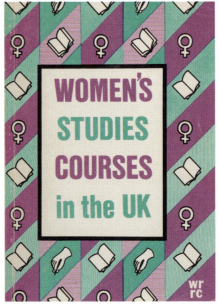

Unfinished Business

These choices, forged in secondary school and channelled through universities, directly translated into jobs. In 1966 the top professional careers for women, i.e. the kinds of roles grammar school graduates were preparing for, were social service oriented: nurses, radiographers and teachers. Conversely, women accounted for less than 1 per cent of engineers, 6 per cent of chemists, and 8 per cent of scientists.[22] The very few women who did go on to higher education in this period were most likely to be found at the University of London, in Welsh and Scottish universities, and in the smaller, civic universities.[23] As one female undergraduate student explained in 1966 when asked why she didn't apply to Oxford or Cambridge: 'Oxbridge do not offer social science courses with the vocational bent as other Redbrick Universities do, it is also still extremely masculine by numbers.'[24] Even in the so-called 'meritocratic' age of rising social mobility, girls and women had to adapt to a system designed for men if they wished to derive the maximum benefits from education.

Several things changed in the 1970s to improve education for girls in Britain. During that decade, most state schools became non-selective, comprehensive schools, the majority of which were co-educational.[25] Comprehensive schools offered a broader range of subjects, including the social sciences, which girls liked and did well in.[26] On measures of social and emotional satisfaction, co-education appeared positive for girls.[27] The school-leaving age was raised to 16 in 1972, and by 1975 there was a higher proportion of 17-year-old girls than boys at secondary school for the first time. In the optimistic moment of the 1960s, co-educational comprehensive schools were seen as emblematic of a brighter future. However, from the 1970s, dissenting voices were emerging to restate the case for single-sex education. Feminist sociology demonstrated the ways in which boys tended to dominate co-educational spaces to the detriment of girls.[28] It was also found that girls in single-sex schools were outperforming their counterparts in co-educational institutions, notably in 'STEM' subjects.[29] The question of whether or not to educate girls separately from boys, which some had considered closed by the 1960s, therefore re-emerged in the context of second-wave feminism.

Much of the feminist conversation around girls' secondary education in the 1970s arose from the fact that an earlier generation of women had made significant gains in higher education during this decade. The Women's Liberation Movement was formed in the intellectual milieu of postwar universities, and activists argued for greater access to education for girls and women and resources and courses suited to their interests and needs. Feminists proposed the revolutionary new discipline of Women's Studies, designed to 'move away from the deficit model of women as lesser men'.[30] Women's Studies was most successful as an educational project in adult education, where many women in the 1980s and 1990s turned to catch up on what they'd missed during their schooldays. In January 1983 the Open University (OU) introduced its first Women's Studies course. 'The changing experience of women' combined literature, history, biology, economics, media studies, law and technology, and teaching methods drew inspiration from the consciousness-raising of Women's Liberation workshops.[31] The OU had been founded in 1969 to offer flexible degree-level study to people returning to education later in life. A survey of OU students in 1977 found that the cohort was 40 per cent female and 60 per cent male, with the majority of the women students working and under 39 years of age.[32]

The case of the OU indicates women's vast, unquenched thirst for higher education by the late 1970s. In the 1979/80 academic year, 37 per cent of higher education students in the UK (excluding the OU) were women, whereas by 1995/96 this figure had risen to 51 per cent.[33] Over the crucial decades of the 1980s and 1990s the enhanced quality of secondary education for girls, especially in relation to exams and staying on, had made accessing university easier, while deindustrialising and changing labour markets and the gradual erosion of workplace discrimination had all contributed to university becoming a realistic and worthwhile option for women for the first time. In many ways, therefore, second-wave feminist demands for the opening up of higher education for women were riding the tide of a set of complex social trends already in motion.

Since the turn of the millennium, women have overtaken men in higher education participation in the UK. This gender gap is still widening in the twenty-first century.[34] Yet even as focus has shifted more squarely onto social class and ethnicity, and the underperformance of boys in secondary education, feminist activism and research remains critical. It continues to highlight gender inequalities in university culture and assessment methods, as well as revealing how much more important educational qualifications are for women than for men in reaching the top jobs.[35] Spectacular gains in accessing education over the past 150 years have given women the tools, credentials and voices to critique educational institutions from within. Given these platforms, we must continually point out how gendered cultures and practices might still hold girls back from achieving their future potential.

1. Mary Wollstonecraft, *A Vindication of the Rights of Woman, with Strictures on Political and Moral Subjects* (1792) [https://www.gutenberg.org/ebooks/3420, accessed online 28 June 2019].

2. Jane Martin, 'Entering the Public Arena: The Female Members of the London School Board, 1870–1904', *History of Education*, 22, 1993, pp. 225–40.

3. Carol Dyhouse, *No Distinction of Sex? Women in British Universities, 1870–1939* (London: Taylor & Francis, 2003), p. 239.

4. Shirley Roberts, 'Jex-Blake, Sophia Louisa (1840–1912)', *Oxford Dictionary of National Biography*, [https://doi-org.ezp.lib.cam.ac.uk/10.1093/ref:odnb/34189, accessed 28 June 2019].

5. Dyhouse, *No Distinction of Sex?*, p. 7.

6. Ibid., p. 242.

7. Annemarie Turnball, 'Learning Her Womanly Work: The Elementary School Curriculum, 1870–1914', in *Lessons for Life: The Schooling of Girls and Women 1850–1950*, Felicity Hunt ed. (Oxford: Basil Blackwell, 1987), pp. 83–100.

8. Catherine Manthorpe, 'Science or Domestic Science? The Struggle to Define an Appropriate Science Education for Girls in Early Twentieth-Century England', *History of Education*, 15, 1986, pp. 195–213.

9. Sir W. H. Hadow, *Report of the Consultative Committee on Differentiation of the Curriculum for Boys and Girls Respectively in Secondary Schools (The Hadow Report)* (London: HMSO, 1923).

10. Brian Harrison, 'Wilkinson, Ellen Cicely (1891–1947)', *Oxford Dictionary of National Biography*, [https://doi-org.ezp.lib.cam.ac.uk/10.1093/ref:odnb/36902, accessed 30 June 2019].

11. *The Times*, 13 October 1937, p. 10.

12. Carol Dyhouse, *Students: A Gendered History* (London; New York: Routledge, 2006), pp. 92–3.

13. British Medical Association, *Becoming a Doctor: A Guide to Careers in Medicine* (London: BMA, 1962).

14. Ministry of Education, *Children and their Primary Schools (The Plowden Report)* (London: HMSO, 1967).

15. Eileen Elias, 'Fifteen Points to Think About When Your Daughter Goes to Primary School', *Where, Supplement Sixteen: Educating Girls* (London: Advisory Centre for Education, 1968), pp. 6–7.

16. James Douglas, Jean Ross, and Howard Simpson, *All Our Future. A Longitudinal Study of Secondary Education* (London: Peter Davies, 1968), pp. 29–34.

17. Ministry of Education, *Statistics of Education 1962, Part One* (London: HMSO, 1963), pp. 30–1.

18. Ministry of Education, *Half our Future (The Newsom Report)* (London: HMSO, 1963), pp. 627–75. In 1967 63.6 per cent of secondary modern schools were co-educational, compared to 35 per cent of grammar schools, *Statistics of Education 1967, Volume One* (London: HMSO, 1968), pp. 2–3.

19. Peter Mandler, 'Educating the Nation: III. Social Mobility', *Transactions of the Royal Historical Society*, 26, 2016, pp. 1–23.

20. Phillida Bunkle, 'The 1944 Education Act and Second Wave Feminism', *Women's History Review*, 25, 2016, pp. 791–811.

21. *Statistics of Education 1962*, p. 66.

22. In 1966, 90 per cent of nurses were women, 67 per cent of radiographers and 57 per cent of teachers. Women were 0.2 per cent of civil, structural and municipal engineers, 0.4 per cent of electrical engineers, 0.7 per cent of electronic engineers, 6 per cent of chemists, and 8 per cent of physical and biological scientists. These figures come from Economic Activity Part 1 Sample Census 1966, which was based on a sample of 10 per cent of the population. Table reproduced in Sue Keable, 'Women in the Professions', *Where, Supplement Sixteen: Educating Girls* (London: Advisory Centre for Education, 1968), p. 29.

23. From the Robbins Report (1963) and cited by Dyhouse, *Students*, p. 82. In Cambridge, 10 per cent of the students were female, 15 per cent in Oxford, compared to an average of 35 per cent in smaller civic universities, 25 per cent in larger civics, and 30 per cent in Wales, Scotland and London.

24. This quote comes from a member of the 1946 British birth cohort, formally known as the 'National Survey of Health and Development', see https://www.nshd.mrc.ac.uk/, accessed 3 July 2019. The quote is taken from an original survey questionnaire, researched by the author for the ESRC-funded project 'Secondary education and social change in the United Kingdom since 1945', see https://sesc.hist.cam.ac.uk/, accessed 3 July 2019.

25. Over 85 per cent of comprehensive schools were co-educational by 1982, Ministry of Education, *Statistics of Education Schools 1982* (London: HMSO, 1983), pp. 9, 13.

26. Peter Mandler, 'Educating the Nation: IV. Subject Choice', *Transactions of the Royal Historical Society*, 27, 2017, pp. 1–27.

27. R. R. Dale, 'Are They Happier?', in *Where, Supplement Sixteen: Educating Girls* (1968), pp. 11–12.

28. Sara Delamont, *Interaction in the Classroom* (London: Methuen & Co Ltd., 1976); Jennifer Shaw, 'Education and the Individual: Schooling for Girls, or Mixed Schooling – A Mixed Blessing?', in Rosemary Deem ed., *Schooling for Women's Work* (London: Routledge & Kegan Paul, 1980), pp. 66–75.

29. Gaby Weiner, 'Sex Differences in Mathematical Performance: A Review of Research and Possible Action' and Jan Harding, 'Sex Differences in Performance in Science Examinations', both in Deem ed., *Schooling for Women's Work*.

30. Mary Hughes and Mary Kennedy eds., *New Futures: Changing Women's Education* (London: Routledge & Kegan Paul, 1985), p. 26.

31. Diana Leonard, '"The Changing Experience of Women" at the Open University', in Hughes and Kennedy eds., *New Futures*, pp. 135–42.

32. Moira Griffiths, 'Women in Higher Education: A Case Study of the Open University', in Deem ed., *Schooling for Women's Work*, pp. 133–4.

33. Department for Education and Employment, *Higher Education in the Learning Society (The Dearing Report)* (London: HMSO, 1997), graph 3.6.

34. 'Why is Martha Doing Better than Arthur?', *Times Higher Education*, 10 May 2018, pp. 36–42.

35. Erzsebet Bukodi, 'Education, First Occupation and Later Occupational Attainment: Cross-cohort Changes among Men and Women in Britain', *CLS Cohort Studies Working paper 2009/4*, (2009); Alice Sullivan, Heather Joshi and Diana Leonard, 'Single-sex Schooling and Academic Attainment at School and Through the Lifecourse', *American Educational Research Journal*, 27, 2010, pp. 6–36.

STEMETTES

Established in 2013, Stemettes aims to inspire young women to take up STEM careers, through events, mentoring, hackathons and exhibitions. Fewer than 22 per cent of the people working in core science, technology, engineering and maths (STEM) occupations in the UK in 2018 were female. Stemettes aim to raise this to 30 per cent. In 2019 the Stemettes launched the Stemette Society - a closed, global network for young women to access career opportunities on demand and receive career advice.

Reimagining Education

— **PROFESSOR ANN PHOENIX**

Brightly illustrated, with clever keyword reading schemes, the Peter and Jane 'learn to read' pocket books have sold over 80 million copies worldwide since they were launched by Ladybird in 1964, and some remain in print. Yet these books exemplify the manner in which educational systems have reflected pernicious social inequalities across race, class and gender. Peter, Jane, Mummy and Daddy, with Pat the dog, were white, middle-class beneficiaries of the self-assurance common at the tail-end of the British empire and American imperialism, and reinforced the rigidly idealised image of the 1950s nuclear family. In their early productions, the children played at 'cowboys and Indians', while a 'golliwog' peeped from a toy shop window; meanwhile, British explorers mastered the world in Ladybird's Adventures from History series.

Such ideologies of white male superiority were even starker in Dr Truby King's *Mothercraft as an Educational Process*, a child-rearing model which became globally influential in the middle part of the twentieth century. King's in some ways visionary ideas about preventing child mortality were unhappily conditioned by his colonial, patriarchal mindset in early twentieth-century New Zealand. Establishing the Society for the Promotion of the Health of Women and Children (known as the Plunket Society) there in 1907, he entwined arguments that mothers should be trained in regimes of strict, chilly childcare with eugenic notions of 'the perils of unfitness' and what he saw as 'impending race suicide'. His 1917 'Save the Babies' week featured the slogan 'The Race marches forward on the feet of Little Children'. This of course also implies a world in which people with disabilities are hardly welcome.[1]

Many of Truby King's ideas are now discredited, and the Peter and Jane books have been revised several times since the 1970s to challenge the worst stereotypes they originally promoted.[2] Along with them, a plethora of alternative, inclusive and multicultural educational practices and tools have been developed in the last fifty years, including those by various radical and multicultural publishers and bookshops. Yet these necessary changes would not have happened without the creativity of teachers, writers, policy-makers, parents, inspectors and educational activists who courageously resisted ideologies of inferiority and exclusion. This has been despite the deep class, gender, racialised and ableist institutional structures which have kept women, minority ethnic groups and people with disabilities out of positions of power in existing educational systems.

In the 1950s and 1960s, for example, teachers from the Caribbean struggled to gain employment in education, despite being eminently qualified. Beryl Gilroy (1924–2001), a Guyanese teacher who came to study at the University of London in 1952, became the UK's second black headteacher as well as a writer, teacher, psychotherapist and founder member of the Camden Black Sisters group in the early 1980s.[3] She was initially rejected from teaching positions and, like many highly qualified Caribbean migrants, found unskilled employment in domestic service, dishwashing and factory work. Between 1967 and 1971 she produced a series of books titled Green & Gold Readers for Guyana which, compared to standard British texts used in Guyanese schools, explicitly referenced Guyanese culture. She moved on to more pioneering ideas in seven children's stories, written for the progressive Nippers series, at the encouragement of John La Rose from the black publisher and book shop, New Beacon Books, in Finsbury Park, London. Published between 1973 and 1975, its characters come from Indian, Pakistani, Caribbean, Greek

Opposite: Play with Us, a 1964 title from the Ladybird reading series showing children playing at being native Americans, is an illustration of how education could be both sexist and imperialist.

Mind: Education

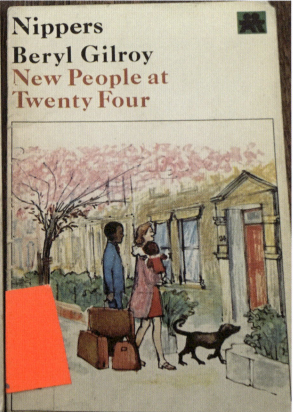

Cypriot and white working-class backgrounds, and live in realistic streets and shared houses, attractively illustrated by Shyam Varma. *A Visitor from Home* demonstrates Gilroy's subtle exploration of the struggle for identity and acceptance alongside the high esteem in which black children and families held education, contrary to the stereotype that they were generally unmotivated.[4] Her autobiographical *Black Teacher* (1976) made an important contribution to challenging racist exclusions, and she published adult novels from the 1980s onwards.

    Gilroy's work can be set in a wider movement of resistance to the intersection of racism and classism in the educational attainment of black children in the British education system. The early Black Education Movement and the Black Supplementary Schools Movement from the 1960s onwards were based in North London, particularly the Borough of Haringey. Building on existing 'supplementary education' organisations established in the 1960s, the Black Supplementary School was a form of self-help designed to counter the prejudice of the formal schooling system, its inadequate care for the needs of black children and the assumption that they had lower IQs than white children. They sprung up in several areas of London, and in Birmingham, Huddersfield, Manchester and other cities. Black teachers and parents came together to counteract the biased and false view that black children were being given of their own history, culture and identity, in order to raise their self-esteem and increase their academic skills.[5] In 1971 Bernard Coard published *How the West Indian Child is Made Educationally Sub-normal in the British*

Below: Handwritten notes from the OWAAD's third conference, at which education and the establishment of supplementary schools were a key focus.

Opposite: Part of the Nippers reading series, *A Visitor from Home* and *New People at Twenty Four* by Beryl Gilroy, both published 1973.

School System, which provided quantitative and qualitative evidence of the widespread mistreatment of children of Caribbean backgrounds. Coard's work inspired a generation of activists.

Black Women's Movements from the 1970s wove ideas about gender equality into campaigns against the educational inequalities experienced by black children. Organisations such as the Brixton Black Women's Group (formed in 1973), OWAAD, the Organisation of Women of African and Asian Descent (1978–83), and the Abasindi Black Women's Cooperative in Manchester (formed in 1980) were partly created in recognition of what Kimberlé Crenshaw has since called intersectionality – that black women were frequently rendered invisible in the (white) Women's Liberation Movement and in the male-dominated black consciousness and Black Power movements of the time. All made educational rights and equality core demands. They set up Saturday schools and summer schools, produced educational literature, and challenged local education authorities to improve provision. They also brought fun, community and pride into their ideas of education. Abasindi, for example, built on Victoria McKenzie's pioneering publications in patois to champion the value of Caribbean languages, and ran workshops in pan-African drumming and dancing. Hair plaiting both raised money and provided a space for discussions.

Mind: Education

ABASINDI CO-OPERATIVE

'SI ZALELWE UKUSINDA'
We Were Born to Survive

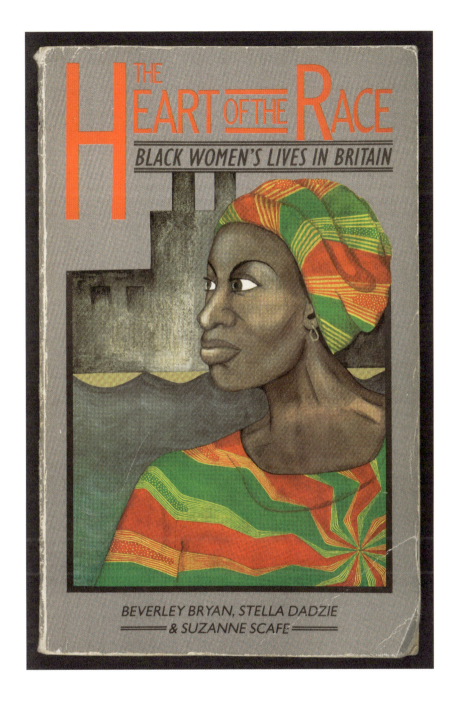

Opposite: Abasindi Co-operative newsletter, 1985. The Abasindi Co-operative was started in 1980 in Moss Side, Manchester. Abasindi means 'survivors'. The Co-operative was established as a 'social, supportive base for Black women' and included a resource centre where they could meet to develop new skills. Activities included a Saturday and summer school for young people. The Saturday school focused on maths and English and the summer school focused on culture, arts and crafts.

Above: First published in 1985, *The Heart of the Race* by Beverley Bryan, Stella Dadzie and Suzanne Scafe reclaimed and recorded black women's history. It detailed their everyday struggles and the political and personal battles they had to fight, as well as documenting their relationship with Britain and its long history of empire, slavery and colonialism.

Mind: Education

Like the London-based Women's Research and Resources Centres established in 1975, these initiatives, including bookshops and publishers, were grassroots, often run by volunteers. They were also invaluable resources for burgeoning Women's Studies and Black Studies courses and degrees. Part of their importance is that they combined activism and theory, as well as providing supportive meeting places. Abasindi was closely involved with the Manchester Black Access Course, for example, which came into being after the 1981 uprising in Moss Side, when local communities protested against police 'stop and search' harassment, racism and the pressures of unemployment. The Manchester Black Access course was linked to the local polytechnic and colleges of higher education, and students who were successful gained automatic entry to a degree programme. Most of the teaching staff and management were black, and the course incorporated a politicised approach including Black Studies and class consciousness, which allowed students to begin from, and theorise, their own experiences.[6]

One of the distinctive contributions of black women activists was to spotlight the way that boys as well as girls lost out in education, and the particular impacts of police racism on minority ethnic men and boys. It is important to take an intersectional perspective in that inclusion and attainment in education are simultaneously related to gender, social class and ethnicity. For example, at GCSE level (age 16) today, the attainment gap associated with social class is twice as large as the biggest ethnic gap and six times as large as the gender gap. However, white working-class boys and Black Caribbean boys attain the least well, and for the middle classes, only Indian students attain better than white British students.[7] Women constitute a large proportion of the teaching profession, particularly in primary schools. Yet, men continue to be more likely to be headteachers, and there continues to be a dearth of black and Asian school teachers. Among university teachers, white male academics are by far the most likely to be professors, while black women hardly feature, and white women are less likely to be professors than white men. The relative figures in 2017/18 were 15,595 male professors and 5,345 female professors. In the same year 16 per cent of academic staff at all levels were recorded as 'Black and Minority Ethnic'. Campaigns for equality in higher education are as important as those in schools.[8]

Yet, here again, there are pressures pushing for change. Athena SWAN (Scientific Women's Academic Network) is a charter established in 2005 and managed by the UK Equality Challenge Unit (now part of Advance HE) to recognise and celebrate good practice in higher education and research institutions. In 2015 the charter was expanded to include non-STEM departments including arts, humanities, social sciences, business, law and professional, support and technical staff as well as trans staff and students. It now recognises work designed to address gender equality in general, rather than only barriers to progression that affect women. Universities that sign up to the charter are expected to plug the 'leaky pipeline' of women failing to progress to senior roles in science, and to ensure equal pay and mainstream support at all levels. There are funding incentives that have led many universities to seek the charter mark, and in 2011, the UK Chief Medical Officer made it a requirement for academic departments applying for funding from the UK National Institution of Health Research to hold the Athena SWAN silver award. In parallel, the Race Equality Charter is designed to challenge the entrenched under-representation of minority ethnic academic staff in higher education – though the separation of these two awards suggests that there remains a need for a truly connected approach, despite Athena SWAN's commitment to intersectionality since 2015.[9]

Such institutional mechanisms for more equal education marks vital progress. But the long history of community self-education and access movements continues to inspire more holistic change. The importance to contemporary activism of documenting educational activism has become clear. Education activist Stella Dadzie, a founder member of OWAAD, has made invaluable contributions to this process by donating papers from the Black Women's Movement to the Black Cultural Archives (BCA) in Brixton, London, as has Jan McKenley, also an OWAAD member, who helped develop the SHINE leadership programme for aspiring headteachers from black and minority ethnic backgrounds. The BCA also holds the 2009–10 oral history project, The Heart of the Race, themed around the 1985 book of the same name by Beverley Bryan, Stella Dadzie and Suzanne Scafe. This captured the memories of black women activists in Britain across different sectors and regions, whose educational struggles were frequently central to their narratives. The history of the Supplementary Education movement is documented in The George Padmore Institute (GPI), an archive, research and information centre of materials relating mainly to the histories of people of Caribbean, African and Asian descent in Britain and Continental Europe.

However, our knowledge of such histories remains precarious, with continual funding challenges for community archives. In times of nationalistic backlash the documenting and publicising of such histories are crucial to challenging exclusive, hierarchical and intolerant perspectives for future generations.

---

1 Philippa Mein Smith, 'Truby King's Women: Four Australian Case Studies', *Social History of Medicine*, vol. 32, iss. 2, 2017, pp. 357–76.

2 Caroline Lowbridge, 'Ladybird Books: The Strange Things We Learned', BBC News, 6 March 2015, https://www.bbc.co.uk/news/uk-england-leicestershire-30709937 (accessed 16 August 2019).

3 'Beryl Gilroy', Peepal Tree Press, https://www.peepaltreepress.com/authors/beryl-gilroy (accessed 16 August 2019).

4 Karen Sands-O'Connor, *Children's Publishing and Black Britain, 1965–2015* (New York: Palgrave MacMillan, 2017), pp. 43–9.

5 George Padmore Institute, 'The Black Education Movement', Collection Ref No.: GB 2904 BEM, Date range: 1965–88, https://www.georgepadmoreinstitute.org/collection/black-education-movement (accessed 16 August 2019).

6 Diane Watt and Adele Jones, *Catching Hell and Doing Well: Black Women in the UK – The Abasindi Cooperative* (Stoke on Trent: Trentham Books, 2015), p. 154.

7 Steve Strand, *Ethnicity, Deprivation and Educational Achievement at Age 16 in England: Trends Over Time*, Department for Education, 2015, report available at https://ora.ox.ac.uk/objects/pubs:609618 (acessed 16 August 2019).

8 Of professors, 26 per cent were female in 2017/18: https://www.hesa.ac.uk/data-and-analysis/staff/working-in-he/characteristics (accessed 12 August 2019).

9 Advance HE, 'Intersectionality', https://www.ecu.ac.uk/equality-charters/athena-swan/athena-swan-faqs/intersectionality (accessed 16 August 2019).

MIND: WORK

'To bring **FEMINIST THEORY HOME** is to **MAKE FEMINISM WORK** in **THE PLACES WE LIVE,** the places we work. ...We use our particulars to **CHALLENGE THE UNIVERSAL.**'

SARA AHMED (B.1969)
From *Living a Feminist Life* (2017)

Sara Ahmed's work focuses on how power is experienced and challenged in institutional settings such as the workplace. Her own life experience informs her theoretical work on migration, orientation, difference and mixed identities. She resigned from her professorial post at Goldsmith's and publishes through her blog, feministkilljoys, reaching out beyond academia.

Working Women

— PROFESSOR PAMELA COX

Look back at the women in your own family tree and you will likely find a whole host of work histories. The story of women's paid and unpaid work is rich and varied. It is also the story of a long battle for equality that is far from over.

Women have always worked. The myth that they only 'entered' the workplace en masse during the two world wars needs busting. Our eighteenth-century foremothers worked as farmers, miners, brewers, bakers, seamstresses, spinners, weavers, shopkeepers, market traders, street sellers and more. The Victorian ideal of the woman as the 'Angel in the House' was exactly that – far removed from the everyday experiences of most working people in the past.

Many of these women workers were young, often taking on their first jobs as young children or in their early teens. Those who went on to marry and/or have children often combined paid work with domestic tasks. Their story remains hard to uncover, as it is rarely preserved or archived. Their casual work went unrecorded, as did their contributions as wives and daughters within family homes and firms. Census data captures only a fraction of their economic activity. As women grew into old age, many had little choice but to carry on working, especially in the era before state pensions were set up in the early 1900s.

Although their range of occupations was broader than we might imagine, women workers have been concentrated within particular sectors at particular points in time. In the mid- to late nineteenth century, most were employed in agriculture, domestic service, shops or factories. By the early twentieth century, the balance was tilting towards clerical work, assembly lines and a more diverse retail sector. The rise of the welfare state, a new means of meeting the pressing public need for better health, housing and education, created new public sector jobs in these areas. Alongside this, the prising open of previously male-only professions allowed middle-class women in particular to qualify as teachers, lawyers, doctors and scientists. During the two world wars, women took on many jobs in previously male-dominated fields, although this in itself did not lead to any lasting transformation of women's prospects.

The legacies of this wider history are evident in women's work patterns today. Women make up nearly half of the UK labour force, but remain concentrated in the lower-paid parts of it. Many feel they have no option but to sacrifice their dreams of higher pay or promotion to their need for flexibility. According to the Office of National Statistics, over 40 per cent of female workers work part-time, a statistic driven by the fact that many are still combining paid work with unpaid work.

The story of women's work is told here through personal stories and everyday artefacts. Grace Higgins was employed as a domestic servant for nearly fifty years by artist Vanessa Bell, the sister of Virginia Woolf, and her partner, Duncan Grant. Grace's diary details domestic life at Charleston Farm in Sussex. She was pivotal to the Charleston household and their many guests, overseeing cooking, cleaning, laundry, sewing, provisioning, caring and hosting over many years. She also attended to the family during their vacations, spending months away from her own husband and son. One diary entry lists a recipe for lemon ice cream that she collected during a long trip to France. Like all diaries, this one can be read at many levels. As a source for the history of women's work, it illustrates the many demands made of domestic servants – and their skills in meeting or deflecting these.

Grace's experience of working for one family for almost the whole of her life was rare. Most domestic servants changed jobs much more frequently. Middle-class demand for servants was high, but the supply began to dry up as other opportunities opened up for women in the early twentieth century. Young women swapped service for higher-status jobs in shops and offices in their droves, prompting regular outcries about servant shortages in this period.

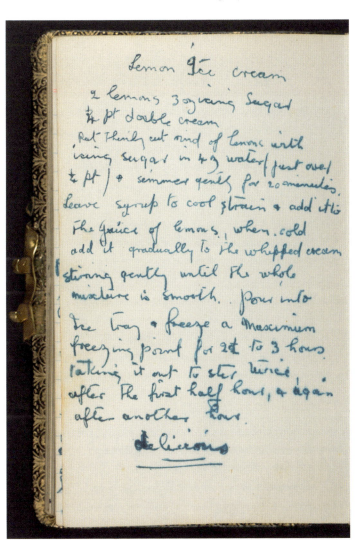

Recipe for 'Lemon Ice Cream' from Grace Higgins' diary.

Mind: Work

IN THE AYAHS' HOME (HACKNEY).

Photograph of ayahs reading and sewing in the Ayahs' Home in Hackney, London, around the start of the twentieth century. The Ayahs' Home provided accommodation and support for Indian ayahs and Chinese amahs (nannies) who were often ill-treated, dismissed or abandoned by their employers, and were unable to find passage home.

Elite families recruited some of their servants from abroad, either to serve in their British homes or their colonial properties. Many British and Anglo-Indian families employed ayahs – Indian women who cared for their children – in large numbers from the mid-nineteenth century onwards. Some ayahs advertised their services in newspapers, and many ayahs moved to Britain with their employers. For some this was an adventure, but, cut off from their own families, they could easily become vulnerable. The Ayahs' Home in Hackney, run by the London City Mission, provided assistance for those who were ill-treated, dismissed or abandoned, while also seeking to convert them to Christianity. As Sumita Mukherjee discusses elsewhere in this volume, these forms of charity were rooted in imperialist thinking and practice.

Servants were frequently called on to provide personal and nursing care to the infant, adult and elderly members of their employers' households. In this sense, the history of nursing is closely connected to the history of domestic service, but also has its own important place in the wider history of women's work. Nursing was one of the first female occupations to become professionalised through approved training and state registration. The Royal British Nurses' Association was set up in 1887, the first in a series of national bodies. The reform of military nursing during the Crimean War (1853–6), pioneered in very different ways by Florence Nightingale and Mary Seacole, laid the foundations of this professionalisation process. A woman of Jamaican–Scottish heritage, Seacole's place in nursing history went largely unrecognised until the 1980s.

UNITED VOICES OF THE WORLD

We are United Voices of the World.

We are predominately migrant women workers and we are unapologetic in our fight for dignity and respect at work.

We cook, clean, change beds, look after the sick and vulnerable, strip, work in retail, serve food, design, create and use direct action and the law to fight back.

We will not stop until we have a living wage, equality and safe workplaces for everyone – women, men and non-binary people.

We are silent no more because when migrant women rise, we all rise.

Left: Photograph of Maureen Cox (née Smith), the author's mother, as a nurse. The Royal London Hospital, c. 1956.

Opposite: First edition of *The Wonderful Adventures of Mrs Seacole*, 1846, the autobiography of a British-Jamaican business woman and nurse who cared for soldiers behind the front line during the Crimean War.

Unfinished Business

By the mid-1950s, thousands of women were employed as nurses. The newly established National Health Service, with its revolutionary 'cradle to grave' ethos, offered care free at the point of use and greatly fuelled demand. That demand was partly met by a generation of postwar school leavers, including my own mother and many of her friends. In order to fully meet that demand, the government ran recruitment campaigns in the Caribbean and other parts of the British Empire and Commonwealth. Many hundreds of women signed up and thereby helped to shore up the NHS. Among them was Beverley Chapman, who migrated from Jamaica to London in 1969, aged 18, to train as a midwife. Today, women continue to make up a large proportion of the health and social care workforce.

The story of women's work is also a story of entrepreneurs, investors and managers. Historians estimate that up to 10 per cent of Britain's businesses, particularly shops and stores, were run by women in the early nineteenth century. The majority of these were small family businesses – but not all of them. The landmark London store Harvey Nichols was formed in 1850 when Anne Harvey, the widow of store owner Benjamin Harvey, went into partnership with James Nichols. In 1930, Laura Bowen became the general manager of the Peter Jones store within the John Lewis Partnership at the age of 24. Thirty years on, young women bosses were behind the 1960s boutiques that revolutionised the aesthetics of how women looked and shopped. Mary Quant's *Bazaar*, Barbara Hulanicki's *Biba*, Celia Birtwell's *Quorum* and Dorothy Owanabae's black cosmetics – to name just a few – enabled women to reimagine themselves and their futures. Women edited magazines and ran publishing houses. Virago, founded in 1973 by Carmen Callil to publish books by women writers, was but one of a plethora of feminist publishers inspired by the Women's Liberation Movement of the period. It also pioneered a feminist approach to business and the boardroom that valued collaboration over competition.

WOMEN'S RIGHTS AT WORK

Modern histories of women's rights tend to focus on women's political struggle for the vote. But their struggles for rights as workers were equally important. Like most of the Victorian labour force, many women worked long hours in poor conditions, but they also did so for wages that could be half to two-thirds of those paid to men. Some took part, at great risk to themselves, in landmark campaigns to address these injustices.

During the Match Girls strike of 1888, 1,400 female employees brought an East End factory to a standstill before winning better conditions. Their action, inspired and co-ordinated by Annie Besant, lit the touch paper for others. The National Anti-Sweating League, whose founders included Mary Macarthur, with Clementina Black as vice-president, pressed for a 'living wage' for the thousands of casual and piece-rate workers, particularly those linked to the garment trade. Employees typically worked in their own homes or informal workshops, and thus fell outside the protections extended to many factory workers

Below, left: Sylvia Pankhurst's painting *The Chainmaker* was part of a series created by the artist during a 1907 tour of worksites in northern England and Scotland witnessing the working conditions and struggles of women.

Below, right: Cradley Heath chainmaker's hammer, with indents made from a woman worker's hand. In 1910, in a strike organised by the trade unionist Mary Macarthur, the Cradley Heath chainmakers galvanised national opinion against women's low pay and sweated labour. As a crucial first test case for minimum wages backed by law, their victory benefited women and men alike.

Opposite: In 1906 the union organiser Mary Macarthur founded the National Federation of Women Workers, which achieved many gains for women. An agitator and campaigner, she founded the union's campaigning newspaper, *The Woman Worker*. Sold for a penny, it changed from a monthly to a weekly paper when it reached 20,000 subscribers.

during this time. Some turned to part-time prostitution to supplement low wages. The League published powerful first-hand accounts, mounted exhibitions exposing scandalous conditions and encouraged consumer boycotts of outlets relying on sweated labour. They succeeded in outlawing some of the worst employer practices. However, the return and survival of these practices in many parts of the world today, including the UK, mean that the struggle against them goes on. Campaign groups No Sweat and the Clean Clothes Campaign are at the forefront of this vital effort in our own times.

In the UK, our right to a minimum wage is rarely contested today – but it was hard won. In the early twentieth century, thousands took part in strikes in order to secure it. Under the 1909 Trade Boards Act, Parliament approved the principle of a minimum wage for specific industries. The chain-making industry was the first in which a minimum rate was set, but many employers attempted to avoid applying it. That summer, union organiser and campaigner Mary Macarthur initiated a ten-week strike by 1,000 women chainmakers. Most male chainmakers worked in a factory setting and were unionised. By contrast, women chainmakers worked in 'chainshops' in the backyards of their homes, often caring for babies and children at the same time. A 1907 painting by Sylvia Pankhurst shows the arduous conditions in which they laboured. As they were isolated from one another, organising as a united front was perceived as impossible, but Mary Macarthur won their trust and the National Federation of Women Workers helped to raise funds for strike pay. Their action received publicity in the local and national press as well as in the Federation's newspaper *The Woman Worker*. The chainmakers' strike became a test case for minimum wage legislation in the UK. They won their strike action and almost doubled their wages. Their success encouraged others to follow suit, with hundreds of other strikes taking place.

The Co-operative Women's Guild also joined the fight. It supported the minimum wage but insisted that this be the same for men and women. Equal work deserved equal pay; perhaps especially in a co-operative movement born of a wider fight for fairness. The Guild's leader, Margaret Llewelyn Davies, was appalled by the fact that while 500 co-op societies had agreed to implement minimum wages for men, only eight had agreed to do the same for women. Women simply could not sustain an independent living on low wages, and should not be forced to rely on a male breadwinner. Her members concurred. As one, a Mrs Wimshurt from Lewes, put it at a district co-op conference in 1909: girls often had to marry because their wages were so low that they felt 'compelled to accept the first offer from a decent man'. The Lewes members enjoyed the joke but also resolved to have the last laugh, supporting Llewelyn Davies' call for greater pay equality. The co-op network rose to the challenge. By 1911, sixty of their local societies had set

Unfinished Business

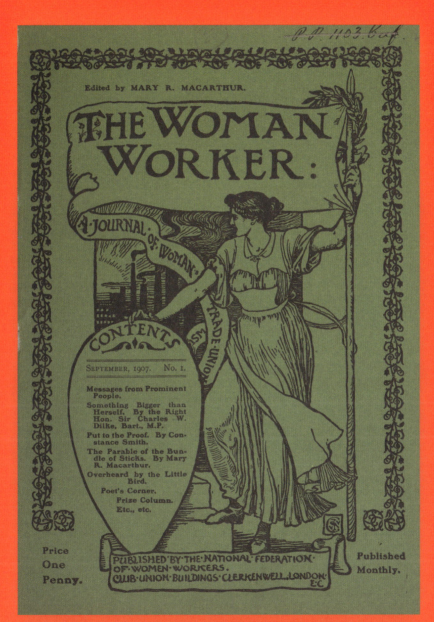

Below: Commemorative plate from 1985 celebrating the success of the Ford Dagenham sewing machinist protests. Strikes started in 1968 in protest against discriminatory pay and grading. Joined by women at Halewood, they halted Ford's UK car production. Their strike ended after Barbara Castle intervened as Secretary of State for Employment. She introduced the 1970 Equal Pay Act banning gender-based pay scales. The machinists won higher pay, overturned union attitudes and changed the law, but they were only re-graded in 1984 after striking again.

Opposite: Glasgow equal pay campaign – one of the biggest equal pay strikes in the UK – in October 2018. More than 8,000 women employed in homecare, schools and nurseries, cleaning and catering services across Glasgow took action supported by male workers respecting picket lines. This ended a twelve-year dispute against discriminatory job evaluations that penalised those working less than thirty-six hours per week. Thousands of women working part-time or on split shifts won compensation.

new minimum wage rates for women, and by 1913, 250 had done so. For all that, these rates did not yet offer equal pay for equal work, and this battle would be taken up by others.

The 2010 film *Made in Dagenham* celebrated the fortieth anniversary of the passage of equal pay legislation and the crucial part that a strike led by women played in securing it. In June 1968, the sewing machinists at Ford's car plant in Dagenham, the European centre of the US motor giant's global business, walked out. They worked on the specialised upholstery for car seats, and were outraged by Ford's re-grading of its workforce, which had placed them on a lower, unskilled grade while men doing very similar work had been placed on a higher one. Lower grades meant lower pay. No upholstery, however, meant no finished products and no car sales. The strike brought Ford's entire UK production to a halt, especially when women at their Halewood plant in Merseyside also downed tools.

This quickly became a national story, but one that would probably have ended quite differently if anyone other than Barbara Castle had been Secretary of State for Employment in the Labour government of the day. One of a handful of women to have held a Cabinet post by then, Castle met with strikers and other equal pay campaigners and used their stories to win support for a pioneering piece of legislation: the 1970 Equal Pay Act. The Act gave all employers five years to make whatever changes were necessary to ensure that they offered all workers equal pay for equal work, a right already won by women civil servants in 1955 and women teachers in 1961. But the fight for equal pay rates to be implemented in practice still goes on. In 2018, for instance, more than 8,000 women employed by Glasgow City Council went on strike to win their twelve-year fight for equal pay after new pay structures resulted in care, cleaning and catering staff – mainly women – earning less than refuse workers, who were mainly men.

Vital as equal pay legislation is, it has failed to wipe out a gender pay gap that persists today. The principle of equal pay for equal work needs to be expanded to include equal opportunities to undertake that equal work. According to the Fawcett Society, women's opportunities to do this are seriously constrained by three factors. First, women continue to carry unequal caring responsibilities and face discrimination, particularly around pregnancy and maternity leave, with over 50,000 women forced to leave their job every year after becoming a mother. Second, our divided labour market means that women are still more likely to be in low-paid and low-skilled jobs, particularly in the care, leisure and retail sectors – a fact closely connected to unequal care roles. Third, men still make up the majority of those in the highest-paid and most senior positions. Fawcett campaigners also point out that although it has been illegal for over forty years to pay a woman less than a man for the same work, this still happens. In 2019, Asda shopworkers (mostly women) won their equal pay dispute, arguing that they should be paid the same as Asda warehouse workers (mostly men).[1]

Discrimination is, of course, intersectional. Workers past and present have faced discrimination on the grounds of their ethnicity, disability, age and sexual orientation as well as their gender. Struggles against this have taken many forms and some are more widely documented than others. The Grunwick dispute was a pivotal chapter in the story of both women's work and wider industrial relations. It involved a new generation of migrant women workers, mostly South Asian women who had come to Britain from East Africa, protesting against degrading conditions in a new industry, a fast-paced mail-order photo processing lab in West London. In 1976, a group of Grunwick workers walked out, led by Jayaben Desai. They had joined a trade union, APEX (Association of Professional, Executive, Clerical and Computer Staff), in defiance of their employers, who initially refused to recognise their right to do so. Their strike, involving controversial secondary action by other unions, lasted for two years, making it one of the UK's most protracted industrial disputes. It ended in 1978 when the Trades Union Congress (the national federation of trade unions) and APEX withdrew their support in a move that divided the labour movement. Desai, who became a national figure in the course of the strike, commented that 'Trade union support is like honey on the elbow – you can smell it, you can feel it, but you cannot taste it'.

The trade union movement has had a troubled history with women workers' rights. When unions were first established in the nineteenth century – at

great personal risk to many involved – their primary goal was to protect the pay and conditions of skilled male workers. Men working in unskilled or casual trades were excluded, as were the majority of women workers. As we have seen, apart from women working in factories and textile mills, most Victorian women workers were concentrated in sectors with weak traditions of labour organisation – in agriculture, domestic service and shop work. In all these cases, their employers were mostly private householders, farmers or small-business owners. So, although a quarter of a million women worked in shops in 1900, for example, they were dispersed across thousands of small private enterprises with very low rates of union penetration. The same was true of domestic servants, nearly a million strong at the time but similarly dispersed across thousands of private family homes.

At the same time, women were barred from most professions, such as law and medicine, and thereby barred, too, from most professional associations. It is not surprising that the professional roles that they eventually carved out for themselves in the late nineteenth and early twentieth centuries, notably in nursing, teaching, welfare, public administration and the civil service, became female dominated.

Mind: Work

Grunwick workers strike and picket line, October 1977.

Yesterday

7.45   Up, get breakfast, get 3 ready for school
         Dress twins
         Do washing up, make beds
10.45-55   Shopping for dinner
11 - 11.45   Cleaning
11.45-12.00   Cook dinner
12.00-1.15   Eat dinner, wash up
1.30   Get twins up (asleep from 11)
         Feed & change
2.15   Make tea
         Hoover upstairs
         Clean window
         Wash net curtains
         Fill oil heaters
3.30   Syr-old home
         Make tea (for children)
4.00-4.30   Get herself ready for work
         Get tea ready (children have it when she's at work)
4.30-5.15   Shopping on way to work
5.15-7.15   Work
7.30   Bath: wash twins & get ready for bed.
         (other 3 put themselves to bed)
8.00-9.00   Ironing
9.00-9.15   Make husband sandwiches & one for herself to eat then.
9.15-10.15   Watch TV & knit
10.15-10.30   H makes scrambled eggs & tea
11.30   Bed.

Cleaning Some every day = whole house esp. - carpet sweep & dust bedrooms, sweep stairs [front room once a wk]
          Wash kit floor.
          One day a wk change all beds (any day she feels in the mood)
          - that day hoovers throughout (no hoovering on other days).
Washing   Every day (either at home or send eldest to launderette)
          either in daytime, or when home from work.
          1hr - sometimes 2hrs.
Ironing   Morning or evening every day
Shopping Big shop Fri afternoon - small shopping every day.

Opposite: Empirical research notes depicting the labour involved in managing a home, from Ann Oakley's landmark study on housework, 1974. Oakley conducted forty in-depth interviews with London housewives. Oakley's research concluded that housewives spent an average of seventy-seven hours per week doing unpaid housework.

In 1974, a group of women civil servants and feminist trade unionists drew up a remarkable document: the Working Women's Charter. The Charter emerged from grassroots debates in local women's groups around the country. It stands as a testament to the cumulative challenges faced by generations of women in the workplace and beyond. It listed ten demands for equality: pay, opportunities, education and training, working conditions, legal rights, childcare, maternity leave, contraception and abortion, increased family allowances, and more women in public and political life.

Chris Coates, one of the activists involved, remembers being present when the Charter was presented to a packed conference room at Congress House, the TUC headquarters in London. 'The idea was to then go and mobilise in local areas', she says. 'It was a real coming together [of different activist groups], which was probably the first time we tried to do that. I think that was the strength of the charter: trying to link up the ideas that had come out of women's liberation with the organisational strength of the trade union. It was very exciting.'[2]

Despite this initial enthusiasm, the TUC Congress later that year voted to reject the Charter. Instead, it subsumed its demands into its own initiatives. The organisational strength of the trade union had trumped the ideas of the women's movement. That strength has certainly delivered for women in many respects, yet the wider labour movement remains too focused on securing progressive gains in a labour market that remains geared to white men's interests – the interests that keep that gender pay gap firmly in place.

This tension continues to dog our progressive politics today. In 2015, a diverse group of feminists established a new political party – the Women's Equality Party (WEP). Modelled on similar parties found across the EU, and using suffragette brand colours of purple, white and green, its founding manifesto had six demands: equal representation in politics and business, equal representation in education, equal pay, equal treatment of women by and in the media, equal parenting rights, and an end to violence against women. These demands are supported to a greater or lesser degree by all our mainstream political parties. The Labour Party remains wary of campaigning alongside WEP activists on them, however, arguing that – once again – the labour movement alone can deliver women's equality. The underlying cause of this unproductive tension lies in the blurred lines between paid labour performed outside the home and unpaid labour performed within it.

UNPAID AND INFORMAL WORK

In 1974, the same year as the Working Women's Charter appeared, Ann Oakley published two lightning-bolt books. *Housewife* and *The Sociology of Housework* offered the first academic account of women's work in the home as unpaid domestic labour. They were based on interviews with forty urban English housewives and presented their views on housework and their conflicting feelings of monotony, fragmentation and satisfaction. Oakley took a historical approach, tracing the gradual separation of home and work over time. Her approach fuelled the notion that women and men came to occupy 'separate spheres', with women increasingly confined from the nineteenth century onwards to the private domestic sphere, while men were propelled into the public sphere of work. This idea has since been much contested, not least by historians of women's work and entrepreneurialism, who have stressed that the majority of women worked for wages (albeit meagre ones), particularly when they were young. The key point here, perhaps, is that they also worked for free in the home across their whole life course, from girlhood to old age.

It can be difficult to capture the extent and scale of domestic tasks. One effective way to do this is to return to records of the lives of domestic servants – those who were paid to undertake these tasks. Servant manuals from the nineteenth and early twentieth centuries were used by masters, and particularly by mistresses, to structure the working day of their domestic staff. Mrs Beeton's *Book of Household Management*, first published in the 1860s and running to many editions, timetables the long list of tasks to be completed by a single servant in a single day. Manuals like these made domestic labour visible and also attributed a monetary value to it. When people had to pay for their domestic service, they were more willing to view this as a job. When they did not, and the work was undertaken by a wife or daughter, they were much less likely to see it as a job than as a calling, as a natural extension of femininity, as 'what wives and daughters did'.

Mind: Work

The idea that housework would only be valued once it was (re)monetised has a common sense to it, as expressed in a 1937 Women To-day article, but was given powerful depth in 1970s Wages for Housework campaigns. These campaigns reimagined Marxist ideas of alienated labour to join together housework, care and sex work, informal street economies and migrant exploitation through modern slavery. In parallel, a sex workers' rights movement developed, largely focused on economic motivations and solutions to the difficulties of the trade. The fight for sex workers' rights continues through organisations such as the Sex Worker Advocacy and Rights Movement.

Naturally these connections raise complex questions about political strategy and our understandings of love, care, sexuality, identity and power, all much debated by different parts of the women's movement. Yet the long history of thinking through the economics of women's work across class, race and ethnicity remains highly instructive. Consider the 1920s research by the Co-operative Women's Guild and feminists within the Fabian Society into the means by which working-class mothers stretched their time and scant resources. Their studies went on to shape calls for the introduction of family allowances, or state welfare payments, to mothers to enable them to better support their families. The first family allowances were introduced in 1945, championed by Eleanor Rathbone. Rathbone had built her case over decades, drawing on her 1918 book, The Disinherited Family. She faced down howls of protest from other politicians and many trade unionists, who feared that granting cash allowances to women would undercut the wages paid to men. How could a man demand a living wage, if that wage was not to be the sole means by which he would meet his family's needs? These fears proved to be misplaced. Family allowances in and of themselves had no negative impact on the longer term wage trends of men or women.

In 2018, the Office of National Statistics put the value of cooking, cleaning and childcare at a staggering £1.24 trillion pounds – an equivalent of £19,000 per person, and more than the value of the UK's retail and manufacturing output combined. And yet this unpaid work, largely carried out by women, is rarely factored into political efforts to raise our collective game when it comes to our productivity, infrastructure and social equality.[3]

Suffrage campaigners demanded 'deeds not words'. Their struggle to secure votes for women succeeded. But, over a century on, our wider struggle for work equality continues. How might the historical dreams and demands documented here translate into deeds for our own times? Over to you…

---

1   The Fawcett Society, 'Close the Gender Pay Gap', https://www.fawcettsociety.org.uk/close-gender-pay-gap (accessed 13 August 2019).

2   Emine Saner, 'The Working Women's Charter: Forty Years On, Women are Still Struggling', The Guardian, 10 November 2014, https://www.theguardian.com/lifeandstyle/2014/nov/10/working-womens-charter-forty-years-still-struggling (accessed 13 August 2019).

3   Kevin Rawlinson, 'British People Do More than £1tn of Housework Each Year – Unpaid', The Guardian, 3 October 2018, https://www.theguardian.com/society/2018/oct/03/british-people-do-more-than-1-trillion-of-housework-each-year-unpaid (accessed 13 August 2019).

Above: Photograph from 1982 of members of the English Collective of Prostitutes with Labour MP Tony Benn and educationalist Caroline Benn. The ECP occupied Holy Cross Church, King's Cross, for twelve days. Their protest was against police targeting of prostitutes and the legal response to the murders of thirteen women in Yorkshire, which distinguished between 'innocent' victims and prostitutes. Their cause drew widespread support.

Right: T-shirt fom the Sex Worker Advocacy and Resistance Movement (SWARM), a sex worker's collective supporting the rights and safety of everyone who sells sexual services. They advocate decriminalisation of consensual adult sex work. Some feminists believe prostitution objectifies women and oppose its legalisation, while Amnesty International, the World Health Organisation and Anti-Slavery International are convinced by evidence that criminalisation exposes sex workers to increased violence and discrimination. 85 per cent of the 73,000 sex workers in the UK are women.

Opposite: Mother's Money, a special Mother's Day publication for the International Wages for Housework Campaign, spring 1978.

Mind: Work

MIND: POLITICAL PRESENCE

"Well, you're the only one who thinks we're a sexist organisation."

© Gizelda

'The point is not for women simply to take power out of men's hands, since that wouldn't change anything about the world. It's a question precisely of **DESTROYING** that **NOTION OF POWER.**'

SIMONE DE BEAUVOIR (1908–1986)
From *The Second Sex* (1949)

Simone de Beauvoir was a French feminist, novelist, philosopher, activist and social theorist. *The Second Sex* inspired post-Second World War feminists. It remains relevant in understanding women's oppression because it describes how women have been oppressed throughout history by being categorised as the 'Other'.

Race, Publicness and Imperial Feminism

— DR SUMITA MUKHERJEE

Below: In 1915 *The Suffragette*, the organ of the Women's Social and Political Union, was renamed *Britannia*. The name made clear that the political allegiance of the militant rebels now sat with the war effort and the fight to protect Britain and its empire. The rights and freedoms of colonised women, who then lived under British rule, were not the concern of Christabel Pankhurst's new Women's Party, which took a resolutely pro-empire line.

Opposite: Sophia Duleep Singh used her celebrity and wealth to support campaigns for women's suffrage in the UK; she donated money to the militant WSPU's 'war chest' and refused to pay tax with the Women's Tax Resistance League.

As women in the UK and Ireland increasingly fought for more rights in the nineteenth century, their demands and dreams were bound up with their understanding and experience of the British and Irish nations, as well as the British empire. In campaigning for political representation, for example, ideas of who should be included as a 'British woman' often left out non-white or Irish women who were perceived as subjects of the empire, rather than citizens of the nation. The British women's movement was beset with racial and imperial ideologies and hierarchies, which intersected with other issues. Their politics, therefore, had direct repercussions on women of colour in Britain and for colonised women in other parts of the British empire, who were sometimes used as ideological tools in their fights, and sometimes ignored to their detriment.

The women's movement has historically had and still has problems with its elite leadership; it has also been criticised for its white and Eurocentric focus. British feminists often presented their activities as the only legitimate form of feminism, peddling assumptions about the status and centrality of British women to the feminist movement at large. As the idea of 'the nation' and British nationalism became more potent in the nineteenth century, this was bound up with possession of an empire. British women also furthered the idea that the British were morally and culturally superior to other cultures and nations and drew on eugenicist and Darwinist evolutionary theories to augment such claims. In the nineteenth and early twentieth centuries, British women involved in activism were predominantly pro-empire. This included well-known suffrage activists such as Christabel Pankhurst, whose paper *Britannia* explicitly aligns women with the imperial project. This seemingly inherent contradiction – of fighting for human or women's rights while ignoring the rights of colonised women – is often described as imperial feminism: a feminism that was also imperialist.

However, women of colour were engaging in political activism in multiple and innovative ways in this period, despite British women's ignorance or suppression of the agency of colonised women around the world, and their emphasis on white women's moral leadership. Women from the colonies, because of the imperial relationship, were bound to British politics and so their movements were often tied closely to British women – it was not easy to sever those imperial bonds. In addition, travel routes to the empire over centuries of imperial expansion had brought colonised people, who were British subjects, to Britain; these numbers increased in the nineteenth century as technology for travel improved. Such women were not only the elites from colonised societies but also included servants and nursemaids, such as Indian ayahs, whose passports we can see.

British women too often had unwelcome views about the empire, and also exhibited crass ignorance about slavery. Problematic analogies between slavery and the position of women were common before and after the nineteenth century. Mary Wollstonecraft, a founding feminist theorist, for example, compared the status of women to slavery in *A Vindication of the Rights of Woman* (1792). She was partly inspired by the growing uprising against slavery, including the successful self-liberated rebellion by enslaved peoples in San Domingo (now Haiti) the

Mind: Political Presence

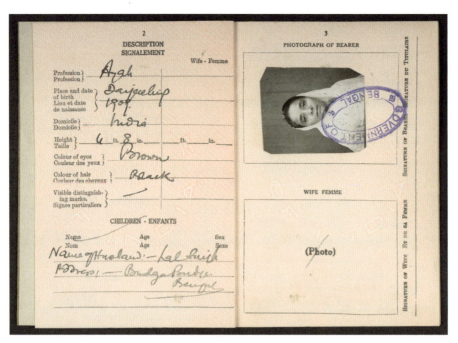

Examples of ayah's passports archived at the British Library's India Office Records archive. Many ayahs travelled with the families they worked for from economic necessity, working their passage from India to Britain and back. Others came because of their attachment to the children they cared for. Some sought travel and adventure, making the journey frequently. Many ayahs were discharged in Britain and had to advertise their services for a return passage. Some settled and found employment in Britain.

Unfinished Business

Right: Sugar produced by enslaved labour was first boycotted by campaigners in 1791. Boycotts were supported by women's anti-slavery associations in Britain, who distributed thousands of pamphlets door-to-door. This handout was produced by the Sheffield Female Anti-Slavery Society around 1825–33. The abolition of slavery in the British empire owed more to slave rebellions and the Haitian Revolution than to British campaigners. However, women sidelined in the anti-slavery movement were inspired to fight for their own political representation.

Below: In 1833, when slavery was abolished in most British colonies, the state agreed to pay £20 million in compensation to slave owners. Many women claimed compensation, often as widows of slave owners. Dorothy Little's letter to the compensation committee details her dependence on her income from enslaved people she owned. She valued women particularly as they 'doubled their number'.

year before, but she also tended to conflate the distinct – evidently worse – experiences of enslaved black women with the white middle-class women she was largely addressing.[1] Similarly, John Stuart Mill, an early champion of women's rights and an ally to the suffrage movement, also aligned women with slavery in his 1869 publication *The Subjection of Women*. Emmeline Pankhurst infamously declared, 'I would rather be a rebel than a slave' in 1913. American commentators constantly used similar comparisons, while some American suffragists such as Elizabeth Cady Stanton and Susan B. Anthony expressed open concerns about enfranchising African-Americans. In doing so, they assumed that women's rights should first or even only apply to white women.

This raises questions about how British women who campaigned prominently for abolition understood their own relationship to enslaved women, and to their own legal status. In some ways there is much to celebrate in the way that women in the early anti-slavery campaigns developed pioneering campaigns such as the sugar boycott and were able to repurpose such techniques for women's struggles. Many abolitionist women, for example, went

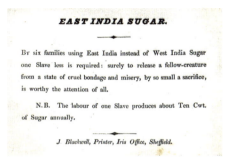

on to challenge the pernicious Contagious Diseases Act and then to campaign for female suffrage. But these later campaigns were too often white-focused. Furthermore, many British women had benefited from the slave trade, and continued to do so, even after legal abolition, including through the policy of compensating former slave owners. Dorothy Little is just one example of a woman who petitioned vigorously for compensation.[2] Following official abolition in 1833, the position of women of African descent in Britain and across the empire did not necessarily improve materially, nor in relations with white British women. Mary Prince, born into an enslaved household in Bermuda in 1788, came to Britain in 1828 and technically worked as a free domestic servant from 1829, but very little is known of her life after 1833, following the publication of her *The History of Mary Prince* in 1831. At large, formerly enslaved peoples and subsequent generations were made to feel they should be grateful for their freedom.

Over the course of the nineteenth century a shift occurred in Britain's imperial preoccupations, from the Caribbean to the prominence of the Indian subcontinent. British feminists soon turned their saviour-complex attention to Indian women, depicting them as weak and in need of saving, as they had portrayed enslaved women in the Caribbean before them. Clearly, the political situation was different: Indian women were

Mind: Political Presence

Below: Photograph of Rukhmabai (1864–1955) with other students at the London School of Medicine for Women: back row, second from left.

Opposite: The Indian barrister Cornelia Sorabji (1866–1954) making a radio broadcast.

not subjected to bondage slavery. Degrading and racialised language nevertheless saturated women's campaigning. Although British women sought to 'improve' the position of colonised women, they did not question the validity of imperial intervention, or their role within it. They were quick to revert to and rely on racial stereotypes about polygamy or veiling, describing Indian women as 'silent' and 'suffering', but did not engage with colonised women directly. British women also started to focus their criticisms on colonial society and cultural traditions rather than the patriarchy – or imperial patriarchy – at large.[3]

There are many examples of philanthropic associations set up by British women that were dedicated to social reform in the empire. Often associated with religious or political groups, they usually focused on imperial unity and self-sacrifice. In 1870, prior to Disraeli's proclamation of Queen Victoria as Empress of India in 1877, the National Indian Association (NIA) was founded by Mary Carpenter (1807–77). Carpenter was an educational reformer who had visited India four times between 1866 and 1876. The NIA's minute book shows how they took pride in 'female uplift' and education, strengthening imperial ties rather than political reform. British women involved in imperial reform thus were able to position themselves as superior in contrast to the victimised non-Western women they set out to 'save'.

The education system in India was modelled on Britain's, not merely in structures and governance but also in curricula, however inappropriate to the history and cultures of India. Moreover, until the 1920s, many of the professions in India were only open to individuals who had British degrees, which compelled aspiring, well-connected Indians to travel to Britain for further study. In order to help Indian women study in Britain, many well-off British women tried to raise funds for scholarships. In the early twentieth century, the Indian Women's Education Association was set up in London and run by British and Indian women to sponsor Indian women to take up teacher training. Prior to this, more ad hoc arrangements were made for lucky individuals. For example, a fund was raised for Rukhmabai to travel to England to study medicine in 1889. Rukhmabai had come to the

Unfinished Business

attention of sections of the British public when she was married aged 11 to the 19-year-old Dadaji Bhikaji. When Rukhmabai refused to move into the marital home eight years later, the case was brought to court and covered in the British press. By travelling to Britain, Rukhmabai was able to remove herself from the ongoing legal situation. She enrolled in the London School of Medicine (whose photo we have here) and qualified as a doctor in 1894, having also studied at the Royal Free Hospital. She then returned to India and worked as the head of a women's dispensary in Surat.

Another notable example is Cornelia Sorabji, who was one of the first Indian women to study for higher education in Britain, but she faced considerable hurdles.[4] Having gained first place in her final degree exams in the Deccan College of Poona, she was not granted the government scholarship that was automatically awarded to the highest-placed student in the Presidency because she was a woman. Lord and Lady Hobhouse (members of the NIA) helped to raise funds for her to enter Oxford University in 1889. Sorabji maintained a lively correspondence with her family while a student at Oxford, but also faced racial stereotyping; British ladies would approach her in the streets and try and convert her to Christianity, without realising that she was of Christian faith. She was the first woman, of any ethnicity or nationality, allowed to study law at Oxford although she was not allowed to officially accept her degree, or be called to the bar, until 1922. Before this, she returned to India and set up her law practice focusing on *purdahnashin* (secluded women) cases.

Below: In late 1906 Sophia Duleep Singh visited India, with the British government's permission but under their surveillance. During the visit her interest in Indian nationalism was stimulated after hearing Lala Lajpat Rai, an activist who was involved in the 'self-sufficiency' movement, speak. In her diary for 17 February 1907 she describes Rai's speech as 'beautiful' and celebrates him as a 'wonderful speaker. A noble and unselfish man'.

Opposite: These surveillance records for Sophia Duleep Singh indicate that the British State was irritated and threatened by Singh's activities, but could not prevent her activism.

Sorabji was not allowed to be a barrister initially because the professions were not opened to women in Britain until 1919, when the Sex Disqualification (Removal) Act was passed. One of the first women to be called to the bar in 1921 was an Indian woman and suffragist called Mithan Tata. The British suffrage movement involved a very small number of women of Indian ethnicity, but generally did not include women of colour residing in Britain at the time. One of the most notable exceptions is Sophia Duleep Singh, but her involvement should not suggest that the British suffrage movement was racially inclusive. British suffrage journals regularly depicted the imperial burden of British women who needed to improve the lives of colonised women, especially Indian women, as one of the justifications for giving women the vote in Britain.

Sophia Duleep Singh was a member of the Women's Social and Political Union (WSPU) and the Women's Tax Resistance League (WTRL). She was born in Norfolk in 1876, the daughter of the exiled and deposed prince of the Punjab, Duleep Singh, and was goddaughter to Queen Victoria. As an adult she was given a 'grace-and-favour' home in the grounds of Hampton Court Palace, and it was through her wealth and royal connections that she was able to bring much-needed publicity to the suffrage cause. As a member of the WTRL, she was able to refuse to pay taxes, and then allow the WTRL to publicise the auctions where her goods could be bought back. However, as a suffragette, goddaughter of Queen Victoria and one of the daughters of an exiled prince, she was kept under surveillance by both the government and the royal household (as shown here in the 1913 surveillance records). In late 1906 she visited

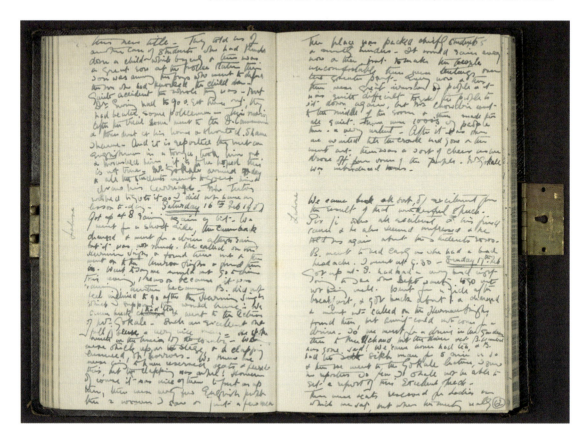

India, with government permission, stimulating her interest in Indian nationalism, which we see in her diary entries from 1907. Duleep Singh visited India again in 1911, where she met Mithan Tata and her mother Herabai. She encouraged the Tatas to get involved in women's suffrage in India, which they did, and which brought them to Britain in 1919 to petition the government for the Indian women's vote.

The issue of the vote for women in other parts of the empire, such as India, was not encouraged by most of the British movement. This was despite the growing Indian suffrage movement from 1917 and the growing power and reach of women's associations in India, such as the Women's Indian Association, founded in 1917, which campaigned on issues including suffrage, education and health, and later the All-India Women's Conference, founded in 1926. *Stri Dharma*, the journal of the Women's Indian Association, was started in 1918 and distributed in Britain, with reports often reproduced in internationalist suffrage periodicals such as *Jus Suffragii* (overleaf).

Below and opposite: The All India Women's Conference (AIWC), established in 1926, was one of several women's associations in India who campaigned on issues such as suffrage, education and health. The card below was sent to the AIWC from British women's groups active in the 1920s; it indicates the public influence of feminism in both Britain and India after the First World War, and a shift in the register of colonial relations from 'salvation' to solidarity. Opposite is the front cover of the souvenir programme for the AIWC's 1973 conference.

It is only from the late 1920s onwards that British women turned their attention more fully to places like India, with which there was this special historical relationship, and supported their women's associations. We see this with the foundation of a liaison group of British and Indian women's associations in the 1930s, and increased travel and contact between India and Britain for British and Indian women activists, especially through the All-India Women's Conference, with contact continuing well into the 1970s, as we see in this 1973 souvenir volume. However, focus was largely on Indian women and their activities rather than consideration of other equally vibrant and path-breaking women's movements in other parts of the empire and world.

Formerly colonised nations are now independent and self-governing, but a new 'neo-imperial' feminism has been fostered through powers that use and twist women's equality for other ends. Just as nineteenth-century European imperialism often used the position of 'degraded' women as a justification for imperial expansion as part of a 'civilising mission', the West has continued to use the justification of protecting women as a pretext for invading countries. The white West's exploitation of Arab women's situation and struggle to justify the so-called 'war on terror' today is but one example. Fortunately, increasing communications and connections between women's movements through global conferences and digital activist networking have allowed for women's voices from around the world to be heard more loudly, for stronger awareness of the ways in which liberation involves thinking about connections between class, race, sexuality, disability and religion, and for white women to slowly acknowledge that their privileges do not give them an automatic right to speak on the behalf of others or dictate how women's activism should be conceived and acted out.

---

1. Moira Ferguson, 'Mary Wollstonecraft and the Problematic of Slavery', *Feminist Review*, vol. 42, iss. 1, 1992, pp. 82–102; *The Interesting Narrative of the Life of Olaudah Equiano, or Gustavus Vassa, the African*, (London: printed for and sold by the author and twelve others, 1789).

2. Hannah Young, 'Dorothy Little – slave owner', *Untold Lives Blog*, 28 June 2013, https://blogs.bl.uk/untoldlives/2013/06/dorothy-little-slave-owner.html (accessed 10 August 2019).

3. Clare Midgley, 'Anti-Slavery and the Roots of Imperial Feminism', in Midgley, ed., *Gender and Imperialism* (Manchester: Manchester University Press, 1998), pp. 161–79; Antoinette Burton, *Burdens of History: British Feminists, Indian Women, and Imperial Culture, 1865–1918* (Chapel Hill: University of California Press, 1994).

4. http://www.open.ac.uk/researchprojects/makingbritain/content/cornelia-sorabji

INTERNATIONAL ALLIANCE OF WOMEN

Souvenir

ALL-INDIA WOMEN'S CONFERENCE

Central Office: 6, Bhagavan Das Road, New Delhi.

Women in Public Life

— **DR CAITRÍONA BEAUMONT**

Mary Wollstonecraft Godwin.

140

Unfinished Business

Contending for the rights of woman, my main argument is built on this simple principle, that if she be not prepared by education to become the companion of man, she will stop the progress of knowledge [...] how can woman be expected to co-operate unless she know why she ought to be virtuous? unless freedom strengthen her reason till she comprehend her duty, and see in what manner it is connected with her real good?[1]

In this extract from the first edition of *A Vindication of the Rights of Woman* (1792), Mary Wollstonecraft laid claim to the rights and duties of female citizens. Responding to political debates about the citizenship rights of men in the wake of the French Revolution (1789) and of people of colour enslaved in colonised lands, Wollstonecraft insisted that women, like men, had a contribution to make to public life. She argued that for women to achieve their potential and to participate in local and national affairs, girls must be given access to the same standard of education as boys. Moreover, Wollstonecraft asserted that the domestic labour carried out by wives, mothers and daughters in the home must be valued equally with the public work of men engaged in politics, business and the professions.

This groundbreaking text of modern feminist thought didn't go so far as to demand the right to vote for women, a right denied to many men at this time. Wollstonecraft was, however, radical in arguing that despite their different roles men *and* women had a right to live independent lives and had an equal duty to participate actively in public life. This chapter will trace some of the ways in which women demanded a public voice, political representation and legal rights in Britain throughout the nineteenth and twentieth century.

Long before women won the right to vote in parliamentary elections in the UK, individual campaigners and groups of women engaged in political activism. For example, in the mid-nineteenth century women played an active part in key social and political reform movements such as the anti-slavery movement, the temperance movement, the Anti Corn Law League and Chartism. Yet the idea that women should have the same political rights as men remained far-fetched. Women were explicitly excluded from the 1832 Reform Act, which extended the parliamentary franchise (being able to vote) to eligible middle-class men. A cartoon by the caricaturist and illustrator George Cruikshank, published in his 1853 *Comic Almanack*, vividly depicts the probable 'effects of female enfranchisement' (overleaf). Here male and female voters flock in support of the dashing 'Ladies Candidate' who, if elected, will guarantee 'Parliamentary Balls once a week'. The 'Gentlemens Candidate, Screw Driver, the great political economist', appears with no supporters and a banner advises 'Do not vote for ugly, old Stingy'.

The idea that women's political engagement would be framed by their interest in dances and handsome men belied the true nature of female political activism. Throughout the late 1800s, for example, Josephine Butler and the Ladies National Association campaigned against the Contagious Diseases Acts (for more information see Challis

Opposite: Frontispiece portrait of Mary Wollstonecraft, from *Memories of the Author of A Vindication of the Rights of Woman*, by William Godwin, 1798.

'The Rights of Women, or, The Effects of Female Suffrage', satirical cartoon by George Cruikshank, published in *The Comic Almanack*, 1853. The gentleman's candidate, the dour political economist Screw Driver, stands ignored. In contrast, the lady's candidate, the dashing Mr Darling – with his offer of weekly parliamentary balls – receives adoring doe-eyed glances from the women. Although satirical, the cartoon highlighted the widespread belief that women were too frivolous to consider weighty political matters.

in this volume). This campaign is just one case of women's willingness and ability to act to protect the citizenship rights of women, long before the parliamentary vote was won.[2]

By the end of the nineteenth century women who met the property and marriage criteria were eligible to vote and stand in local elections. In 1900 over 1,000 poor law guardians, 200 school board members and 200 parish councillors were women.[3] They were also able to participate through supporting established political parties in ancillary groups such as the Conservative Primrose League (1884), the Women's Liberal Federation (1887) and the Women's Labour League (1906). Membership of religious, philanthropic and voluntary associations, for example the Mothers' Union (1885), the Young Women's Christian Association (1887) and the Co-operative Women's Guild (1883), ensured that women acquired the organisational skills, confidence and networks necessary for contributing effectively to public life.

It was amid these vibrant and diverse expressions of female political activism that the women's suffrage movement emerged. Its history is now well known through the many excellent accounts of suffragist (constitutional/law-abiding) and suffragette (militant/direct action) organisations and campaigners.[4] Best known among the numerous suffrage groups are the constitutional National Union of Women's Suffrage Societies (NUWSS, 1897), led by Millicent Garrett Fawcett, and the militant Women's Social and Political Union (WSPU, 1903), led by Emmeline and Christabel Pankhurst. Despite their differences both groups were united in the belief that for women to participate fully in public life, and to benefit from democratic citizenship, they had to be able to vote in national elections.

Not everyone agreed. In response to the growing suffrage movement, an anti-suffrage movement emerged, leading to the establishment in July 1908 of the Women's National Anti-Suffrage League. In a diary entry dated Thursday 5 November 1908, Albinia Yate-Lee recounts her attendance at the inaugural meeting of the League's South Kensington branch. Here she writes that the prominent anti-suffrage campaigner Violet Markham 'spoke very well': Markham's view was that the 'spheres of men and women were different, and therefore they [women] ought to have a different share in the management of the State'.[5] This 'different share' meant that women were best suited to participate in local government, while men were better qualified to deliberate on national and international issues, for example the economy and foreign policy.

Unfinished Business

By 1909 the Anti-Suffrage League had recruited approximately 10,000 members in comparison with a membership of around 5,000 for the WSPU and 50,000 for the NUWSS. The publication of illustrations and cartoons in the journals of each group (*The Suffragette* (WSPU), *The Common Cause* (NUWSS) and *The Anti-Suffrage Review*) and in the popular press was an effective way to publicise their respective views. Anti-suffrage cartoons and postcards frequently characterised suffrage campaigners as unattractive, aggressive and bespectacled women who were the antithesis of traditional ideals of femininity. Pro-suffrage cartoons and artwork often represented women in heroic roles or portrayed exploited women workers and exhausted mothers who would benefit most from having female representation in Parliament.

In her diary Yate-Lee noted her disapproval of the actions of militant suffragettes. She wrote on 26 March 1909 that it was 'hateful to see women degrading themselves like this'. The actions of militant suffragettes caused alarm, particularly during the years 1908 and 1913. It was during this time that the WSPU became increasingly frustrated with the unwillingness of the Liberal government to extend the parliamentary vote to women. Extreme tactics, such as window breaking, destruction of property and bombs left on trains, escalated in direct response to the reaction of the authorities to the methods of the WSPU. Women arrested during suffrage demonstrations, for example on 'Black Friday' in November 1910, were roughly treated with accusations made by those detained of physical and sexual abuse at the hands of the police. Sasha Roseneil discusses the legacy of this style of activism elsewhere in this volume, while Sumita Mukherjee's discussion of race rights struggles at this time tells how Sophia Duleep Singh's suffrage activism occasioned government surveillance.

Approximately 1,000 suffragettes were sent to prison between the years 1905 and 1914. For those who went on hunger strike this included repeated bouts of forcible feeding. Their stoicism in the face of this form of torture reveals the suffering many endured to win political representation for women.[6] One such woman was the artist Olive Wharry, who documented her experiences in a beautifully illustrated prison scrapbook. Wharry, a member of the WSPU, was sentenced to Holloway prison for eighteen months on 7 March 1913 for setting fire to the tea pavilion in Kew Gardens. In her scrapbook she pasted in newspaper reports of the 'Kew refreshment pavilion outrage'. She also recorded her release date of 8 April, following thirty-two days on hunger strike, during which she lost over two stone.[7]

Below: Engraving from the *Illustrated London News*, 8 March 1912. The original caption reads 'Glass-Smashing for Votes! Suffragettes as Window-Breakers'.

Opposite: Anti-suffrage postcard depicting a group of suffragists as sour-tempered and unattractive old maids, with the text 'Suffragettes who have never been kissed', 1900.

Mind: Political Presence

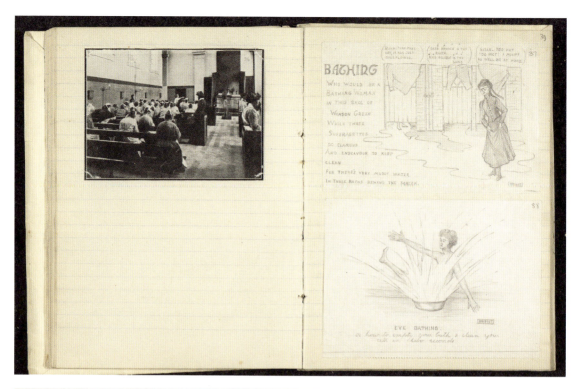

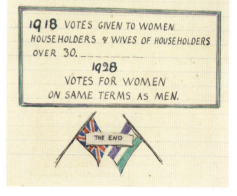

Scrapbook items recording the activities of suffragette Olive Wharry (1890–1947) while in prison. Wharry served at least six prison sentences for her suffragette activities between 1911 and 1914, one of which was for setting fire to the pavilion at Kew Gardens. The scrapbook contains poems, limericks, sketches, newspaper clippings and photographs written by Wharry and her fellow suffragette inmates.

Mind: Political Presence

The great contest at Plymouth for the honour of sending the first woman M.P. to the House of Commons, showing Lady Astor consulting Lord Astor (the late M.P.) over a map of the constituency, and the various stages of her campaign.

Constance Markievicz, in the uniform of the Irish Citizen Army, 1914.

The passing of the 1918 Representation of the People Act extended the parliamentary franchise to women aged over 30 who were either local government electors or married to one. In November of the same year women over the age of 21 were given the right to stand for Parliament. The first woman elected was the charismatic and controversial Constance Markievicz. A member of the Irish Republican Party, Sinn Fein, Markievicz was serving a sentence in Holloway prison at the time of the election. She refused to take the oath of allegiance to the King, and so declined to take up her seat in Westminster. Following a by-election in November 1919 Nancy Astor became the first woman to enter the House of Commons. A member of the Conservative Party, Astor was outspoken on equal voting rights, the employment of additional women police and civil servants, and a host of social welfare reforms that would improve the lives of all citizens.

The winning of the partial franchise in 1918 was a real and symbolic victory for women. It confirmed what Wollstonecraft had argued for in 1792 – that women, like men, had a right and a duty to contribute to public life. However the vote was always a means to an end. From the nineteenth century the women's movement had campaigned for gender equality on a wide range of issues and this continued long after the vote was won. Emmeline and Christabel Pankhurst, having disbanded the WSPU, set up a Women's Party (1917–19) to appeal to the 8.4 million newly enfranchised women. In February 1918 the party called on these voters to raise the 'social conditions of the masses of the people' and support the war effort – controversially in light of Sylvia Pankhurst's (Christabel's sister's) contrasting work with the International Women's Peace Congress and alliance with socialist and labour parties.

The idea that the women's movement went into decline after 1918 and only re-emerged in the late 1960s has been debunked. A number of important legislative reforms passed in the 1920s did improve the lives of women, for example the 1919 Sex Disqualification (Removal) Act, the 1923 Matrimonial Causes Act and the 1925 Guardianship of Infants Act. Nevertheless women faced ongoing discrimination in the workplace, and many were denied access to adequate housing, healthcare and educational opportunities. Despite the introduction of equal voting rights in 1928, women remained under-represented in local and national politics. Between 1919 and 1945 only thirty-eight women were elected to the House of Commons.

Female political representation may have remained marginal during the interwar years, but outside of formal politics significant numbers of women were politically engaged, including in movements for peace, workers' rights and social policy reform. Popular women's organisations, for example the Mothers' Union, Women's Institutes (1915) and the Townswomen's Guilds (1932), recruited hundreds of thousands of women. These groups played a key role in campaigning on behalf of wives and mothers, and were instrumental in encouraging women to become active citizens who used their vote wisely. Family allowances, equal pay, maternity services and pension rights were just some of the issues championed by these groups.[8]

At the end of the Second World War the former suffrage campaigner and Labour MP Ellen Wilkinson wrote an election pamphlet entitled *Plan for Peace*. Here she praised the contribution of 'every man and woman in the country' to the war effort, and set out the new Labour government's vision for postwar Britain, also acknowledging the new United Nations as an international political force relevant to women.

Above: Constance Markievicz, the first woman elected to become a Member of Parliament, photographed in 1914 in the uniform of the Irish Citizen Army. A member of the Republican Sinn Féin party, Markievicz did not take up her seat.

Opposite: Front page coverage in *The New Illustrated* of Nancy Astor becoming the first woman MP, November 1919.

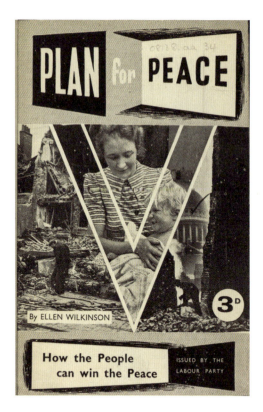

Ellen Wilkinson co-wrote Labour's 1945 election manifesto and, as chair of Labour's National Executive, she guided it through conference, following which Attlee appointed her Minister of Education. Before that, Ellen had headed the Jarrow Crusade and led anti-fascist campaigning. In Parliament, she worked with Nancy Astor to champion legislation that would extend women's rights. The pamphlet *Plan for Peace* sets out her vision.

Throughout the 1950s and 1960s the women's movement continued to demand greater equality and political representation for women. Some progress was achieved, with equal pay introduced in the public sector from 1954 and women admitted to the House of Lords in 1958. Housewives' associations, women's sections of the major political parties, trade unions and feminist pressure groups (for example the Fawcett Society) together made up this postwar women's movement. These initiatives have been sometimes overshadowed by accounts of the Women's Liberation Movement, which sprang up in the late 1960s. However the latter, in conjunction with parallel movements for black civil rights, gay and lesbian equality and disability rights, presented radical new challenges to traditional gender roles and highlighted the hidden cultural conditions which held women back from public life.

Despite the major social and economic changes occurring in late twentieth-century Britain, women remained under-represented in politics and public life. The election of the first female prime minister in the UK, Margaret Thatcher, in 1979 was significant but did little to increase the number of women elected to national and local government. In 1980 the all-party 300 Group was set up by Lesley Abdela to campaign for 50 per cent parliamentary representation. Training was provided for potential candidates in 'political schools', and over forty regional networks established to support female politicians. This has come closest in the 2019 general election, where a record 220 female MPs were elected, but still only representing 34 per cent of all MPs.

Over the course of the nineteenth and twentieth centuries the political representation of women in the UK increased significantly, but we are still far from parity, with particular under-representation of minority ethnic groups. For the twenty-first century it is crucial that female political representation continues to grow. This was the dream of activists in the nineteenth century, and remains the demand of millions of women today who seek global gender justice.

---

1 Mary Wollstonecraft, *A Vindication of the Rights of Woman, with Strictures on Political and Moral Subjects* (1792), p. vii.

2 Other examples of reforms supported by female activists include the 1857 Divorce Act and the 1870 and 1882 Married Women's Property Acts.

3 Helen Jones, *Women in British Public Life, 1914–1950: Gender, Power and Social Policy* (Harlow: Pearson Education Limited, 2000), p. 9.

4 See for example: Maroula Joannou and June Purvis (eds), *The Women's Suffrage Movement: New Feminist Perspectives* (Manchester: Manchester University Press, 2009).

5 *Post*, Thursday 5 November 1908.

6 June Purvis, 'The Prison Experiences of the Suffragettes in Edwardian Britain', *Women's History Review*, vol. 4, iss. 1, 1995, pp. 103–33.

7 Elizabeth Crawford, *The Women's Suffrage Movement: A Reference Guide 1866–1928* (London: Routledge, 2000), p. 707.

8 Caitríona Beaumont, *Housewives and Citizens: Domesticity and the Women's Movement in England, 1928–64* (Manchester: Manchester University Press, 2015).

FAWCETT

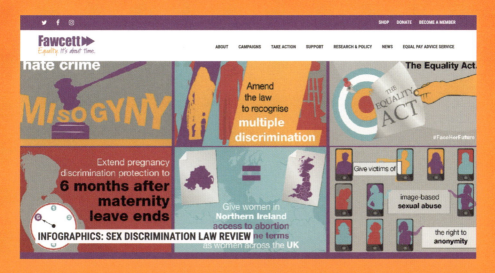

SOCIETY

The Fawcett Society is the UK's leading membership charity focused on gender equality and women's rights. We are the only national organisation rooted in the suffrage movement and named after Millicent Fawcett who led the constitutional campaign for votes for women. Our vision is a society in which women and girls in all their diversity are equal and truly free to fulfil their potential.

voi

Despite all attempts to silence and misrepresent them, women have found radical ways to make themselves heard in different spheres. Sasha Roseneil details the tools of protest that women have deployed and the ingenious ways in which they have expressed themselves, demanded change and insisted the world take notice. Women may have been agitating for change for hundreds of years, but they have not done it alone. Along the way, as Nicholas Owen explores, they have been helped and supported by men and boys who have recognised the injustice of sexual inequality and have understood that everyone stands to benefit from a fairer and more just world. In their chapter looking at historical recovery and rediscovery, D-M Withers explores how feminist libraries and archives uncovered, celebrated and created women's history as a discipline and subject. Mercedes Aguirre turns attention to art and literature, noting how women in the past found ways to write despite being discouraged from doing so and how the reissuing of lost literary texts by women has flourished since the 1970s. For Gabriele Griffin, feminist cultural output since the nineteenth century has been marked by 'do-it-yourself' strategies, with women taking over the means of production from print media to music-making to publishing as a political act and a means of imagining a womanist, feminist future. Speaking of the future, the last chapter by Sheila Rowbotham looks at how women have dreamed of utopian times in literature, art, poetry and through the radical imaginings of the Women's Liberation Movement, which aimed to transform the world.

— **DR POLLY RUSSELL**

VOICE: PROTEST & PARTNERSHIP

© Kate Evans

156

'I choose to re-appropriate the term 'feminism' ... to be 'feminist' in any authentic sense of the term is to **WANT FOR ALL** people, female and male, **LIBERATION** from sexist role patterns, domination, and oppression.'

BELL HOOKS (B.1952)
From *Feminism Is For Everybody* (2000)

The work of American academic bell hooks has focused on the intersection of race, gender and class, and the question of how to make feminism more inclusive. She has exposed racism within feminist approaches and also written on black masculinity. She stresses that overturning racist and sexist oppression involves both men and women.

Creativity and Invention

— **PROFESSOR SASHA ROSENEIL**

Women's Sunday March, June 1908. Organised by Emmeline Pankhurst's Women's Social and Political Union to persuade the government to support votes for women, it is believed to have been the largest ever demonstration held in the UK at that time.

Necessity is the mother of invention

— Old English proverb

Women's exclusion from full and equal citizenship has given rise to a huge variety of innovative forms of protest over the past 150 years. Lacking access to the normal channels of political claims-making, women have had to find unconventional ways of articulating their demands. Working around the mainstream media's failure to grant them fair coverage, women have developed a range of creative interventions that stir the emotions, capture the imagination and disrupt everyday life. This has meant assembling unorthodox political toolkits from the resources available to them. At times it has involved acting on the edges, and even in direct contravention, of the law.

There have been many radically inventive moments in the history of women's struggles. These include the suffragettes, Reclaim the Night, the Greenham Common Women's Peace Camp and, recently, Sisters Uncut, who together tell of a connected, cumulative repertoire of feminist protest. Collective occupation of public space, the direct mobilisation of women's bodies – often breaching both gendered convention and the bounds of legality – and the use of music, song and poetry have all been distinctive methods of political engagement across three waves of feminist organising.

THE SUFFRAGETTES

Feminism did not begin, or end, with the campaign for votes for women, but many of the methods of protest employed by later generations were trialled by the activists of the early twentieth century. Through more than a century and a half of feminist politics, the occupation of public space by large groups of women has been one of the most powerful ways of demonstrating dissent. Marches, rallies and demonstrations are particularly significant actions for women, who have not historically been sanctioned to gather together visibly and loudly in their own name. The gendered division of social life into public and private domains, in which the former is associated with masculinity and the latter with femininity, and which still retains its grip in contemporary Britain, reached its peak in the nineteenth century.[1] The Victorian ideology of 'separate spheres' underpinned the confinement of middle- and upper-class women within the domestic sphere, and justified the exclusion of economically active working-class women from the legal and political rights that had been won by working-class men (see also Cox in this volume). So, when women suffrage campaigners – frustrated by the lack of progress from more conciliatory 'indoor tactics' of drawing-room meetings, garden parties, signing petitions and lobbying Parliament – started to take to the streets in increasingly loud and obtrusive parades and gatherings, a new energy was unleashed.

The Women's Social and Political Union (WSPU) was founded in 1903. Its members came to be known, initially pejoratively, as 'suffragettes', and they organised numerous noisy demonstrations, and then, on 21 June 1908, one of the largest gatherings of women in UK history.[2] The Women's Sunday March comprised seven separate processions from different parts of London that converged on Hyde Park, for a rally of up to half a million women and their male supporters. They had travelled in specially chartered trains from all over the country, many carrying elaborate hand-crafted

Voice: Protest & Partnership

159

Above: The Women's Freedom League banner, 1908.

Opposite: Score of Ethel Smyth's 'The March of the Women'. This became the official anthem of the Women's Social and Political Union. The song, with words by Cicely Hamilton, was first performed on 21 January 1911 by the Suffrage Choir to mark the release of activists from prison. Smyth became the first woman composer to be awarded a damehood when she received the honour in 1922.

banners, for example the Women's Freedom League banner shown here. One of the most striking aspects of this spectacular event, at which more than eighty women speakers were given a platform, was the clothing worn by the women marchers. This was the first occasion at which the 'suffragette colours' – purple, white and green – were displayed, as tens of thousands of women appeared in white dresses, accessorised with purple and green hats, sashes, scarves, rosettes, badges and ribbons, activating the everyday in the cause of votes for women. From then on, the suffragette colours were worn by activists as much as possible, both at public demonstrations and while going about their ordinary lives.[3] Suffragette colours were always specified by the WSPU for the breakfast parties that greeted suffragette prisoners on their release from prison.

Music and song played an important role in the suffrage movement. There were brass bands at many gatherings and marches, and singing together built a sense of community and lifted the collective spirits. 'The March of the Women', composed in 1910 by Ethel Smyth with lyrics by feminist writer Cicely Hamilton, was adopted as the official anthem of the WSPU. The Suffrage Choir first sang the song to welcome Emmeline Pankhurst on her release from prison in 1911, and it was later often sung by suffragettes when they were in prison.

The slogan of the WSPU – *Deeds Not Words* – highlights the key difference between their direct, militant approach to winning votes for women and the rest of the suffrage movement. Between 1908 and 1914, the suffragettes committed thousands of acts of civil disobedience, using their bodies as tools: they threw stones to smash the windows of government buildings and expensive shops, attempted to 'rush' (invade) the House of Commons, chained themselves to railings, cut telephone lines, set fire to letter boxes and cut up the turf of golf courses. Most famously, Emily Wilding Davison walked out in front of the King's horse at the Epsom Derby, later dying from her injuries. Hundreds of activists were arrested and imprisoned, often repeatedly, for offences including obstruction, criminal damage, arson and conspiracy. In response to the government's refusal to recognise them as political prisoners, many went on hunger strike. But neither the introduction of a brutal regime of forced feeding, nor the 'cat and mouse game' of releasing and then re-imprisoning them, crushed their determination. Indeed, the suffragettes' refusal to be silenced can be seen in the harnessing of one of the few objects available to them in prison – toilet paper – as a means of communication (see overleaf).[4] Probably dating from 1921, the poems illustrated here were written on prison toilet paper by Sylvia Pankhurst when she was convicted of seditious activity relating to supporting revolutionary tactics in Britain following the Russian Revolution. Pankhurst was arrested numerous times, initially for her campaigning for suffrage, and was first imprisoned aged 24. A number of poems included in this collection are about the plight of women in jail and the poverty which drove them there, and are illustrative of Pankhurst's life-long commitment to social and political justice as well as women's rights.

Below: Sylvia Pankhurst's poems written on prison toilet paper while serving a prison sentence in 1920.

Opposite, above: In May 1958, at the height of the Cold War, a dozen feminist peace campaigners, led by writer Dora Russell, travelled by caravan to Communist countries in Eastern Europe. The caravan visited women's and peace groups from Edinburgh to Moscow, collecting signatures and artworks from those who embraced their gesture of friendship and solidarity. The journey symbolises the spirit of peaceful protest and feminist internationalism that blossomed in the twentieth century.

Opposite, below: Piece of souvenir Greenham Common fence wire.

RECLAIM THE NIGHT

Many decades later, in the late 1970s, as the second wave of the women's movement swept across Britain, the occupation of public space again became a feminist protest tactic as women took to the streets to 'Reclaim the Night'.[5] Against the backdrop of the murders of women in Yorkshire, attacks that were being attributed to the 'Yorkshire Ripper', and police advice that women should stay at home to avoid the threat of sexual violence, there was an upswell of activism about rape and sexual violence against women. Refusing their banishment to the domestic sphere, where they were not guaranteed safety from violence anyway, the first Reclaim the Night marches in November 1977 brought thousands of women into twelve town and city centres late at night, carrying torches to light up the dark, shouting, singing, dancing, holding hands, chanting, banging saucepan lids and beating drums. Noisily inserting their bodies into places where they were told they should not be, and where they often feared to be, was a collective act of brazen, angry defiance that challenged the fear of violence with which women were living (and still do).[6] Reclaim the Night marches continued through the 1980s, then were revived from 2004 and continue to take place across the UK today.

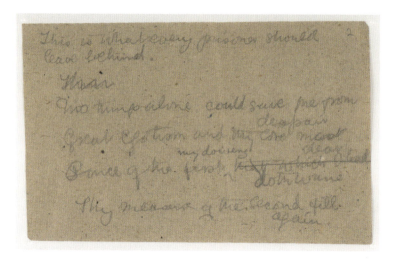

GREENHAM COMMON WOMEN'S PEACE CAMP

In the early 1980s the United States Airforce base at Greenham Common in Berkshire, England, became the focal point of a mass mobilisation of women opposed to the installation of a new generation of intercontinental nuclear weapons at the base. The Women's Peace Camp came into being at the end of a long walk from South Wales to Greenham Common in 1981. This had been initiated by a small group, Women for Life on Earth, to draw attention to their concerns as women about the threat posed by this intensification of the Cold War. Angry at the scarce media interest in their walk or in what they had to say about the nuclear arms race, four women chained themselves to the airbase gates, echoing the actions of the suffragettes, and requested a televised debate with the Secretary of State for Defence. No debate was granted,

Unfinished Business

and the women decided to set up camp in front of the base to continue protesting against nuclear militarism and women's exclusion from matters of foreign and defence policy. For well over a decade afterwards, despite court orders and injunctions, new legislation making their camps illegal, and thousands of attempts to evict them, women continued to camp around the 9-mile perimeter fence. The symbolism of women making their home together – without men, outdoors in all weathers, in the shadow of the missiles, overseen by the overwhelmingly male forces of the state – politicised everyday life at Greenham in a way that captured the imagination of people around the world. Their presence drew ongoing attention to the issue of cruise missiles, and ensured that the women's peace movement was widely known and discussed.

The women who lived at the camp called regular mass protests at the base, inviting others to join them. The Embrace the Base demonstration in December 1982 saw 30,000 women gather to join hands along the perimeter fence, covering the fence with personal messages, political banners, photographs of loved ones, flowers and even tampons. The Close the Base protest the next day involved several thousand women sitting down to blockade the base gates. Such bodily blocking of military operations resulted in hundreds of arrests for obstruction. But over time, weary of the injuries they sustained, women developed surprising non-violent direct action tactics that protected them from bruises and broken bones. They climbed over the fence at dawn on New Year's Eve 1983, and danced and sang on the missile silos. They occupied the sentry box and the air traffic control tower. They cut through the perimeter fence with bolt-cutters, and entered supposedly impenetrable military buildings. Thousands of such actions over the years resulted in many hundreds of arrests, court cases and prison sentences.

Voice: Protest & Partnership

Greenham Common protest,
12 December 1982.

Below: This Greenham Common strike shawl consists of dozens of individual spider web patterns crocheted by the women protestors and sewn together. The motif of the spider's web became a common sight at Greenham Common. Webs symbolised strength. They highlighted the unity and perseverance of the protestors, along with the interconnectedness of all peace movements.

Opposite: Sisters Uncut protesting at the 2015 opening night of *Suffragette* at the BFI London Film Festival in London.

Greenham was a place of great creativity and humour, including in the ways that women lived together on the Common. Most evenings, around the campfire after dinner, there was political discussion, storytelling and singing, with new songs composed to capture a mood or record a moment, and then passed down through the generations of campers in a shared culture. Women who had skills with textiles would weave webs of wool over groups of women blockading the gates or lying in front of diggers, symbolising the strength of nonviolence and women's networks. They made banners to hang on the fence, sewed a four-mile patchwork dragon for a summer equinox festival, created fur-fabric costumes for a teddy bears' picnic inside the base, and crocheted this collectively made shawl, which also incorporates the spider's web symbol. While Greenham's anarchist ethos meant there was no prescribed uniform in the manner favoured by the suffragettes, badges, posters and banners often made self-conscious use of purple, green and white. Women also learned less traditionally female skills, including building 'benders' in which to sleep – shelters made from bent-over saplings draped with sheets of plastic or tarpaulin.

SISTERS UNCUT

Sisters Uncut, founded in 2014, is an intersectional feminist direct-action collective focused particularly on defending domestic violence services under threat from austerity economics.[8] Seen as part of the 'third wave' of the women's movement, Sisters Uncut came to the public's attention in 2015 when they intervened in the premiere of the film *Suffragette* in Leicester Square, in central London. In a manner that echoed both the suffragettes themselves and the women of Greenham, they broke through metal barriers to let off purple and green smoke bombs, and lay down on the red carpet. Dressed in black, their trousers were embroidered in purple and green with the words *Sisters* and *Uncut,* with tops which read 'two women killed every week' and 'dead women can't vote'. Another powerful action involved walking slowly through central London as if on a funeral procession, blocking roads and bridges, chanting: 'They cut. We bleed'. This ended with a gathering in Trafalgar Square, where the water in the fountains was dyed bright red. And, intervening in the everyday site of the London Underground on International Women's Day 2019,

Fund Refuges not Prisons

Theresa, theresa what have you done?
We know there is money, but you say its gone,

Survivors of violence need more than new laws,
Your DV Bill pledges are littered with flaws,

Prisons don't work, so stop telling lies,
Only DV services can really save lives,

If you care about safety, stop cutting our cash,
Give power to survivors, it's as simple as that.

Subversive Poems of the Underground Sisters Uncut is a feminist direct action group which fights against cuts to domestic violence services

  @SISTERS UNCUT   #TimesUpTheresa   24-hour National Domestic Violence Helpline 0808 2000 247

Poem posted on the London Underground by Sisters Uncut for International Women's Day 2019.

the North London Sisters Uncut group posted fourteen different poems written by survivors of domestic violence and state violence on the tube. These posters were perfectly designed to mimic the officially sanctioned Poems on the Underground series, and successfully inserted their critique into the daily commute of thousands of Londoners.

UNLEASHING POSSIBILITIES

Not all of these forms of protest have been embraced by every feminist activist. Indeed many gradualist reformers who have preferred the softer tactics of letter-writing, petitioning, leafleting, lobbying, rallies and speeches, and who have sought to work through conventional political channels, have often distanced themselves from the more emotionally expressive, in-your-face, legally suspect and sometimes blatantly disobedient actions discussed here. Every social movement contains moderate and radical tendencies, often operating in tension and even conflict with each other, and each plays a vital role in securing social change. But the women activists of the past who have pushed the boundaries of acceptable protest, challenging ideas about how women should properly behave, have opened up cultural possibilities for future generations of women, and have created an array of political options for those who came after them.

---

1 Leonore and Catherine Davidoff, *Family Fortunes: Men and Women of the English Middle Class 1780–1850* (Abingdon: Routledge, 2002).

2 On the suffragettes, see: Andrew Rosen, *Rise Up, Women! The Militant Campaign of the Women's Social and Political Union* (London: Routledge, 1974); Sandra Holton and June Purvis (ed.), *Votes for Women* (London: Routledge, 2000); Antonia Raeburn, *The Suffragette View* (David & Charles: Newton Abbot, 1976); Elizabeth Crawford, *The Women's Suffrage Movement: A Reference Guide 1866–1928* (London: Routledge, 2001).

3 Diane Atkinson, *Purple, White and Green: Suffragettes in London 1906–14* (London: Museum of London, 1992).

4 The 1913 Prisoners (Temporary Discharge for Ill-Health) Act allowed for the release of hunger-striking women whose health was severely compromised in order to allow them to recover sufficiently to be re-arrested and complete their sentences.

5 Finn Mackay, 'The March of Reclaim the Night: Feminist Activism in Movement' (PhD thesis, University of Bristol, 2013).

6 The early phase of Reclaim the Night was accused of racism for choosing to march through areas with significant black and minority ethnic populations. See Kum-Kum Bhavnani and Margaret Coulson, 'Transforming Socialist-Feminism: the Challenge of Racism', *Feminist Review*, 23(1), 1986, pp. 81–92, and a discussion and refutation by Finn Mackay, 'Mapping the Routes: An Exploration of Charges of Racism Made Against the 1970s UK Reclaim the Night Marches', *Women's Studies International Forum*, 44, May–June 2014, pp. 46–54.

7 Sasha Roseneil, *Disarming Patriarchy: Feminism and Political Action at Greenham* (Buckingham: Open University Press, 1995).

8 http://www.sistersuncut.org/ (accessed 14 August 2019).

WOMEN FOR REFUGEE WOMEN

Women for Refugee Women is a London-based charity that supports women seeking asylum in the UK and challenges the injustices they experience. We run activities for refugee and asylum-seeking women to build their confidence and skills to speak out and advocate for themselves. We also lead the #SetHerFree campaign against the detention of asylum-seeking women in the UK.

Men in Feminism?

— **DR NICHOLAS OWEN**

170

Unfinished Business

Since the earliest formulations of women's demands for equality, at least some men have been willing to offer support and act as allies to women in their struggles for rights and recognition. In a world in which power and authority have belonged disproportionately to men, such support has often been useful in getting these demands adopted and implemented. However, men's engagement has, at times, been fraught with difficulty. Three problems have arisen repeatedly.

First, there has been the problem of identity and definition. Feminism has not only aimed to improve things for women as they now are. It has also wanted to consider afresh what it means to be a woman, and what women might be, need or want. Men, lacking most or all of the relevant experiences, needs and desires, have had only theory to contribute. Men have also sometimes tried to co-opt women's demands for existing struggles. This has sometimes been useful, broadening their appeal and raising their chances of success. Sometimes, however, it has simplified or postponed women's demands. Liberal men have offered women equal rights, but in a world still made by men. Socialist men have explained to women why their demands cannot be satisfied until the class revolution is achieved.

Second, there has been the problem of agency: that is, of who acts in pursuit of women's demands. Women have often wanted to win their own struggles for themselves. That is not because it is always the quickest way of winning. It is because acting for oneself is symbolically important in pursuit of other goals, such as building women's confidence as political actors, and strengthening the bonds of solidarity between women. For example, men's presence on a 'Reclaim the Night' march might be useful in conveying the breadth of support women's demands have secured. But it might also weaken the march as a demonstration of women speaking and acting for themselves, without male protection.

Third, there has been the problem of the personal. Feminists have often insisted that 'the personal is political'. Matters such as sexuality, intimate relationships, the emotions and the body do not lie in a separate sphere, beyond politics. This has required two things of men wishing to support feminism. They have had to extend their understanding of politics to include issues they have usually regarded as merely personal. And they have been expected to bring their personal lives into line with their politics. Their political commitment to feminism must be visible not only in their public lives, but also in their private lives: in whether they share household tasks equally, whether they give their daughters the same opportunities as their sons, and how they treat their sexual partners.

John Stuart Mill was a strong advocate of women's freedom. His book *The Subjection of Women* (1869), written with the help of his wife Harriet Taylor, denounced the legal and social inequalities endured by Victorian women, especially those who married. 'No slave', Mill wrote, 'is a slave to the same lengths, and in so full a sense of the word, as a wife is.'[1] As the cartoon caption – 'a Feminine Philosopher' – suggests, those expressing such views were often teased as unmanly. Mill's most distinctive argument was that no one could yet know what women were, or wanted, since they lacked freedom. The argument was qualified, however, by his assumption – one shared by many women – that free women would tend to choose the home, marriage and motherhood.[2]

In 1867, Mill, as an MP, proposed women's suffrage on the same terms as men, and over the next fifty years, male parliamentarians were necessary allies if women's suffrage legislation were to pass. Since

Opposite: Vanity Fair cartoon from 1873 of John Stuart Mill, titled 'A Feminine Philosopher'.

Below: Men's League for Women's Suffrage badge, 1918.

Opposite: Letter from Frederick Pethick-Lawrence to Sylvia Pankhurst. Emmeline and Frederick Pethick-Lawrence were ardent campaigners for women's rights. Three years after Emmeline's death in 1954, Frederick remarried. In this letter he mentions his second wife, Helen Craggs, herself a former suffragette, noting 'I find that I bailed her out some 45 years ago!'

many working men could not vote, extending the suffrage could be the 'common cause' of both sexes. However, as the women's suffrage movement became more militant, men's participation seemed to contradict another part of the campaign: the winning, by women, of their own freedom.[3] Unlike the longer-established National Union of Women's Suffrage Societies, the militant organisation the Women's Social and Political Union (WSPU) was a women-only movement. The single exception was Frederick Pethick-Lawrence, married to one of its leaders, Emmeline Pethick-Lawrence. He provided financial, legal and editorial advice, and also underwent the seizure of his assets, imprisonment and forcible feeding.

Such acts of solidarity were welcomed by many militant women suffragists. Even so, both the Men's League for Women's Suffrage, and the Men's Political Union which undertook militant acts in support of the WSPU, never entirely avoided giving the impression that chivalrous men wanted to fight other men on behalf of the 'weaker sex'. The expulsion of the Pethick-Lawrences from the WSPU in 1912 was the result of several considerations, including differences over strategy, but one was Christabel Pankhurst's determination that the organisation should be free of male influence. The estrangement of Sylvia Pankhurst from her family was also at least partly over the place of men in the movement, as well as ideological differences. Sylvia's close relationship with Keir Hardie, though an alliance born out of their shared socialism, was believed by the militants to compromise her feminism. Sylvia 'will never be an Amazon', the composer and suffragette Ethel Smyth told Emmeline Pankhurst in 1913. 'If it is not J.K.H. [Hardie] it will be someone else.'[4]

Unfinished Business

TELEPHONE: 7087 HOLBORN.
TELEGRAMS: "PETHLAWRO-HOLB, LONDON".

11, OLD SQUARE,
LINCOLN'S INN, W.C.2.

Saty Feby 23. 57.

My dear Sylvia

I was so pleased to get your cable of good wishes. I expect you knew Helen Craggs in the WSPU. I find that I bailed her out some 45 years ago! For the present we are going on living here. She has two married children living in California. Already Comm! TV has roped her in to do a piece next Monday.

With loving wishes

Fred.

THE FREEWOMAN

A WEEKLY FEMINIST REVIEW

No. 1. Vol. I.   THURSDAY, NOVEMBER 23, 1911   THREEPENCE

[Registered at G.P.O. as a Newspaper.]

Joint Editors:
DORA MARSDEN, B.A.
MARY GAWTHORPE

CONTENTS

	Page		Page		Page
1. Bondwomen	1	5. Feminism Under the Republic and the Early Empire. By AMY HAUGHTON	7	9. The Illusion of Propagandist Drama. By ASHLEY DUKES	13
2. Notes of the Week	3	6. Contemporary Recognition of Polygamy. By E. S. P. H.	9	10. The Psychology of Sex. By J. M. KENNEDY	14
3. A Definition of Marriage. By EDMUND B. D'AUVERGNE	5	7. The Spinster. By ONE	10	11. A University Degree for Housewives? By EDUCATIONIST	16
4. Der Bund für Mutterschutz. By BESSIE DRYSDALE	6	8. The Fashioning of Florence Isabel. By E. AYRTON ZANGWILL	11	12. The Sheltered Life. By W. H.	18

BONDWOMEN.

IT is a wholly pertinent matter that the temerarious persons who launch THE FREEWOMAN should be asked, "Who are the Freewomen?" Where are the women of whom and for whom you write who are free? Can they be pointed out, or named by name? There must be, say, ten in the British Isles. The question is pertinent enough, but it is difficult to answer, because its answer must of necessity become personal. We might, perhaps, hazard the name of one Freewoman who has become a sufficiently national figure to make her mention impersonal—Ellen Terry. There at least is one, and for the rest the inquisitors must be content with being enabled to arrive at the conception of Freewomen by way of a description of Bondwomen. Bondwomen are distinguished from Freewomen by a spiritual distinction. Bondwomen are the women who are not separate spiritual entities—who are not individuals. They are complements merely. By habit of thought, by form of activity, and largely by preference, they round off the personality of some other individual, rather than create or cultivate their own. Most women, as far back as we have any record, have fitted into this conception, and it has borne itself out in instinctive working practice.

And in the midst of all this there comes a cry that woman is an individual, and that because she is an individual she must be set free. It would be nearer the truth to say that if she is an individual she *is* free, and will act like those who are free. The doubtful aspect in the situation is as to whether women are or can be individuals—that is, free—and whether there is not danger, under the circumstances, in labelling them free, thus giving them the liberty of action which is allowed to the free. It is this doubt and fear which is behind the opposition which is being offered the vanguard of those who are "asking for" freedom. It is the kind of fear which an engineer would have in guaranteeing an arch equal to a strain above its strength. The opponents of the Freewomen are not actuated by spleen or by stupidity, but by dread. This dread is founded upon ages of experience with a being who, however well loved, has been known to be an inferior, and who has accepted all the conditions of inferiors. Women, women's intelligence, and women's judgments have always been regarded with more or less secret contempt, and when woman now speaks of "equality" all the natural contempt which a higher order feels for a lower when it presumes bursts out into the open. This contempt rests upon quite honest and sound instinct, so honest, indeed, that it must provide all the charm of an unaccustomed sensation for fine gentlemen like the Curzons and Cromers and Asquiths to feel anything quite so instinctive and primitive. With the women opponents it is another matter. These latter apart, however, it is for would-be Freewomen to realise that for them this contempt is the healthiest thing in the world, and that those who express it honestly feel it; that these opponents have argued quite soundly that women have allowed themselves to be used, ever since there has been any record of them; and that if women had had higher uses of their own they would not have foregone them. They have never known women formulate imperious wants, this in itself implying lack of wants, and this in turn implying lack of ideals. Women as a whole have shown nothing save "servant" attributes. All those activities which presuppose the master qualities, the standard-making, the law-giving, the moral-framing, belong to men. Religions, philosophies, legal codes, standards in morals, canons in art have all issued from men, while women have been the "followers," "believers," the "law-abiding," the "moral," the conventionally admiring. They have been the administrators, the servants, living by borrowed precept, receiving orders, doing hodmen's work. For note, though some men must be

Below: Written in 1893, George Bernard Shaw's play *Mrs Warren's Profession* struggled to get past the theatre censors. This proof copy includes Shaw's own amendments, highlighting his attempts to make his point while staying within the law.

Opposite: 1911 edition of *The Freewoman: A Weekly Feminist Review.*

There was also the question of how far men shared feminist women's perspectives on questions 'beyond the vote', such as marriage, motherhood, educational and working opportunities, and sex. Men were contributors to *The Freewoman,* a periodical in which such questions were keenly discussed by both sexes.[5] Male and female perspectives overlapped, but there were also some notable differences. Men often favoured reforms which promised to support women in their roles as traditional mothers, supportive wives and carers. They were more equivocal about supporting women in roles which broke from tradition, such as working to support themselves, or living without dependence on men. Notions such as the 'maternal instinct', a household economy based on a male breadwinner, and distinct male and female sexualities went largely unquestioned. These reservations did not prevent co-operation between men and women, because many women felt them too. But they defined the limits of men's support. Women who did not accept them found few, if any, male allies.

A further, and persistent, limit arose over feminist criticism of men's aggressive (hetero-) sexuality, and its expression in sexual violence against women and children. Male allies could be found to share feminists' anger against 'bad' men, such as those who controlled women working as prostitutes. They were less willing to concede that there was a general problem with 'good' male sexuality. For example, men, more than women, held that 'normal' male sexuality, outside marriage, created a largely unalterable demand for prostitution. Prostitution should therefore be approached as an economic conundrum. This was the message of George Bernard Shaw's play *Mrs Warren's Profession*.

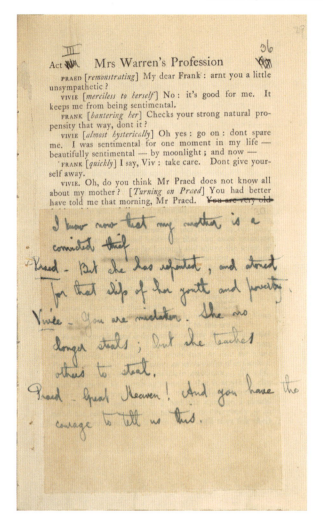

Shaw's solution to prostitution was to relax hypocritical Victorian codes. If women were educated and better paid, they would not be tricked or forced into selling themselves. If men could marry earlier, and divorce more easily, and have easier access to artificial contraception, then the demand for paid sex would diminish. Some feminists, however, thought such solutions condoned rather than condemned men's sexual incontinence. Their purity campaigns advocated celibacy outside marriage, and self-restraint within it.[6]

Some men were prepared to pledge themselves to purity, through youth organisations such as the Alliance of Honour.[7] However, such organisations worked separately from women's purity campaigns. They depicted young men's sexuality as an internal enemy to be conquered by a male hero pledged to revere and protect women, guided by a patriarchal father figure. Women were portrayed either as innocent virgins, dangerous temptresses or sacred mothers. As so often, differences over male sexuality proved the sticking-point for alliances.

Voice: Protest & Partnership

175

Activist and academic Stuart Hall and an unidentified man providing childcare at the Women's Liberation Movement Conference creche, Ruskin College, Oxford, 1970.

In the Women's Liberation Movement (WLM) of the 1970s, men were much less present than they had been in the suffrage movement.[8] Local WLM groups were either women-only from the start, or rapidly became so. Men were soon excluded from the national conferences – a few had spoken at the first one in 1970 – although they sometimes helped to provide the crèche at conferences, as can be seen in this photograph featuring the sociologist Stuart Hall. They were also encouraged to take on a larger share of domestic tasks to make it easier for women to participate in WLM activism.[9] Men also ceased to march alongside women on the annual women's day demonstrations. The emerging institutions of the WLM – women's centres, welfare clinics, refuges – were almost all women-only spaces, as were the movement's newsletters and publications.

The exclusion of men was, perhaps surprisingly, not a consequence of men's opposition to the formal demands of women's liberation. On the contrary, social surveys of the 1970s suggested that men were not much less favourable than women to demands for equal pay, equal opportunities and more nurseries. They were even slightly more in favour of state-provided birth control and abortion on demand.[10] Some, especially socialist feminists and black women's rights activists, therefore argued that men's participation was worth encouraging. At least some men were fellow victims. Capitalism and racism exploited both sexes. It treated working-class men and black men as emotionless providers of cheap labour and profits to others, and women as underpaid nurturers of present and future generations. Socialist feminists and black women activists were also anxious that the WLM should not become isolated from other social struggles in which men were dominant.

However, this position was strongly and successfully countered by radical feminists. Men, they argued, whatever their formal commitment to feminist goals, were reluctant to surrender their privileges. Male politicians were willing to allow certain 'women's issues' to be added to party or trade union manifestos, but only if they were not too critical of male sexism. Even the most sympathetic men seemed unable to hear the radical nature of women's new demands, especially when they extended beyond the workplace into 'his' home and social life.

Indeed, men's support for the formal WLM goals could also mask differences of perspective. Men, for example, were at least as keen as women on state provision of childcare. But this was as much to relieve domestic tensions as to challenge the social norm that childcare was women's work. Men also favoured free access to the contraceptive pill and abortion on demand, at least as much as women did. But reliable contraception and easier terminations also served heterosexual men's interests in making sex less risky and women more sexually available to men. Whether men also supported the feminist demand for women to control their own bodies was less clear.

There was also an important exception to the broad pattern of men's support for the demands of the WLM: sexual violence. Men were no less punitive than women on questions like rape sentencing. But they tended to see sexual violence as a problem of individual 'bad men', rather than – as did increasing numbers of feminist women – the nature of male heterosexuality itself. Men were also more tolerant than women of pornography, and accordingly harder to recruit to support feminist campaigns against it.[11]

As before, men were also excluded from the WLM in the interests of female agency. Men's domineering styles of arguing, which tended to

Autumn 1994 edition of *Achilles Heel* magazine.

silence the exploratory formulation of new demands, were an often-cited prompt towards women-only consciousness-raising groups. The WLM wanted to alter personal relationships with men as husbands, fathers, brothers, sons and lovers. Increasing numbers of feminists experimented with women-centred lifestyles, creating women-only or women-led households, workplaces, discos, holidays and sex lives. But for women still living with men, the problem of the personal remained a persistent one.

Many of the men close to feminist women therefore set up men's groups, modelled on the consciousness-raising groups of the WLM. They explored their initiatives in magazines like *Achilles Heel*, which first appeared in 1978. It was written by a collective of mostly university-educated young men, living in or near London, and influenced by socialism, community politics and therapeutic work. *Achilles Heel* explored the implications of feminism for men's lives and identities, in society, the workplace and the home. It covered topics such as how boys were brought up, the poverty of men's emotional lives, and the many unsatisfactory aspects of their relationships with women.[12] Some men's groups focused on anti-sexism, uncovering their own exploitation of women. However, the consequent guilt could be paralysing, and anti-sexist men's groups never achieved the same success as the women's groups. They also found it hard to accept a relationship of service and accountability to the women's movement. Other men, in investigating the origins of sexism, found themselves to be victims too, especially of the many ways that patriarchy, across classes, ethnicities and religions, prescribed what it meant to be a man. Some therefore focused on 'men's liberation' – the exploration and celebration of more affirmative masculinities. This approach also failed to achieve close co-operation with the women's movement.[13] Gay men sometimes allied successfully with feminists, but found it easier to identify a common patriarchal enemy than common goals.

In 1977, a small group of revolutionary feminists proposed that a strategy of 'separatism' from men was needed in the same way that national liberation or Black Power movements had used it, to enable women to fight patriarchy without distraction. All males must be regarded as enemies, and feminists should adopt 'political lesbianism', abandoning men as sexual partners, and identifying only with women. Anti-sexist men were regarded as especially pernicious, because they made it hard to see all men as enemies. These views were not held by the majority of feminists, but nonetheless became divisive in the WLM.

Before the 1990s, debates over men's participation in women's movements could rely on widely accepted and secure definitions of 'men' and 'women'. These definitions were based more on society's ideas of gendering than 'natural' biological sex differences. But they nonetheless established a strong binary division between men and women. Questions such as whether men could be admitted to women's spaces relied on the possibility of making such clear distinctions.

More recently, however, increased awareness of the concept of gender fluidity has made such distinctions unreliable and difficult to maintain. For some, the loss of clarity over who is a woman and who is not makes it harder to establish sex and gender as the ground on which to base an active, campaigning feminist politics. For others, however, the decoupling of sex, gender identity, gender expression and sexual orientation have created many new possibilities for alliances.[14] The search for alliances with other disadvantaged groups, such as Black and Minority Ethnic (BAME) struggles and the disability rights movement, carries on.

Men have engaged more successfully with some feminisms than others. They have found it easiest to support campaigns with shared goals, such as the Edwardian suffrage 'common cause', which united women and working men who themselves could not vote. Men have also supported campaigns which aim to improve things for women in traditional roles such as mothers, housewives or sexual partners for heterosexual men. However, campaigns to make women more independent of men – financially, domestically and sexually – have attracted less male interest. Sometimes, too, when motivated by the need to define their interests for themselves, or female self-empowerment, or their own solidarity, women have rejected men's involvement. Men's support has been most acceptable, and most successful, when it has respected the autonomy of the women's movement.

---

1   John Stuart Mill, Alan Ryan (ed.), *On Liberty* and *The Subjection of Women* (London: Penguin Classics, 2006), p. 166. See Sumita Mukherjee's article in this book for a discussion about the racial politics of discussing white women's position as 'slavery'.

2   Barbara Caine, 'John Stuart Mill and the English Women's Movement', *Historical Studies*, 18(70), 1978, pp. 52–67.

3   Angela V. John and Claire Eustance (eds) *The Men's Share? Masculinities, Male Support and Women's Suffrage in Britain, 1890–1920* (London: Routledge, 1997).

4   Quoted in Barbara Winslow, *Sylvia Pankhurst: Sexual Politics and Political Activism* (London: UCL Press, 1996), pp. 7–8.

5   Dora Marsden (ed.), *The Freewoman: A Weekly Feminist Review* (London: Stephen Swift and Co. Ltd., 1911–12).

6   Lucy Bland, *Banishing the Beast: English Feminism and Sexual Morality, 1885–1914* (London: Penguin, 1995).

7   Gregory A. Page (ed.), *The Alliance of Honour Record* (London: Morgan & Scott, 1911–14).

8   Nicholas Owen, 'Men in the 1970s British Women's Liberation Movement', *The Historical Journal*, 56(3), 2013, pp. 801–26; Lucy Delap, 'Uneasy Solidarity: The British Men's Movement and Feminism', in Kristina Schulz (ed.), *The Women's Liberation Movement: Impacts and Outcomes* (New York: Berghahn Books, 2017).

9   Jan McKenley interviewed by Margaretta Jolly, Sisterhood and After: The Women's Liberation Oral History Project, 2010–13. British Library Sound & Moving Image Catalogue reference C1420/15, transcript p. 23/track 01 © The British Library.

10 See the social survey data at http://paper-darts.com/men-and-the-demands-of-womens-liberation [accessed 23 August 2019].

11 See http://paper-darts.com/men-and-the-demands-of-womens-liberation. For more positive engagement with feminist perspectives, see Pete Six and Five Cram, interviewed by Lucy Delap, *Unbecoming Men: Interviews on Masculinities and the Women's Movement*, 1970–91. British Library Sound & Moving Image Catalogue reference C1667/30.

12 Victor Seidler, *The 'Achilles Heel' Reader: Men, Sexual Politics and Socialism* (London: Routledge, 1991).

13 Amanda Goldrick-Jones, *Men Who Believe in Feminism* (Westport, Conn: Praeger, 2002).

14 Nicholas Owen, *Other People's Struggles: Outsiders in Social Movements* (New York: Oxford University Press, 2019).

VOICE: RECOVER

'RE-VISION – the act of looking back, of seeing with fresh eyes, of entering an old text from a new critical direction – is for woman more than a chapter in cultural history: it is AN ACT OF SURVIVAL.'

ADRIENNE RICH (1929–2002)
From *On Lies, Secrets, and Silence* (1979)

American poet and scholar Adrienne Rich exposes how patriarchal culture enforces heterosexuality as 'normal' and turns women against each other. Ranging from the politics of language, through racism, history, motherhood and lesbianism, Rich's inspirational work refuses the myth of female passivity, and aims to recover women's role in history.

Recovering Traditions, Inspiring Action

— DR D-M WITHERS

Below: Celebration of the life and work of the Trinidadian-born feminist, activist, communist and community leader Claudia Jones (1936–1964), published by Camden Black Sisters Publications, 1988.

Opposite: Frontispiece from *Josephine Butler: Her Work and Principals and Their Meaning for the Twentieth Century*, by Millicent Fawcett, 1928. Fawcett's celebration of Butler was published to mark the centenary of Butler's birth in 1828. Fawcett admired Butler for her moral qualities and commitment to 'social purity' and 'moral hygiene'; these ideas were not embraced by all feminist movements of the early twentieth century.

Denied a place in official history and often absent from literature, art, music and in print, for over a century women have politicised the act of recovering and documenting their histories, connecting generations and celebrating foremothers. Josephine Butler (1828–1906), a prominent reformer and advocate of social and moral purity active in the Victorian age, was an inspirational figure for many suffrage campaigners in the early twentieth century. Marion Holmes of the Women's Freedom League, for example, extolled Butler's life as one 'replete with deeds of charity, kind love and stainless days',[1] in reference to her campaigns to repeal the Contagious Diseases Act. Millicent Fawcett echoed such adoration. In a publication that marked the centenary of Butler's birth in 1928 she argued that Butler 'should take the rank of the most distinguished woman of the nineteenth century'.[2]

For women active in Black feminist movements,[3] Claudia Jones, a Pan-African communist who settled in Britain after being deported from the US for her political activism in 1955, has repeatedly been heralded as an inspirational figure.[4] Camden Black Sisters Group (CBSG), one of many Black women's groups that formed in Britain after the first Organisation of Women of African and Asian Descent conference in 1979, produced a booklet and exhibition in 1988 to revitalise the memory of Jones' life and work. For CBSG, Jones was emblematic of the 'strength and the courage of Black Women struggling all over the world'. Their publication celebrated Jones' life but also paid tribute to 'the millions of Black Women whose lives can no longer continue to be denied'.[5]

In the late 2000s another remarkable community activist, Olive Morris, who died in 1979, was recovered by a new generation of Black feminist activists, the Remembering Olive Collective (ROC). Their project, 'Do You Remember Olive Morris?', was a call to action as the collective worked to revive the deeper history of radical Black activism in Brixton and beyond, guided by Morris' life and the people who recalled her. Activating the memory of figures like Jones and Morris is a strategic act with significance far greater than the celebration of individual Black women's lives; it is how varied traditions of collective political and

Voice: Recover

Below: Poster for the stage play *Emilia*, 2018.

Opposite: Photograph of the activist Olive Morris. In 1986 activists successfully campaigned to name a Lambeth council building in honour of Morris. A commemorative plaque was attached to the wall of Olive Morris House. The building was demolished in 2019, but the plaque was acquired by the Remembering Olive Collective, a group who keep the memory of Morris, and the causes she believed in, alive.

cultural resistance are kept alive, as radical foremothers are mobilised to encourage activism in the present.

The work to combat the erasure of community memory is, however, an ongoing struggle waged against powerful capitalist forces. Grassroots memory activism resists the redefinition of places through gentrification which threatens to demolish locations where alternative cultures and political realities have thrived. It also fights back against austerity, as over-stretched community archives are forced to compete for ever-squeezed funding streams in order to sustain their organisations and preserve valuable collections. In 2019 ROC relaunched as ROC 2.0 in response to Lambeth Council's plans to redevelop Olive Morris House, a building named by local activists to honour Morris' life in 1986. The new collective aims to challenge the Council's plans that risk removing all reference to Morris' life in Brixton's public spaces.[6]

Recovery can also be a creative strategy used by artists to reimagine stories and give excluded figures a new cultural life. Morgan Lloyd Malcolm's play *Emilia* (2018) centres on the life of poet Emilia Bassano who, as the reputed muse and 'dark lady' of Shakespeare's Sonnet 130, has been an ever-present fixture in the cultural imagination for over 400 years. Despite this, few are familiar with the life, work and legacy of Bassano – a considerable poet in her own right. The play explodes this silence by showing Bassano as a girl, young woman and fiercely wise older woman. The three Emilias perform on stage together, witnessing each other's experiences. *Emilia* tells multiple stories that challenge received wisdom about race, gender and literary genius, and Britain as a diasporic, multi-ethnic nation, enriched by centuries of migration. *Emilia* also gives witness to the power of integrating feminist generational experience by allowing women at different stages in their life to speak to each other, rather than placing their lives in opposition.

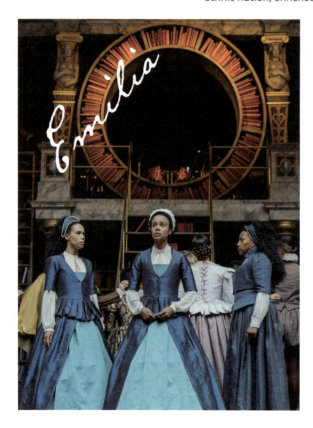

Remembering and forgetting, recovering and displacing: 'There's this peculiar thing isn't there, about women's movements, that they come and go and somehow or other so often women's movements have to reinvent themselves,' reflected Virago Press editor Ursula Owen in 2011. 'In some ways you have to reinvent yourself because it's such a personal thing, because feminism is extremely personal. And you have to do it yourself.'[7] Activists in the women's liberation movements (WLMs) of the 1970s may have claimed their politics to be radically 'new', an epochal Year Zero for feminism, but they were equally earnest in stating the political and cultural stakes of recovering women's place in history and society.

Women's liberationists were motivated by the idea that women's histories were 'hidden' and had to be found, and there were varied attempts to recover and (re)construct women-centred traditions, imagery and culture. This happened most notably in the fields of oral and folk song, captured in the recordings of Frankie Armstrong, Sandra Kerr and Peggy Seeger,

Unfinished Business

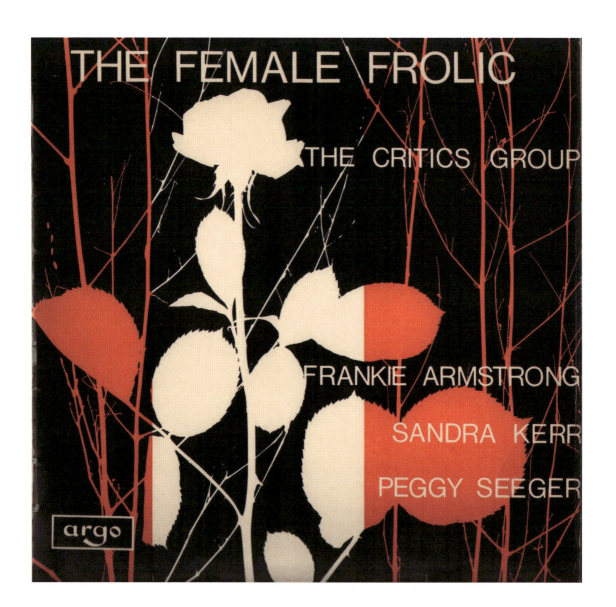

Below: Card catalogue from The Feminist Library, London. Feminist archives and classification systems made a fundamental intervention into how knowledge is organised and categorised. As a result, issues became visible and topics discoverable for researchers longing to find information about women.

Opposite: Cover of *The Female Frolic* by the Critics Group, 1968.

among others, as well as the reclamation of matriarchal spirituality embodied in Monica Sjöö's commanding painting *God Giving Birth,* viewed as controversial due to its depiction of God as an androgynous black woman giving birth, and the grassroots activities of the Matriarchy Study Group. Reclaiming women's traditions acquired mainstream recognition through Virago's Modern Classics series, as Mercedes Acquirre discusses elsewhere in this book.

Women's liberationists were often conscious of the fact they were *making* as well as recovering history. Some activists set up archives and libraries to ensure a legacy was created so future generations had the opportunity to reclaim and build on their actions. The Feminist Archive was established in 1978 by a group of activists living in Shepton Mallet, Somerset. Initially housed in an attic, it soon outgrew these premises and moved between various locations in Southwest England from the 1980s to the 2000s. The Feminist Archive was the first archive in Britain to specifically collect materials from the various feminist movements that blossomed internationally from the late 1960s onward.

An important intervention of feminist archives in this period was the attention they paid not just to collecting materials, but also to their cataloguing and classification. Feminist Archive founder Jean Freer developed an idiosyncratic version of feminist information science based on separatist principles, for example by insisting on the use of 'womyn' or 'wimmin' in catalogue descriptions, while attempting to integrate feminist witchcraft and numerology in the scheme. Freer's actions ran in parallel with those of librarian Wendy Davis, whose library classification scheme was adopted by the Feminist Library, and information specialists in the US and Europe who devised the 'Women's Thesaurus' and 'European Women's Thesaurus', cataloguing schemes now widely used by institutions which collect feminist and women-centred materials. The aim of feminist classification systems was to create new methods for discovering women, and the issues that affected them, in archive and library collections. Sometimes it simply meant creating a category for a subject – 'Jewish Women', 'Temperance', 'Afro-Asian', 'Wombyn-only', 'Bisexual', 'Menopause', 'Transgender' – that would help those searching for information to pull out individual items from a mass of possibilities.

Establishing a collection dedicated to women's lives was not, of course, an idea invented by women's liberationists in the 1970s. The Women's Library, based in London, had its roots in the suffrage campaigns of the late Victorian era. Originally called the Women's Service Library, it began to formalise its collections in 1926. Its mission at that time was to provide resources and information to women able to enter public life following legal reforms to the voting system (1918) and the legal professions (1919).

Now at LSE, the Women's Library has led a nomadic existence across its nearly 100-year history, and over this period its collections have grown substantially. In 1977 the Library faced a crisis, and the collection was nearly broken up. It was able to survive, however, and found a new home at the City of London Polytechnic Library and, importantly, a skilled librarian who helped develop its collections. Rita Pankhurst – Sylvia Pankhurst's daughter-in-law – gave form and order to the Women's Library's holdings during the 1970s and 1980s: a time when feminist print culture was rapidly expanding due to the explosion of publications in and around the WLM.[8]

Collections housed in feminist archives and libraries are the building blocks from which future acts of recovery are made. They are also important community spaces. The Feminist Library in London, which evolved from the Women's Research and Resources Centre established in 1975, remains embedded in the community, acting as a hub for activist meetings and campaigns. In recent years the Feminist Library has worked with artists and art institutions to activate its collections in inventive ways, creating imaginative contexts in which debate and exposure to feminist history can take place. The Glasgow Women's Library, established in 1991, is a multi-faceted cultural institution that promotes community cohesion, understanding and gender equality through its walking tours, literacy initiatives, archives and historical and artistic exhibitions. The GWL, now based in permanent premises that enable it to fulfil its pioneering work and commitment to the community, is the only Accredited Museum in the UK dedicated specifically to women's lives.

The twentieth century was punctuated by increasingly visible struggles to recognise women's rights and freedoms. Some of these histories were ephemeral and everyday, others monumental and dramatic. Centenaries and anniversaries, as well as annual events such as International Women's Day on 8 March, are vital pawns in the cultural battle to mobilise memory; time and time again the power of the calendar is used to ensure political issues remain relevant and topical.

2018 was a landmark year in Britain for recognising significant events in women's history as towns and cities marshalled state- and crowd-sourced funds to observe the centenary of the 1918 Representation of the People Act. Debate about women's contribution to politics in the past and in the present took place throughout the centenary year. Often the focus fell on the comparative lack of statues of women in public spaces, as activists highlighted that men outnumbered women by sixteen to one – a statistic that would be significantly worse if you took away all the statues of Queen Victoria. A wave of activism focused on public monuments led to statues of Millicent Fawcett in Parliament Square, Emmeline Pankhurst in Manchester, Alice Hawkins in Leicester, Emily Davison in Morpeth and Annie Kenney in Oldham being created, as suffrage footsoldiers and leaders alike were celebrated by local communities and politicians. A year on from the 1918 centenary, new statues of women continue to be campaigned for and unveiled, including one of comedian Victoria Wood, now immortalised in her home town of Bury.

The significance of statues is, of course, in their monumental presence. Yet the suffrage statues erected in 2018 – and wider calls for monuments about women's history to be instated in towns and cities – are meaningful because they have been rooted in participatory, often grassroots, campaigns. More widely, the suffrage centenary generated new exhibitions, TV and radio programmes, workshops, artistic interventions, debate, reflection and dialogue on a scale that is unprecedented for women's history. This proliferation of activities,

GLASGOW WOMEN'S LIBRARY

Established in 1991, Glasgow Women's Library houses archive, library and museum collections dedicated to women's history in the UK. The collections represent the diversity of women's lives and voices, ranging from archives that document women's activism to objects charting the lives of women who did war work or campaigned for women's suffrage. Glasgow Women's Library is the only Accredited Museum in the UK dedicated to women's lives, histories and achievements. It delivers innovative programmes of public events and learning opportunities, and is a multi-award winning, unique organisation visited by people from all over the world.

Unfinished Business

Opposite: Bronze statue by the artist Gillian Wearing commemorating the life of the suffragist Millicent Fawcett. The statue is located in London's Parliament Square and was unveiled in 2018 as part of the centenary of the 1918 Representation of the People Act, which gave some women over the age of 30 the right to vote. The statue's plinth includes the names of fifty-five women and four men who supported women's suffrage.

grounded in the recovery of activist histories, enabled a new generation to recover and activate a rebellious archive of militant activism and conscientious social reform as their own. As we surge through the twenty-first century, paradoxically we move further away from landmark moments in women's history but closer to their epic memorialisation. New centenaries and anniversaries come into view, bringing with them novel opportunities for reuse and recovery, activating sentiments of progressive social movements in the process: equality, self-determination, peace, freedom, transformation, liberation. Recovery has, at least since the early twentieth century, been an important element in the toolkit of activists, the state, communities, artists and entrepreneurs. The trick is to know *when* to use it.

1 Marion Holmes, *Josephine Butler: A Cameo Life-Sketch,* 8th edn (London: Women's Freedom League, 1913), p. 16.
2 Millicent Garrett Fawcett, *Dame Josephine Butler: Her Work and Principles, and Their Meaning for the Twentieth Century, etc.* (London: Association for Moral & Social Hygiene, 1928).
3 'Black' is capitalised here to signal the political use of 'Black' by British people of African, Afro-Caribbean, South and East Asian descent in the 1960s to 1980s.
4 Beverley Bryan, Stella Dadzie and Suzanne Scafe, *Heart of the Race: Black Women's Lives in Britain* (London: Virago, 1985), pp. 136–9; Diana Watt and Adele D. Jones, *Catching Hell and Doing Well: Black Women in the UK – the Abisindi Cooperative* (London: IOE Press, 2015), pp. 6–7.
5 Yvonne Joseph and Louisa Jean-Baptiste, *Claudia Jones 1915–1964: A Woman of Our Times* (London: Camden Black Sisters Publications, 1988).
6 'Olive Morris Collective Says Memorial Must Not Be Lost', https://www.brixtonblog.com/2019/06/olive-morris-collective-says-memorial-must-not-be-lost/?cn-reloaded=1 (accessed 7 August 2019).
7 Ursula Owen, interviewed by Rachel Cohen, Sisterhood and After: The Women's Liberation Oral History Project, 2010–2013, British Library Sound & Moving Image Catalogue reference C1420/36/04 (The British Library and The University of Sussex, 2011).
8 Rita Pankhurst, 'Collection Development and Women's Heritage: The Case of the Fawcett Library', *Women's Studies International Forum*, vol. 10, iss. 3, 1987, pp. 225–39.

Recovering Women's Writing

— **DR MERCEDES AGUIRRE**

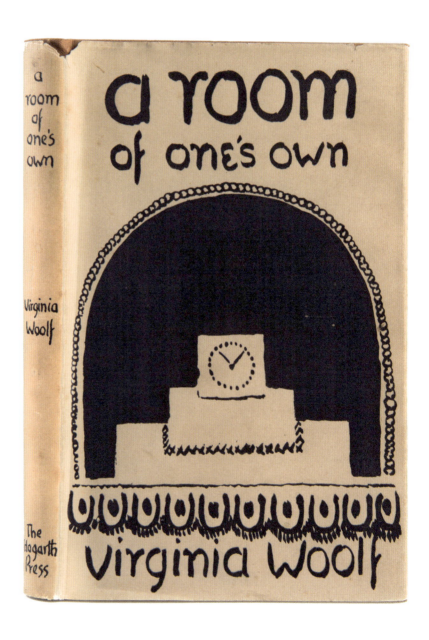

> **I would venture to guess that Anon, who wrote so many poems without signing them, was often a woman.**
>
> – Virginia Woolf, *A Room of One's Own*

What would have happened to Shakespeare's sister Judith, had she been born with her brother's genius for words? Virginia Woolf argues in her 1929 essay *A Room of One's Own* that, unlike her brother, Judith would not have received a formal education. She would not have been taught grammar, logic and Latin through the texts of Horace and Virgil. Her family would have expected her to marry young. Had she run away to London to follow her passion for the theatre her plans would have been met with incredulity and derision – women could not be actors. Finding herself unmarried and pregnant by actor-manager Nick Greene, Woolf continues, Judith would have committed suicide. But Judith Shakespeare is a fictional character, the creation of Woolf's imagination. Looking at the bookshelves of the British Museum Library and noting the absence of seventeenth-century female playwrights, Woolf employs Judith to hypothesise what the fate of a talented woman writer would have been in early modern Britain. 'It would have been impossible', she concludes, 'for any woman to have written the plays of Shakespeare in the age of Shakespeare'.[1]

A Room of One's Own originated in lectures Woolf gave in two women's colleges at Cambridge University, Newnham and Girton, in 1928. She was speaking to a group of young students who would not be awarded a degree even if they passed their examinations, as it wasn't until 1948 that Cambridge permitted women to graduate (men could graduate in 1209). 1928 was also the year the Representation of the People Act had extended the suffrage rights of the 1918 law, giving the vote to all women over the age of 21 on equal terms with men. Woolf's essay is a foundational text of feminist literary criticism and addresses many of its core questions: how social and financial constraints have shaped women's ability to write and publish, how women have been represented in works of fiction written by men, and the idea of a female literary tradition.

'BY A LADY': WOMEN WRITERS AND ANONYMITY

Becoming a professional writer in the nineteenth century involved particular challenges for women authors. As Alexis Easley argues, women writers 'often faced social censure, received substandard pay, and fell subject to a critical double standard'.[2] Writers such as Charlotte Brontë, Jane Austen or Mary Shelley chose to publish their works anonymously or under a male pseudonym. This was not uncommon: until the early nineteenth century the majority of British novels had been published anonymously,[3] and, as John Mullan states, 'guessing at the gender of an unknown author became part of the pleasure of reading'.[4] Men and women writers have historically chosen to hide their authorship for different reasons, from following the convention of modesty, to faking an eyewitness account or feeding speculation among readers. Women writers had additional reasons to conceal their authorship. Becoming a public writer rendered women more vulnerable to social disapproval. Particularly

Opposite: Front cover of the first edition of Virginia Woolf's *A Room of One's Own*, 1929.

Below: Draft manuscript for George Eliot's *Middlemarch*, 1871–2.

Opposite: First edition of Jane Austen's *Sense and Sensibility*, which was first published anonymously in 1811. The title page declared it was written 'By a Lady'.

at a time in which debates about what constituted respectable work for women proliferated, many women writers had to carefully manage their social reputation and their professional ambitions.[5] Writing under a pseudonym also freed women from having to follow the standards of a narrowly defined feminine literary style and helped them avoid prejudiced critical reviews. Charlotte, Emily and Anne Brontë deliberately chose gender-ambiguous pseudonyms for their works – Currer, Ellis and Acton Bell – as Charlotte Brontë revealed in the 1850 preface to the joint edition of *Wuthering Heights* and *Agnes Grey* after the deaths of her sisters. Brontë cites avoiding critical bias against women writers and condescending reviews as their main reason to publish under a pseudonym: 'we had a vague impression that authoresses are liable to be looked on with prejudice',[6] but their ambiguous pen names also had the effect of prompting excited speculation about their authorship.

Jane Austen's first novel, *Sense and Sensibility,* was published anonymously in 1811. Its title page declared it was written 'By a Lady', the conventional attribution for a woman writer, concealing Austen's name but revealing her gender. The novel's first edition sold out, and when *Pride and Prejudice* was published it was announced as 'by the author of Sense and Sensibility'. None of Austen's novels published in her lifetime appeared under her name, though the secret was revealed soon after her death. Mary Anne Evans took the masculine pen name George Eliot in 1857, having published other works anonymously before that date. While Eliot, who lived for many years with a married man, the philosopher George Henry Lewes, may not have wanted to draw attention to their extramarital relationship, a primary concern was the implication of being labelled a 'woman writer'. In 'Silly Novels by Lady Novelists', published anonymously in the *Westminster Review* in 1856, George Eliot criticised the formulaic romantic novels written by women which were bestsellers at the time, and their effect on society's ideas of what constituted women's writing. The essay points out how women are subjected to different standards by critics, who offer patronising praise to mediocre women writers but refuse to recognise good writers. Eliot does not argue here that women writers should adopt traditionally masculine subjects or style. 'Silly Novels by Lady Novelists' stresses that there have been very fine women novelists, and gestures towards the idea of a female literary tradition: 'A cluster of great names, both living and dead, rush to our memories in evidence that women can produce novels not only fine, but among the very finest; novels, too, that have a precious speciality, lying quite apart from masculine aptitudes and experience'.[7] By the time *Middlemarch* was published as a serial between 1871 and 1872, the identity of its author was widely known by the public, but Eliot still chose to continue writing under a masculine pen name.[8] George Eliot is one of the few novelists still known by their pseudonym.

SENSE
AND
SENSIBILITY:

A NOVEL.

IN THREE VOLUMES.

BY A LADY.

VOL. I.

London:
PRINTED FOR THE AUTHOR,
By C. Roworth, Bell-yard, Temple-bar,
AND PUBLISHED BY T. EGERTON, WHITEHALL.
1811.

Above: Cover of Omenala Press's 1986 re-edition of Buchi Emecheta's *In the Ditch* (first published in 1972).

Opposite: 1890 manuscript journal of Michael Field, the name used by Katharine Harris Bradley and her niece Emma Cooper to hide their identity.

For other writers, a male pseudonym hid more unconventional arrangements. Katharine Bradley (1846–1914) and Bradley's niece and romantic partner Edith Cooper (1862–1913) wrote poetry under a single male name, Michael Field. In 1884, when Cooper was 22 and Bradley 38, they published their first volume under that pseudonym, containing the verse dramas *Callirrhoë*, about a classical Greek nymph's erotic transformation, and *Fair Rosamund*, a historical drama about Henry Plantagenet's mistress, both of which were enthusiastically reviewed. Both writers were concerned about their identity being discovered and the effect it would have on their ability to publish. As Bradley wrote in a letter to their friend and mentor Robert Browning in 1884, in which Bradley asked him not to disclose their identity to critics, 'the report of lady-authorship will dwarf and enfeeble our work … [W]e have many things to say the world will not tolerate from a woman's lips'.[9] Their identity was revealed to the press soon afterwards. While critics have pointed out that Michael Field's outmoded style and preference for the genre of the closet drama was unfashionable for the time,[10] the discovery of their female authorship affected the reviews of Field's later works, which were never as enthusiastic.[11] However, Bradley and Cooper continued to use their joint pen name, writing more than thirty works together as Michael Field, and co-writing several volumes of a journal of Michael Field entitled *Works and Days*.

While stereotypes of what constitutes female authorship may look outdated, in our own age the perception that women writers are only able to speak about women's experiences rather than universal ones still persists. Perhaps the most famous recent example is that of J. K. Rowling, author of the Harry Potter books, who was advised by her publishers to choose her initials rather than her name Joanne Rowling to conceal the fact that she was a woman for fear that it would alienate young male readers.

RECOVERING WOMEN'S WORDS

Do women have a literature of their own? In *A Room of One's Own*, Woolf writes about the need for a woman writer to trace a female literary tradition: 'we think back through our mothers if we are women'.[12] Throughout literary history, writers have traditionally related themselves to their predecessors, heirs to a literary tradition or rebels against it. For women writers, identifying their foremothers and recovering their histories has served to defend their own right to write. As Gilbert and Gubar have argued, the woman writer 'searches for a female model … because she must legitimise her own rebellious endeavors'.[13] There are many examples of women writers who have set out to record the lives and recover the works of their forerunners. Elizabeth Gaskell famously wrote a biography of her friend Charlotte Brontë, published in 1857 and considered the first British biography of a female novelist by a female novelist. Virginia Woolf and Sylvia Townsend Warner explored the legacy of Jane Austen in the twentieth century.[14] But not all genealogies emerge in a linear way. As Sandra Courtman has argued, the success of Andrea Levy's historical novel *Small Island* (2004), which narrates the stories of Jamaican immigrants in postwar Britain, has served to highlight the neglected works of pioneering women writers of the Windrush generation, including Beryl Gilroy's *In Praise of Love and Children* (1959).[15] A sense of literary heritage is crucial for anyone trying to break through into public culture. Contemporary women writers have acknowledged their debt to the writers who broke both racial and gender barriers. Reacting to the news of the death of British-based Nigerian writer Buchi Emecheta, Chimamanda Ngozi Adichie stated: 'We are able to speak because you first spoke.'

The recovery of women's writings by feminist scholars and writers in the 1960s and 1970s, closely connected to the activism of the Women's Liberation Movement and their radical focus on culture, and the ensuing academic field of gender studies, has happily transformed the literary canon and the curriculum today. Feminist publishing also played a critical part. British feminist publishers, such as the Women's Press, Sheba Feminist Publishers, Onlywomen Press, Pandora and, most notably, Virago, have uncovered swathes of lost treasures. Perhaps the best known of these is the Virago Modern Classics series, which began in 1978 with the reprinting of Antonia White's 1933 work *Frost in May*, followed by Sylvia Townsend Warner's *Mr Fortune's Maggot* and *The True Heart* in the same year, and went on to include nineteenth-century women's travel writing, children's writing and landmark biography such

Voice: Recover

197

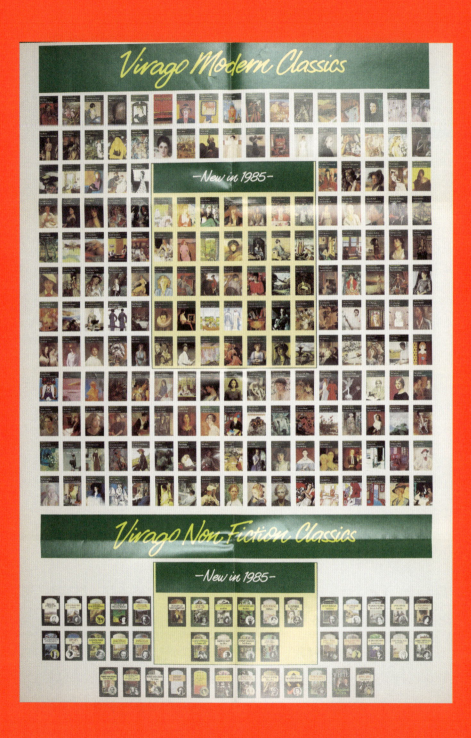

as Vera Brittain's protest against the slaughter of the First World War, *Testament of Youth*. In 1977 Virago republished *Life as We Have Known It,* an extraordinary collection of working-class women's testimonies which had first been published by the Hogarth Press in association with the Co-operative Women's Guild in 1931, and included an introduction by Virginia Woolf herself. In 2019, the Virago Modern Classics list contains 687 titles.

Putting these works on the map has helped force a rethinking of the twentieth-century literary canon, and redefined ideas of aesthetic value, period and literary schools. However, such works also illuminate the skill and vision of women in the publishing business, including their own struggles to succeed in the traditionally white, class-bound 'gentleman's profession'. Margaret Busby became Britain's youngest and first black woman publisher when she co-founded Allison & Busby with Clive Allison in the late 1960s. Allison & Busby published notable men and women authors including Rosa Guy, C. L. R. James and Buchi Emecheta, whose novel *The Slave Girl* (1977), which won the *New Statesman*'s Jock Campbell Award, is dedicated to Busby 'for her believing in me'. Emecheta's son Sylvester Onwordi continues to preserve his mother's legacy, reprinting her works under his imprint Omenala Press.

The recovery of black British women writers has often required a transnational approach, drawing on a long tradition of women writers from the African diaspora, and challenging limited ideas of national as well as gendered heritage. In 1992, Margaret Busby edited the groundbreaking anthology *Daughters of Africa,* reuniting the works of women writers of African descent, including Beryl Gilroy, Audre Lorde, Nancy Morejón, Claudia Jones and Jackie Kay. Reflecting on the works of the writers included in the anthology, Busby states:

> Throughout these women's words runs the awareness of connectedness to a wider flow of history, to the precursors, our foremothers. Our collective strength, like that of a chain, derives from maintaining the links.[16]

2019 has seen the launch of her *New Daughters of Africa,* a new anthology of over 200 past and contemporary writers of African descent. Published by the independent, women-led Myriad Editions, it is a marker of the ongoing work of those finding practical and creative ways to develop and challenge our understanding of British literary history.

Opposite: Poster from 1985 depicting *Virago Modern Classics* titles.

---

1. Virginia Woolf, *A Room of One's Own* (London: Hogarth Press, 1929), p. 70.
2. Alexis Easley, 'Making a Debut', in Linda H. Peterson, *The Cambridge Companion to Victorian Women's Writing* (Cambridge: Cambridge University Press, 2015), pp. 15–28.
3. Peter Garside and James Raven, eds., *The English Novel, 1770–1829: A Bibliographical Survey of Prose Fiction Published in the British Isles* (Oxford: Oxford University Press, 2000), p. 41.
4. John Mullan, *Anonymity: A Secret History of English Literature* (London: Faber, 2007), p. 76.
5. Joanne Shattock, 'Becoming a Professional Writer', in Linda H. Peterson, *The Cambridge Companion to Victorian Women's Writing* (Cambridge: Cambridge University Press, 2015), pp. 29–42.
6. Charlotte Brontë, 'Preface', *Wuthering Heights and Agnes Grey* by Ellis and Acton Bell (Smith, Elder, and Co.: London, 1850), p. ix.
7. George Eliot, *Silly Novels by Lady Novelists* (London: Penguin, 2010), p. 33.
8. The relationship between Mary Anne Evans, one of the canonical great English women novelists, and the masculine authorial persona of George Eliot that Evans adopted, has long been a subject of interest for literary critics. For a discussion of the implications of using gendered pronouns when writing about Eliot and the narrators in Eliot's novels, see J. Hillis Miller's *Reading for Our Time: 'Adam Bede' and 'Middlemarch' Revisited* (Edinburgh: Edinburgh University Press, 2012) pp. 3–4, and Grace Lavery's 'Down With These So-Called "Gender Categories"!' in her newsletter *The Stage Mirror* [https://grace.substack.com/p/down-with-these-so-called-gender]. Accessed on 7 November 2019.
9. Katharine Bradley and Edith Cooper, in Marion Thain and Ana Parejo Vadillo, *Michael Field, The Poet* (Toronto: Broadview, 2009), p. 311.
10. Joseph Bristow, 'Michael Field in Their Time and Ours', *Tulsa Studies in Women's Literature*, 29(1), Spring 2010, p. 163.
11. Sharon Bickle, 'Victorian Maenads: On Michael Field's Callirrhoe and Being Driven Mad', *The Michaelian*, 2, December 2010, p. 1.
12. Virginia Woolf, *A Room of One's Own* (London: Hogarth Press, 1929), p. 114.
13. Sandra M. Gilbert and Susan Gubar, *The Madwoman in the Attic: The Woman Writer and the Nineteenth-Century Literary Imagination* (New Haven: Yale University Press, 2000), p. 50.
14. Virginia Woolf, *The Common Reader. First Series* (London: Hogarth Press, 1925) and Sylvia Townsend Warner, *Jane Austen, 1775–1817* (London: Longmans, Green & Co., 1951).
15. Sandra Courtman, 'Women Writers and the Windrush Generation: A Contextual Reading of Beryl Gilroy's *In Praise of Love and Children* and Andrea Levy's *Small Island*', *EnterText*, vol. 9, 2012, p. 100.
16. Margaret Busby, 'Introduction', *Daughters of Africa: An International Anthology of Words and Writings by Women of African Descent from the Ancient Egyptian to the Present* (London: Jonathan Cape, 1992), p. xxxxviii.

VOICE: EXPRESS

'I have come to believe over and over again that what is most important to me **MUST BE SPOKEN**, made verbal and shared, even at the risk of having it bruised or misunderstood.'

AUDRE LORDE (1934–1992)
From 'The Transformation of Silence into Language and Action' (1977)

Writing as a black 'lesbian, mother, warrior, poet', Audre Lorde used her creativity to confront racism, sexism and homophobia, and to inspire in women the courage to speak out. Her poetry burns with anger against injustice and her scholarship examines difference, identity, illness and mortality with the aim of transforming our world.

Sistahs Doing It For Themselves

— PROFESSOR GABRIELE GRIFFIN

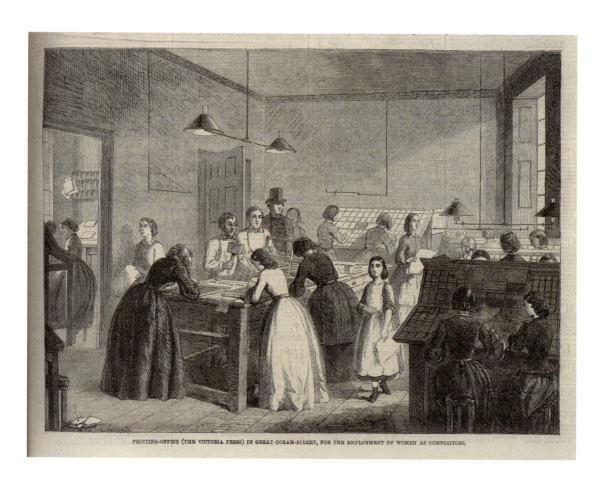

PRINTING-OFFICE (THE VICTORIA PRESS) IN GREAT CORAM-STREET, FOR THE EMPLOYMENT OF WOMEN AS COMPOSITORS.

Above: Emily Faithfull, 1891.

Opposite: Women compositors at The Victoria Press Printing Office in London's Great Coram Street. The Victoria Press was started by the feminist activist Emily Faithfull in 1860 and was created as a way to encourage more women into a career in printing.

During second-wave feminism (1960s to 1980s) the notion of women 'doing it for themselves' became prominent across continents, as a reaction against men's dominance in the public sphere and their unwillingness to take up women's concerns. From Audre Lorde's assertion that 'The master's tools will never dismantle the master's house',[1] and bell hooks' injunction for black women to agitate on their own behalf rather than be spoken for by others (white women), to Monique Wittig's outright refusal of the word 'woman' as being a patriarchal construction, and Radicalesbians' statement that 'a lesbian is the condensed rage of all women to the point of explosion', the prevailing mood was that women should empower themselves and each other through collective action on behalf of themselves.

This call to active engagement by 'women-identified women', based on an antagonistic relation to men and their hegemony, had antecedents dating back to the mid-nineteenth century, at the very least. At that time women of dissenting and middle-class backgrounds such as the Langham Place group sought to improve women's status in society through campaigning for women's suffrage. Meeting at 19 Langham Place, this all-female group included, among others, Barbara Leigh Smith Bodichon (1827–1891), Emily Davies (1830–1921), Bessie Rayner Parkes Belloc (1829–1925) and Emily Faithfull (1835–95). Importantly, the group sought to expand educational and employment opportunities for women. In 1859 they co-founded the Society for Promoting the Employment of Women. One such possible employment was publishing, at the time a male-dominated domain. In 1860 Faithfull founded the Victoria Press as an all-female printing establishment. This was a contested move because it challenged the male dominance of the print trade. It offered remunerated industrial employment to women, training them to become compositors, and thus setting them up as producers rather than mere consumers of published work. It challenged prevailing working conditions, which were cited as reasons why the print trade was unsuitable for women. Faithfull also founded the *Victoria Magazine,* which she edited until 1880. Concerned that women should be able to undertake remunerated labour which would render them financially independent of men, she sought respectability through a close and public association with Queen Victoria, indicated in her use of the Queen's name for her various enterprises and the dedications to the Queen in the early editions of the *Victoria Magazine.* In these moves Faithfull showed a powerful understanding of the importance of public – in her days print – media as a tool to further her cause. Faithfull was duly rewarded by being appointed Printer and Publisher Ordinary to Her Majesty in 1862, and from 1889 she received an annual civil list pension of £50. Together with Emma Paterson, she co-founded the Women's Printing Society (1876–1913). Providing employment for women, the press published, among other things, feminist tracts – notably the reports of the Central Committee of the National Society for Women's Suffrage.

Voice: Express

Below: The feminist activist, educationalist and writer Stella Dadzie illustrated Womanopoly – a tongue-in-cheek, consciousness-raising game. Players experience how racialised gender stereotypes determine life's chances.

Opposite: Una Marson (1905–1965) broadcasting to British troops in the West Indies from a theatre in London, February 1942.

In 1864 Faithfull was embroiled in the Codrington Scandal. Admiral Henry Codrington sued his wife Helen for divorce. It has been suggested that Faithfull had a lesbian relationship with her. The Langham Place group withdrew its support from Faithfull following this scandal, but she continued a successful career as a printer, publisher, public speaker and explicit supporter of women's work, never marrying and accompanied through her life by various female companions. The point here is that Faithfull's commitment to women, their fiscal independence from men, and her participation in female collectives engaged in improving women's lives was also bound up with a personal life that was dedicated to women. Such dedication has been one of the hallmarks of feminist moves to empower women by becoming active participants in the public sphere.

Another woman who also sought to empower other women through her interventions in the world of publishing was Una Marson (1905–65), who came to London from Jamaica in 1932. She already had a history as the first black female editor in Jamaica of publishing magazines there, having set up *The Cosmopolitan*. This magazine published on feminist topics as well as poetry, but ceased in 1931 due to financial problems. In London Marson initially lodged with Harold Moody, founder in 1931 of the League of Coloured Peoples. Through the League of Coloured Peoples she became involved with *The Keys* journal (1933–9), its official publication. Its first edition featured Marson's poem 'Nigger', which detailed her response to racist verbal abuse on the streets of London. Like many colonials in the metropole Marson had to negotiate prevailing stereotypes about black people. She did this through her writings and through work she conducted for the League of Coloured Peoples seeking to support figures such as Haile Selassie, who were lobbying the British government for better conditions in, and support for, the colonies. From 1938 she worked for the BBC as a producer on the *Calling the West Indies* programme, designed to enable soldiers from there who had enlisted in the British Army to send messages home. She transformed this programme into *Caribbean Voices*, a highly influential space for Caribbean poetry.

Both Faithfull and Marson recognised the importance of public media for achieving a presence for marginalised people. But where Faithfull was mainly concerned with improving the employment opportunities for women, not least through providing actual employment for them, Marson was preoccupied with improving the situation of black people in a world of hegemonic whiteness.

The recognition that women needed to do it for themselves, and in as many spheres of life as possible, became a key driver of feminist work in the second half of the twentieth century, especially from the 1970s onwards. Stella Dadzie was one who, like Marson, began from the perspective of black independence movements, but helped forge black British women's organisations which connected civil rights with those of women and children. Her Womanopoly board game recasts Monopoly through a feminist lens, playfully imagining the struggle to win in the game of life against these many challenges.

Voice: Express

Opposite: Northern Women's Liberation Rock Band Manifesto, 1974–6.

A different cultural response was the setting up by women of women-only presses such as Virago (1973–), Onlywomen Press (1974–2010), The Women's Press (1978–2013), Sheba Feminist Press (1980–94), Pandora Press (1980–96) and Persephone Books (1999–), to publish 'forgotten' and new work by women. They also produced magazines dedicated to women such as *Spare Rib* (1972–93), *Trouble and Strife* (1983–2002) and the transnational newspaper *Outwrite* (1982–8).

The pages of these magazines chart the changing preoccupations of the women's movement from early socialist concerns with women's conditions and opportunities in the labour market, through discussions about relations between lesbian and straight women, to debates about race and ethnic relations among diverse female constituencies.

These presses were largely located in London, but through the music scene women from other spaces (the regions, the suburbs) seized the means of production to make their voices heard. The highly politicised Manchester-based Northern Women's Liberation Rock Band (1973–6) featured Angela Cooper and Luchia Fitzgerald as singers, Angie Libman on drums, Carol Riddell on keyboards, Frances Bernstein as lead and rhythm guitarist, Jane Power as occasional rhythm guitarist and Jenny Clegg on bass. NWLRB was, as Angela Cooper put it, 'a mixture of feminists from different class and ethnic backgrounds and political views – Maoists, libertarians, lesbians and heterosexuals and a transsexual – a motley crew reflecting our times! We sprang directly out of the Women's Liberation Movement.'[2] This group made explicit connections between different kinds of oppression – of race, class, sexuality and gender – and played music accordingly, at the same time as being, according to Jenny Clegg, 'against the whole commercialisation of music and its corporatist power hierarchies and we wanted to express the collectivism of the movement against the individualist ego-tripping of "cock rock" superstars'.[3] They expressed their refusal of the male domination of rock and pop music, and of the ways in which women within that scene were constructed as infantilised ('baby', 'doll') wives and mothers directly through their Manifesto. The NWLRB played all their gigs: '"for a cause" as well as for women's socials as part of the women's movement in Manchester and nationally [the Edinburgh Women's Conference; a benefit for *Spare Rib* in London], we also helped promote and raise funds, for example, for the Gay Liberation Front [Lancaster], strikers at Chlorides' in Manchester, and local community groups'. At the same time they were involved in many different forms of feminist activism. In 1976 they disbanded, though different group members continued to set up or be involved in other bands.

The NWLRB disbanded just at the time when punk arrived on the scene (1976–9). They shared a politics derived from a geopolitically infused sense of outrage with the social conditions of the Britain at that time, though NWLRB was women-focused. The politically driven passion, bottom-up approach, deliberate amateurism and anti-music-business attitude that characterised punk also continued into post-punk. Its subcultural status signalled both its counterculturality and its arrival from the suburbs, often of London, such as Bromley. It embraced a do-it-yourself activist culture not unlike that of Emily Faithfull and Una Marson, aided by advancing technologies, punk histories of DIY music production that included concrete instructions on how to do it, and the democratising ethos that anyone could make music, as producers of music and of its material form as records, as well as distribute it themselves.

Northern Women's Liberation Rock Band Manifesto

WHY ARE THERE HARDLY ANY WOMEN'S ROCK BANDS?

Women are held back in the sphere of music as they are in any other sphere of life. They aren't the people who think, create and contribute to society - their place is in the home, looking after their husbands and bringing up kids. Rock music is specially male dominated and prejudiced against women. Women are mostly put down as too birdbrained to get a band together, and besides, only men can handle the complex electronic equipment - women would only electrocute themselves.

IS POP MUSIC INSULTING TO WOMEN?

Pop Lyrics present women as sex objects for men. Nowadays no-one would dare to insult blacks by singing songs about golliwogs, but men think nothing of singing about women as "baby", "doll", "my girl", in other words as their playthings, their possessions. Women are not encouraged to be strong and independent beings in their own right. Instead, commercial pop songs present for them a world in which true love is their only goal and men are the only source of sadness, joy, or meaning in their lives. These songs help to keep women in their accustomed role of wives and mothers, dependent on men, because they hide the real conflicts in women's lives and relationships with men and so prevent them understanding their oppression.

Below: Big Joanie in front of the Salford Lads' Club, May 2017.

Opposite: Ana da Silva of The Raincoats performing at Alexandra Palace, London, June 1980.

Ana da Silva, co-founder with Gina Birch of the post-punk band The Raincoats in 1977, came to London from Portugal. The country had been under a dictatorship until 1974, so the possibility of expressing anti-state sentiments such as the Sex Pistols did in 'Anarchy in the U.K.' and 'God Save the Queen' came as a revelation to her, and inspired her own music-making. The Raincoats were part of a growing number of 'riot grrrl' bands such as X-Ray Spex, enabled by a general climate of demands for social change. As da Silva put it in an interview: 'At this time organisations like Women's Liberation, Gay Liberation, Rock against Racism, [and] Reclaim the Night all expressed the desire and need for resistance and change. All these things made me feel alive and encouraged me in my own desire to do something that was challenging in the visual arts and in music.'[4] The iconic record shop and label Rough Trade brought out their first EP, 'Fairytale in the Supermarket', and later 'Odyshape', 'The Kitchen Tapes' and 'Moving'. All these spoke to women's concerns, fantasies and dreams, setting the mundanity of the everyday but also women's fears against cultural fantasies of difference and desire.

Women's sense of taking and making spaces for themselves in changing cultural scenes continues to the present. The post-punk all-female band Big Joanie, established in 2013, features Stephanie Phillips

(singer/guitarist), Estella Adeyeri (bass) and Chardine Taylor-Stone (drums). The band formed in 2013 and released their first EP 'Sistah Punk' in 2014, the single 'Crooked Room' in 2016, and the album *Sistahs* in 2018. Like Rachel Aggs, who set up the band Trash Kit (2009) with Rachel Horwood, Big Joanie are London-based and represent new metropole queer multi-ethnic identities in an age of rising xenophobia, but also increasing hybridisation where pluralism sits alongside popular nationalism. Paying femage (as opposed to homage) to their feminist ancestors, Aggs, for example has performed the Pauline Oliveros score *To Valerie Solanas and Marilyn Monroe, In Recognition of Their Desperation* (1970) in the Turbine Hall of Tate Modern in 2012.

The context of these bands' work has also changed in technological terms. The opportunities for self-publicising and distribution through the internet, unavailable before the mid-1990s, have been fully grasped by these 'new' post-punk bands and online feminist activists in what has become known as the third and fourth wave of feminism. One dimension of this is the blogs, use of Twitter and Facebook, and zines produced by current generations of musicians and artists. Oomk zine ('One of my Kind') is a striking example of this. Set

Voice: Express

Opposite: Front cover of OOMK, issue 5, 2016

up in 2014, the collaborative work of Rose Nordin, Sofia Niazi and Heiba Lamara, it continues the DIY self-publishing culture that characterised punk. And we can also think back to the much earlier work of the Victoria Press's innovative graphics in the radically stylish design of *gal-dem,* an online and print magazine launched in 2015, to address inequality and misrepresentation in the industry and provide a space for the voices of young women and non-binary people of colour. The ideas of collective action, of anti-capitalism, of a democratised cultural sphere in which women can project their voices through multiple channels, are in evidence here. Sistahs continue to do it for themselves.

1 Audre Lorde, 'The Master's Tools Will Never Dismantle the Master's House', *Sister Outsider: Essays and Speeches* (Berkeley, CA: Crossing Press, 1984; repr. 2007), pp. 110–14.
2 Angela Cooper at Northern Women's Liberation Rock Band in 2012, https://womensliberationmusicarchive.co.uk/n/, accessed 4/9/2019, not paginated.
3 Jenny Clegg, ibid.
4 Ana da Silva, ibid.

ONE OF MY KIND

OOMK

ISSUE FIVE: COLLECTING

Voice: Express

Dreaming and Demanding

— **SHEILA ROWBOTHAM**

Through the centuries in many cultures, women have lamented their fate. Some found solace in dreams of flight; others argued for support in their traditional roles. But, just occasionally, they have expressed bolder visions of change and transformation. The essays in this book tell a powerful tale of how these voices have combined over time and place, and how important it is to learn from each others' experiences.

One early voice is Mary Collier's remarkable poem 'The Woman's Labour' (1739). Collier was a rural worker in Hampshire, trapped in a cycle of toil. She was provoked to write in fury at another rural poet, Stephen Duck, whose 'The Thresher's Labour' (1730) sneers about 'prattling females' and their supposed idleness:

> And from the time that Harvest doth begin.
> Until the Corn be cut and carry'd in,
> Our Toil and Labour's daily so extreme
> That we have hardly ever *Time to dream*.[1]

Just over fifty years later, amid new forms of production and revolutionary ideas of freedom, the governess and schoolteacher Mary Wollstonecraft fundamentally challenged assumptions about women's fate in her book *A Vindication of the Rights of Woman* (1792). Well-versed in philosophic reason, yet also influenced by the early stirrings of Romanticism, Wollstonecraft rejected domestic confinement and argued for women's education and wider opportunities. Directing her feelings in barbed, sardonic prose, she bravely announces:

> A wild wish has just flown from my heart to my head,
> and I will not stifle it though it may excite a horse-laugh.
> I do earnestly wish to see the distinction of sex, confounded
> in society, unless where love animates the behaviour.[2]

Over the course of the nineteenth century women's rights were to surface within movements for social and economic emancipation such as anti-slavery and the 'socialism' of the early Owenite co-operative movement. A young and radical John Stuart Mill also argued for knowledge of birth control. However, by 1832 he decided that when trying to 'persuade the English' it was strategic to avoid proposals of systemic change and tell 'them only of the next step they have to take'.[3] Accordingly the emphasis was to be on rights to education, employment and the vote for middle-class women.

Mill's perspective influenced the mass movements for women's suffrage which developed in the early twentieth century. Yet, regardless of their moderation, women who asserted their claims to vote were mercilessly caricatured.

Just as advocates of anti-slavery, women's and workers' rights had intertwined in the early nineteenth century – albeit not always easily – later rebels seeking the realisation of Wollstonecraft's 'wild wish' sought to connect multiple emancipations. This remained hard to envisage in 1890, when the South African writer Olive Schreiner dedicated her allegorical work *Dreams:* 'To a small girl-child, who may live to grasp somewhat of that which for us is yet sight, not touch'.[4] Schreiner was later to oppose the British government in the Boer War and publish the groundbreaking *Woman and Labour* (1911), which argued for a society in which women could be both mothers and workers.

Opposite: The cartoon 'Mill's Logic' from *Punch* magazine mocks John Stuart Mill's attempts to replace the word 'man' with 'person' in the Second Reform Act of 1867. His proposal was greeted with derisive laughter in the House of Commons and defeated by 76 to 196 votes.

Voice: Express

Below: Sylvia Townsend Warner's *Lolly Willowes* (1926) tells the story of Lolly, a 28-year-old unmarried woman who becomes dependent on her brother and his wife. Unwilling to spend the rest of her life as the maiden aunt, she decides to break free, moves to the small village of Great Mop, and becomes a witch. Subverting gender and family roles, Warner's novel was an immediate success on both sides of the Atlantic.

Opposite: Front cover of Olive Schreiner's *Dreams*, 1891.

During the first half of the twentieth century in countries that had been subjected to imperialism, concepts of equality and 'self-rule' came to acquire a special meaning for many women inspired by national liberation. In a variety of ways women on the left simultaneously sought to oppose both class exploitation and women's oppression. A radical minority argued as well for women's control over their bodies, and more equal personal relationships between the sexes. In guarded terms love between women was also being raised. The writer Sylvia Townsend Warner's fantasy fable of the rebellious spinster witch *Lolly Willowes* (1926) hints at her later discovery of lesbian love and communist activism:

> Is it true that you can poke the fire with a stick of dynamite in perfect safety? [...] Anyhow, even if isn't true of dynamite, it's true of women. Even if other people still find them quite safe and usual, [...] they know in their hearts how dangerous, how incalculable, how extraordinary they are. Even if they never do anything with their witchcraft, it's there – ready![5]

In a letter to the lesbian magazine *The Ladder* in 1957, the African American playwright Lorraine Hansberry linked women's freedom and same-sex loving, observing that 'homosexual persecution' would come to be equated with 'anti-feminism'.[6]

When we began to form women's liberation groups in the 1960s, we had only a sketchy knowledge of what had been done and thought by women in the past. Early in 1969, I wrote a pamphlet, 'Women's Liberation and the New Politics'. Aware that sexual intimacies, like other aspects of

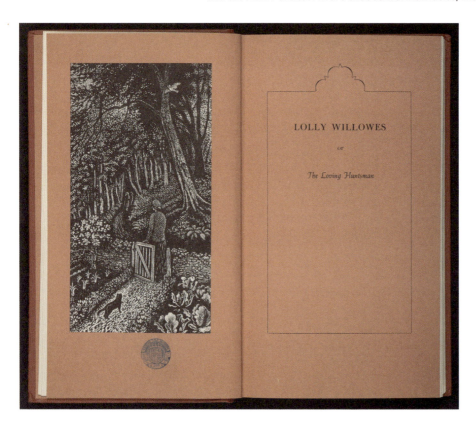

Unfinished Business

human beings' personal experience, are not easily encapsulated in terms of demands for political and economic rights or even democratic control over reproduction, I sought to probe 'the language of silence'. It felt as if new terms, new images and a transformed sense of self in relation to others were needed. I envisaged a new politics emerging from 'how we live with one another and how we feel and regard one another, how we communicate with each other'.[7]

The powerful impulse to transform inner and outer bondages brought into being women's movements far beyond what I could then imagine. Yet our dreams of total transformation also contained snags, for women's wants could be at variance. Some argued for the curtailing of sexual desire, others for its more extreme expression. Some wanted individual and others collective advancement. Some sought equality with men, while others asserted that women embodied an alternative. Did we then aim to become more distinct as 'women' or search for greater gender fluidity?

Much remains unresolved; nevertheless more and more women have defied the contemptuous 'horse-laugh' described by Wollstonecraft and are listening to the silence evoked in Khadija Saye's image (see page 13), making threads through to myriad movements of emancipation and cultural creativity around body, mind and voice. A clue is perhaps there in the Vulva Quilt (see page 49), in which a craft tradition reveals the beauty in what has been concealed. Something old can thus be re-envisaged by making something anew.

This book evokes an echoing chamber conveying dreams, demands and hopes that the young will carry into new spaces.

---

1   Ed. E. P. Thompson, *Stephen Duck, The Thresher's Labour and Mary Collier, The Woman's Labour: Two Eighteenth Century Poems* (The Merlin Press, 1989), pp. 8, 20.

2   Mary Wollstonecraft, *A Vindication of the Rights of Woman, with Strictures on Political and Moral Subjects* (London: Verso, 2010), p. 76.

3   John Stuart Mill, 'The Globe', April 18, 1832, quoted in Richard Pankhurst, *The Saint Simonians, Mill and Carlyle* (London: Lalibela Books, n.d.), p. 74.

4   Olive Schreiner, Elizabeth Jay (ed.), *Dreams* (Birmingham: Birmingham University Press, 2003).

5   Sylvia Townsend Warner, *Lolly Willowes: Or, The Loving Huntsman* (Chicago: Academy Chicago, 1979), p. 249.

6   Lorraine Hansberry, 'Letter signed L.N.', *The Ladder*, 1(11), August 1957.

7   Sheila Rowbotham, 'Women's Liberation and the New Politics', in Sheila Rowbotham (ed.), *Dreams and Dilemmas* (Virago: London, 1983), pp. 8, 31.

LDC COMICS

Established in 2009 as Laydeez do Comics by artists Sarah Lightman and Nicola Streeten. We hold free monthly London meetings with invited guests speaking about graphic works to public audiences. Women-led, welcoming all, informed by feminist strategies with a mission to change the world through comics, in 2018 we launched women-only awards for graphic novels and a festival supported by Arts Council England.

Voice: Express

A SNAPSHOT OF FEMINISM IN THE UK, 1972–93

Created by Dr Zoe Strimpel and The Business of Women's Words team

This map is based on information from *Spare Rib*, the key magazine of the Women's Liberation Movement.

We looked at the listings published each June between 1972 and 1993 to map activities such as events, marches, meetings, performances, screenings and more personal interests such as dating and travel. We combined these with reader letters to map feminist activities, concerns and debates.

As the data reflects just one month of each year, the map is inevitably not exhaustive. It shows, however, the remarkable spread and variety of interests of this period of women's activism in the UK.

No. No. of listings and letters in Spare Rib, June editions, 1972–93

 Talks and lectures

 Personal

 Groups

 Health and therapy

 Arts, entertainment, shopping and leisure

 Bookshops

 Campaigns

ORKNEY
Jun 1985, letter

Dear Friends, I am writing to you about a very offensive poster which I have just seen in my local GP's surgery. I wondered whether you could investigate why such a sexist poster could be produced by the Health Education Council …! The poster depicted an overweight woman in a bikini parading in front of two men…. The first illustration showed the woman with her stomach sagging and breasts drooping. The second depiction showed her pulling in her stomach and lifting her chest …. The caption beneath read 'Do you breathe in every time a man looks at you?' I am appalled that a (presumably) government body should produce such a poster to warn against overweight ……

Yours sincerely, Love, light and peace from Mavis E. Strudwick, Orkney

LEEDS

12　8　10　7　14　3　18

BRISTOL

14　5　2　2　16　1　5

PENZANCE, CORNWALL
June 1992, advert

B&B for gay women

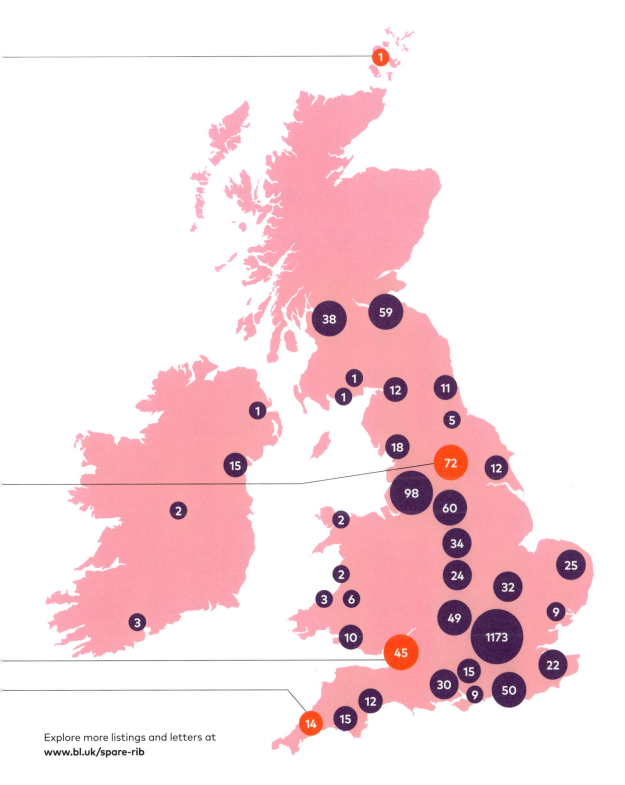

Explore more listings and letters at
www.bl.uk/spare-rib

Map

FINISHING THE BUSINESS?

— **PROFESSOR MARGARETTA JOLLY**

Reviewing this book's exuberant accounts of women's fight for rights, we might feel we have arrived. Consider these markers of progress: free contraception on the NHS; legislation to ensure equal pay for work of equal value; protection from domestic abuse – mental as well as physical; same-sex marriage and paternity leave. We can also glory in a culture which includes prize-winning working-class and black self-portraiture, Muslim Manga cartoons, feminist folk songs, women's football on the telly and bedtime reading for 'boys who dare to be different' as well as 'rebel girls'. We can stroll past public monuments from suffragist Millicent Garret Fawcett to comedian Victoria Wood, or pop into Glasgow Women's Library to browse through some feminist zines.

But the writers who have responded to the objects and stories featured in the *Unfinished Business* exhibition do not conclude that we can relax into 'post-feminism'. Rather, each suggests that the business of women's liberation is unfinished. Pamela Cox, for instance, notes the gargantuan value of women's unpaid domestic work to the UK economy. Anita Biressi reminds us of how quickly capitalism commodifies diversity. Debbie Challis abhors the sexual violence called out by #MeToo. Sumita Mukherjee highlights the unfinished self-education of white, Western feminists in forging inclusive, anti-imperialist politics.

So how do we finish the business? There are clear answers in the rich array of campaigns for rights and representation today. We might volunteer to mentor young women curious about careers in science, technology, engineering and maths. Boycott the diet and fast fashion industries and buy fairly traded, sustainable pleasures. Donate to end period poverty, collect data on Equal Pay Day, reclaim artificial intelligence, demand freedom from detention for refugee women, and start our own feminist publishing social enterprise. We can of course use our hard-won vote.

As Sasha Roseneil reminds us in this volume, there are plenty of ways to make a difference – blockading, creative damage to enemy weapons, and other forms of militant direct action, but clever insider reform too. Both are vital in changing the world. Let's offer respect to those who strive as elected representatives or officers in local government, progressing the great UK tradition of municipal feminism, or who are active in national or international government. For complex oppressions require us to go beyond single-issue politics. Broader, multi-dimensional platforms can help to address entwined inequalities of race, class, sexuality and body as well as gender, and prevent feminism being used selectively by otherwise unfriendly forces.

But simply loving women's community and bringing up children to be tolerant and free are also ways to roll the ball forward. As the poet Audre Lorde provocatively put it, women historically alienated from each other, and from their sexual selves, can find transformative power in erotic knowledge, a power which helps us 'not to settle for the convenient, the shoddy, the conventionally expected, nor the merely safe'. For her, the erotic was 'an assertion of the lifeforce of women; of that creative energy empowered, the knowledge and use of which we are now reclaiming in our language, our history, our dancing, our loving, our work, our lives'.[1]

Admittedly, it is hard to imagine when women in all their different situations will be fully equal and empowered. The 2010s have seen backlash and despair, in which populists peddle patriarchal as well as nationalist solutions to inequality and social crisis. So, for a moment, let us sextrapolate with science fiction.[2] Television's required viewing *The Handmaid's Tale*, based on Margaret Atwood's 1985 novel, offers one frightening vision of a militarised theocracy where women have been denied all rights. The handmaid's red cloak, as Angela Saini describes in this volume, symbolises the bloody treatment of the fertile 'slut' class of baby-makers. Just as scary are the blue cloaks of the privileged wives who abet the rape of their slave-sisters, while grey-robed Aunts enforce domestic oppression.

Atwood wrote her original tale about America under President Ronald Reagan. How frighteningly prescient she was. In the United States nearly thirty-five years later we recoil from new challenges to equal rights, reproductive rights, welfare, migration and racial tolerance – experiences shaping *The Testaments*, Atwood's sequel of 2019. Zoe Fairbairns' 1979 novel *Benefits* has been similarly perceptive in the UK. In its eugenicist future state, a woman prime minister uses welfare benefits to force women back into the nuclear family to reproduce. Based partly on Fairbairns' experiences volunteering for an abortion charity, it anticipates the kind of Brexit Britain which positions feminism as another plot by the metropolitan elite, and where anti-immigration politics are accompanied by calls for higher birth rates by white Britons.[3]

Of course, both Atwood and Fairbairns offer plots of resistance – underground railroads, inventive technology, secret codes and courage – though Fairbairns is also dryly funny about feminists' tendencies towards endless meetings, lesbian shenanigans and leadership panics. Gwyneth Jones, in *Divine Endurance* (1985), sends to her post-apocalyptic future an android cat and angel to sort things out. Naomi Alderman's 2016 *The Power* imagines a more dramatic solution:

Afterword

Gina Miller, shortly after the Supreme Court ruling that the prorogation of Parliament was unlawful, 24 September 2019.

women can electrocute people by touch, create their own doctrinal ideology and even learn how to rape. But Alderman's world is in the tradition of 'women on top' science fiction, which, despite its feminist analysis, provides no feminist solution.[4] Bina Shah's 2018 *Before She Sleeps* arguably provides a more feminist underground through the surprising strategy of offering men intimacy without sex. But what would a feminist utopia look like?

Here, the Bengali feminist thinker Rokeya Sakhawat Hossain's 1905 short story *Sultana's Dream* is a pioneer. Men are confined indoors, while women, under new laws which prevent early marriage and ensure girls' education, reinvent a peaceful, clean civilisation using solar power and ingenious weather control. The women-only world of Whileaway, imagined in Joanna Russ' *The Female Man* in the early 1970s, also describes the tidying effect of women having power – perhaps a little too much![5] In this land, women hunt, explore, govern, have sex and get five years off work after childbirth. Marge Piercy's *Woman on the Edge of Time* (1979) features a bisexual, gender-fluid communal child-rearing society. Octavia Butler's 1993 *Parable of the Sower* proposes a future where humans learn to care for each other and the planets through 'Earthseed', a new religion based on the principle that 'God is change'. This vision evolves from the African-American heroine's inheritance of the condition of 'hyperempathy', where she feels others' pain as if it were her own, bleeds if they bleed.

What these visions show is that gender harmony and liberation involve transcending simplistic biological determinism. Shulamith Firestone's *The Dialectic of Sex* (1970) said the same at the beginning of the feminist revival: 'It is everywhere … feminists have to question, not just all of Western culture, but the organisation of culture itself, and further, even the very organisation of nature.'[6] But, as we come to understand biology as itself both changeable and profound, so a feminist future must therefore engage respectfully with it as well as with social and economic solutions. This becomes clear in the second shared feature of these utopias, which is the importance of the environment and of non-human species. Feminist futures may be techie, yet they are also strikingly ecological.

This future is in fact now. Climate change is a global emergency, threatening disastrous consequences for all species.[7] What any kind of liberation requires, then, is the same focus on connecting causes that women brought when they set up protest camp at the United States Air Force base at Greenham Common in 1981. At the height of the Cold War, women applied feminist and transnational ideas to disarmament to counter the insanity of 'mutually assured destruction' and the apocalyptic threat of nuclear war.[8] But the Greenham experience also offers lessons in where romantic action needs political development. Rebecca Johnson, who lived at the camp for five years, offers one example of how to retune edgy activism in her subsequent life-long work on the Nuclear Non-Proliferation Treaty.[9] As we face up to the one-world challenge of survival, ambitious coalitions and diplomatic skills are vital if we are ever to finish the business of women's rights.

So what might a British Library exhibition one hundred years from now display about women's lives? Possibly a hologram of Baroness Brenda Hale (wearing her spider brooch) announcing the Supreme Court's verdict on whether it was lawful to shut down Parliament in 2019 at the height of a national crisis, next to another of Gina Miller, who launched the case. Perhaps the diaries of the UK's first non-binary prime minister, describing how they brought in the circular economy, four-day working week and five years' paid parental and care leave. The campaign for Sex Robots' Rights would undoubtedly provoke interest.[10] Perhaps we'll see the score of 'Tapdancing on the Glass Ceiling: The Musical'? We'll wonder at the Library's celebrated archive of ancient algorithms, recalling the time before Facebook and Instagram were outpaced by the Women Reinvent the Internet project. We'll puzzle over the 'micro' exhibition of plastic beads, water bottle tops and silicone fillers, happy that the seas have been cleaned and people are too busy decolonising Mars to spend much time on make-up. And how fun it will be to enjoy the British Library's touring exhibition in an eco-hut in rewilded forest. Gibbons, golden frogs and puffins, no longer endangered, enjoy visiting on Tuesdays, the late-night opening for other species.

---

1   Audre Lorde, 'Uses of the Erotic: The Erotic as Power', in *Sister Outsider: Essays and Speeches by Audre Lorde* (Freedom, CA: Crossing Press, 1984, first published 1978), pp. 55, 57.

2   I owe this phrase to Rob Latham in his 'Sextrapolation in New Wave Science Fiction', in *Queer Universes: Sexualities in Science Fiction*, edited by Wendy G. Pearson, Veronica Hollinger and Joan Gordon (Liverpool: Liverpool University Press, 2008), pp. 54–71.

3   Zoe Fairbairns, *Benefits: A Novel* (Nottingham: Five Leaves, 1998), p. ii.

4   Pamela Sargent, 'Introduction: Women in Science Fiction', in *More Women of Wonder: Science-Fiction Novelettes by Women About Women*, edited by Pamela Sargent (Harmondsworth: Penguin, 1979), pp. 11–54.

5   Roz Kaveney, 'The Science Fictiveness of Women's Science Fiction', in *From My Guy to Sci-Fi: Genre and Women's Writing in the Postmodern World*, edited by Helen Carr (London: Pandora Press, 1989), pp. 78–97.

6   Shulamith Firestone, *The Dialectic of Sex; the Case for Feminist Revolution* (London: The Women's Press, 1979), pp. 12.

7   The Intergovernmental Panel on Climate Change (IPCC) Special Report, 2018, at https://report.ipcc.ch/sr15/pdf/sr15_spm_final.pdf.

8   Tom Castella, 'How did we forget about mutually assured destruction?', *BBC News Magazine*, 15 February 2012, https://www.bbc.co.uk/news/magazine-17026538.

9   Rebecca Johnson, *Unfinished Business: The Negotiation of the CTBT and the End of Nuclear Testing* (Geneva: UNIDIR, 2009). See also Rebecca Johnson, interviewed by Margaretta Jolly, Sisterhood and After: The Women's Liberation Oral History Project, 2010–2013. British Library Sound & Moving Image Catalogue reference C1420/34 © The British Library and The University of Sussex. Excerpts and *Return to Sender*, a short film about Johnson and the removal of cruise missiles from Greenham Common, directed by Lizzie Thynne, are available at https://www.bl.uk/people/rebecca-johnson.

10 Kate Devlin, *Turned On: Science, Sex and Robots* (London: Bloomsbury, 2018).

Afterword

ACKNOWLEDGEMENTS

The theme of women's rights is in this light so broad that an exhibition of this scale could only be achieved in close co-operation between curators, academics, activists and other institutions. This book aims to accompany the exhibition and to provide more insight into the historical and cultural context of the exhibits. There are too many people to mention here who have helped with the exhibition and this book; we offer apologies, therefore, for possible omissions.

Moving from the outside in we would like to thank the fantastic members of the exhibition Advisory Board. They provided invaluable advice, subject expertise and critical friendship when the exhibition concept was being developed, particularly in its early stages. We are greatly indebted to the Advisory Board Chair, Jude England, and members Helen Antrobus, Caroline Bressey, Debbie Challis, Lucy Delap, Kelly Foster, Sarah Lasoye and Sumita Mukherjee.

For every activist organisation that has agreed to be represented in the exhibition and book and has shared their story and donated objects: thank you. Your contributions ensured the content of *Unfinished Business* was relevant, urgent and inspiring. In particular we are grateful to Liv Little and all her team from gal-dem; Gabby Eldin; Rachel Grocott and Hannah Whelen from Bloody Good Period; Olivia Marshall and Katherine O'Brien and everyone from bpas and Now for Northern Ireland; Anne-Marie Imafidon and her colleagues at Stemettes; Isabel and the team at United Voices of the World; Hester Liakos Gemma Rosenblatt and Ella Smillie, and everyone at the Fawcett Society; Sam Hudson, Natasha Walter and Nahzley Anvarian at Women for Refugee Women; Sue John, Nicola Maksymuik and colleagues at Glasgow Women's Library; and Nicola Streeten and the team at LD Comics.

Though the exhibition is packed full of wonderful items from the British Library's collections, we have also relied heavily on the generosity of institutions and individuals to loan us their objects. We are hugely grateful to everyone for entrusting their precious objects to us, and for allowing them to be part of the story. Thanks in particular to Jameela Jamil and her amazing I-Weigh team, Niku Archer and Sisters Uncut, Feminist Library South, London Feminist Library, Tate Britain, Museum of London, Sammy Roddick, Margaretta Jolly, Lesley and Chris Mees, Travis Alabanza, Janie Lightfoot, Beverley Chapman, Gillian Wearing, Nicola Green, Lucy Cartledge, the Estate of Khadija Saye, Cambridge University, Women's Library LSE, Richard Saltoun Gallery, Chiara Capraro, Caroline Lucas, Manchester Art Gallery, Susie Orbach, Science Museum, Joy Gregory, Ann Oakley, Sarah Waters, Pragna Patel, Frankie Favia, Southall Black Sisters, Edinburgh University Library, Black Cultural Archives, Brunel University, Hope Powell, Black Country Living Museum, See Red Collective, Stephan Cross, Bishopsgate Institute, Ana da Silva, Big Joanie, Jennifer McCarey and Unison Glasgow City Branch, Sylevester Onwordi, Shoreditch Sisters WI and Sam Jenkins from the People's History Museum in Manchester.

To Steve Rose and Nick Fairclough, thank you for the cups of tea, holding the fort and being excited about this project.

Thanks are also due to Phil Hatfield and colleagues in the Eccles Centre who believed in the exhibition and have provided terrific backing. The Business of Women's Words Project, funded by the Leverhulme Trust and led by the Universities of Sussex and Cambridge in partnership with the British Library, provided wonderful support in kind through the expertise and labour of Margaretta Jolly, Lucy Delap, D-M Withers and Zoe Strimpel.

Curators and Learning colleagues at the British Library were very generous with sharing their time, knowledge and ideas. We are sorry we could not fit everything in. We very much appreciate all assistance and support given us in the process of preparing this book and the exhibition, in particular by Katie Adams, Alison Bailey, David Beech, Helena Byrne, Laurence Byrne, Lucy Evans, Jess Gregory, Tanya Kirk, Stephen Lester, Andy Linehan, Chandan Mahal, Antonia Moon, Richard Morel, Rob Perks, Harriet Roden, Mary Stewart, Jason Webber,

Charmaine Wong and everyone from the European and Americas department.

In addition to BL staff we were lucky enough to be joined for three months by two outstanding PhD students, Alice O'Driscoll and Charlotte James, who contributed ideas and content in equal measure. Many thanks to them.

The exhibition could not have happened without the fantastic work of British Library colleagues in marketing, media communications, content, design, events, fundraising and commercial teams: Jamie Andrews, Stuart Boxall, Sarah Bryne, Michele Burton, Jean-Paul Calvin, Sam Connor, Jon Fawcett, Hannah Gabrielle, Roberto Kusabbi, Vicky Lee, Sue McDonough, Bee Rowlatt, Liz Scase, Susannah Stevenson, Sarah Walsh and Laurie Williams. Some of the many others whose work was vital are the colleagues at the Library's Imaging Studio as well as textile conservator Elizabeth Rose.

Thanks to Alex Whitfield for steering, sometimes corralling, the exhibition board and to Sophie Sabin for seamless administrative support.

Support and tolerance from colleagues in Contemporary British Collections has been seemingly endless – thank you Eleanor Casson, Ian Cooke, Eleanor Dickens, Rachel Foss, Jerry Jenkins, Callum McKean, Helen Melody, Jonathan Pledge, Richard Price and Zoe Wilcox.

Particular thanks to colleagues from the Library's Exhibitions department who have worked so hard to bring this challenging exhibition to fruition. We could not have done it without Howard Batho, Caroline Brown, Susan Dymond, Alex Kavanagh, Cleo Laskarin and Polly Mills or indeed from colleagues at the British Library's Conservation Centre, in particular Alexa McNaught-Reynolds and, from the Loans Registry, Hazel Shoreland and Lesley Thomas.

Thanks to Here Design for creating such a stylish and impactful book, to Lauren Scully and Brian Scully of Plaid London for their innovative exhibiton design, to Margo Lombaert of Margot Lombaert Studio for her versatile and elegant graphic design and to Clay Interactive for creating incredible AV. Crucially, thanks to Sally Nicholls, Abbie Day and colleagues in the Library's Publishing team for their indispensable support throughout.

The work of the exhibition curatorial team has been outstanding and the exhibition and book would never have happened without them. Thank you to Mercedes Aguirre, Greg Buzwell, Debbie Cox, Jo Norledge and D-M Withers for being so wonderful to work with.

Last but not least we would like to express our heartfelt gratitude to the authors of this book who are listed separately with more biographical details. It is first and foremost thanks to their expertise and in-depth knowledge that this book contains a variety of contributions that reflect the great diversity women's history, activism and lives.

— **DR POLLY RUSSELL AND PROFESSOR MARGARETTA JOLLY**

PARTNERS AND SUPPORTERS

Lead Partner

Joanna and Graham Barker

INDEX

Italic page numbers refer to illustrations.

A

Abasindi Black Women's Co-operative 105, *106*, 107, 108
Abdela, Lesley 150
abolitionists 133
abortion 71, 177;
  illegality and decriminalisation 11, 48, 67, 70, *70*, 71
Abortion Act (1967) 71
abuse, domestic 72–5, *74*, 221
Achilles Heel (magazine) 178, *178*
Adeyeri, Estella 209
Adichie, Chimamanda Ngozi 197
advertising 23, 29, *29*, 36, *37*
Aggs, Rachel 209
Aguirre, Mercedes 9, 154–5, 187, 192–9
Ahluwalia, Kiranjit 72
Ahmed, Sara 111
AI (artificial intelligence) 47, 221
Alabanza, Travis *60*, 61
Alderman, Naomi, *The Power* 221–2
Ali, Nimco 48
All-India Women's Conference (AIWC) 137, 138, *138*, 139
Alliance of Honour (youth organisation) 175
Allison & Busby (publishers) 199
Allison, Clive 199
anatomy *see* biology and anatomy
Anderson, Elizabeth Garrett 65
Anderson, G. D. 200
'Angel in the House' ideal 27, 77, 112
anonymous and pseudonymous writing by women 193–7
Anthony, Susan B. 133
Anti-Corn Law League 141
anti-nuclear protests 12, 162–7, 223
anti-slavery movement 133, 141, 213
anti-suffrage movement 144–5

Anti-Suffrage Review, The (journal) 145
any-body.org (body-positive activist website) 38
APEX (trade union) 121
Aphrodite (goddess) 43
archives and libraries, feminist 14–15, 184, 187–8, 189, 221
Armstrong, Frankie 184, *186*
Arshad, Rowena 71
artificial intelligence (AI) 47, 221
Asda (supermarket) 121
Astor, Nancy, Viscountess *148*, 149, 150
asylum-seekers and refugees 53, 169, 221
Athena SWAN (Scientific Women's Academic Network charter) 108, 109
Attlee, Clement, 1st Earl 150
Atwood, Margaret:
  The Handmaid's Tale 47–8, *48*, 221;
  The Testaments 221
Austen, Jane 193, 194, 197;
  Sense and Sensibility 194, *195*
ayahs (domestic servants) 114, *114*, 131, 132, *132*

B

Barker, Victor 56
Bassano, Emilia 184
BCA (Black Cultural Archives) 109
Beaton, Kate, cartoon *62*
Beaumont, Catríona 9, 89, 140–50
beauty contests 22, 23, 24, *24*–5
Beauvoir, Simone de 129
Bechdel, Alison 23
Beeton, Mrs, *Book of Household Management* 125
Bell, Vanessa 113
Belloc, Bessie Rayner Parkes 203
Benjamin, Ruha 71
Berer, Marge 72
Berger, John, *Ways of Seeing* 23, 29
Bernard, Jay 61
Bernstein, Frances 206

Berry, Carro 84
Berwick Street Film Collective 29
Best, George 29
Bhikaji, Dadaji 135
Big Joanie (band) 209, *209*
Biggers, John 59
Billinghurst, Rosa May 26, *26*–7
Billington, Teresa 27
biology and anatomy 42–61, 65
Birch, Gina 209
Biressi, Anita 8, 18, 22–38, 221
birth control *see* contraception
Birtwell, Celia 117
bisexuality 35, 55, 61
Black, Clementina 117
Black Cultural Archives (BCA) 109
Black Lives Matter (activist movement) 71
Black Power movement 105, 178
Black Studies courses 108
Black Supplementary Schools 104, 105, 107, 109
blogs and blogging 36, 111, 209
Bloody Good Period (charity) 12, 53, *53*
Bodichon, Barbara Leigh Smith 203
body-positive activism 36–8
Boston Women's Health Book Collective 83
Boulton, Ernest 'Stella' 55, 56
Bowen, Lauren 117
Boycott, Rosie, Baroness 29
bpas (British Pregnancy Advisory Service) 70
Bradley, Katharine 197, *197*
Brexit (British exit from European Union) 34, 221, 222
Britannia (WSPU journal) *see* *Suffragette, The*
Brittain, Vera, *Testament of Youth* 199
Brixton Black Women's Group 105
Brontë sisters *62*, 194
Brontë, Anne 194; *The Tenant of Wildfell Hall* 72
Brontë, Charlotte 193, 194, 197

Brontë, Emily 194; *Wuthering Heights* 80, 194
Brown, Isaac Baker 48
Brown, Louise 59
Browning, Robert 197
Bryan, Beverley, *The Heart of the Race* 107, *107*, 109
Busby, Margaret 199
Butler, Josephine 65, *76*, 77, 141, *182*, 183
Butler, Judith 41
Butler, Octavia, *Parable of the Sower* 222–3

C

Callil, Dame Carmen 117
Calling the West Indies (radio programme) 205
Cambridge University 93, *93*, 99, 100*n*, 193
Camden Black Sisters Group (CBSG) 103, 183
Campaign Against Pornography 36
Caribbean Voices (radio programme) 205
Carpenter, Mary 134
Carter, Laura 8, 88, 92–100
cartoons 12, *20*, 27, *40*, *62*, *90*, *110*, *128*, 141, *142–3*, 144, 145, *156*, *170*, *180*, *200*, *212*, 221
Castle, Barbara (*later* Baroness Castle of Blackburn) 120
Cathy Come Home (television programme) 67
cervical caps 66, *66*, 67
chain-making 118
Challis, Debbie 8, 19, 64–75, 81, 221
Chapman, Beverley 116, 117
Charing Cross Hospital (London) 56
Charleston Farm (Sussex) 113
Chartism 141
Cheselden, William, *Osteographia* 42, *43*
childbirth *see* pregnancy and childbirth
children's books 97, *97*, *102*, 103–4, *104*
Chiswick Women's Aid 72
Christianity 77, 114, 135, 144

cinema *see* film and cinema
civil rights movement 150
Clapham Maternity Hospital (London) 65, 67
classification schemes, library 187
Clean Clothes Campaign (campaign group) 118
Clegg, Jenny 206
climate change 223
clitoridectomy 48
co-operative movement 213
Co-operative Women's Guild 65, 118, 126, 144, 199
Coard, Bernard 104–5
Coates, Chris 125
Codrington divorce (1864) 205
Collier, Mary 213
comics and graphic novels 217, 221; *see also* zines
Common Cause, The (NUWSS journal) 145
Conran, Shirley, *Superwoman* 35
consent, sexual 84, *85*
Contagious Diseases Acts (1864–9) 65, 75, 77, 133, 141, 183
contraception 11, 65–71, *66*, 67, *68*, *71*, 175, 177, 213, 221
Cooper, Angela 206
Cooper, Edith 197, *197*
Correll, Gemma, cartoon *20*
Cosmopolitan, The (magazine) 205
Courtman, Sandra 197
Cox, Pamela 8–9, 88–9, 112–27, 221
Craggs, Helen 172
Crenshaw, Kimberlé 105
Crimean War (1853–6) 114
Criminal Law Amendment Act (1885) 55, 56
Critics Group, *The Female Frolic* 186
cross-dressing 34, 35, *35*, 55, 81
Cruikshank, George, 'The Rights of Women' 141, *142–3*
Custody of Infants Act (1839) 72

D

da Silva, Ana *208*, 209
Dadzie, Stella 109, 205; *The Heart of the Race* 107, *107*, 109
Daily Mail 34–5, *34*
Daily Mirror 26, 27
Darwin, Charles 43–4, 44–5, 46, 131
Das, Bishamber 36
Daughters of Africa (anthology) 199
Daughters of Eve (non-profit organisation) 48
Davies, Emily 203
Davies, Margaret Llewelyn 65, 118
Davis, Wendy 187
Davison, Emily 160, 188
Dennett, Terry 30
Depo-Provera (contraceptive) 71, *71*
Desai, Jayaben 121
dildos 78, *79*
disability 26, 27, 38, 66, 71, 150
Disraeli, Benjamin (*later* 1st Earl of Beaconsfield) 134
divorce 72, 150*n*, 175
domestic abuse 72–5, *74*, 221
domestic labour 125–6, 141, 221
domestic service 113–14, *113*, 125; ayahs 114, *114*, 131, 132, *132*
Douglas, James 81
Duchamp, Marcel, *Fountain* 98
Duck, Stephen 213
Duncan, Riana, cartoon *110*
Dyhouse, Carol 94

E

Easley, Alexis 193
Edinburgh University 94
education *see* schools and schooling; universities and higher education
Education Acts:
(1870) 93;
(1880) 94;
(1918) 95;
(1944) 95

Index

Elbe, Lili 59
Eliot, George (Mary Anne Evans) 194, *194*, 199n
Ellis, Havelock 55–6, 77
Emecheta, Buchi 196, 197, 199
employment, women's 88–9, 108–9, 110–27, 136, 203
English Collective of Prostitutes (ECP) 127, *127*
Éon, Chevalier d' 55
Equal Franchise Act (1928) 15n, 149, 193
equal pay 108, 118–21, 125, 177, 221
erotica 35, 78–80, 221
eugenics 46–7, 52, 66, 81, 103, 131, 221
Evans, Kate, cartoon *156*
Evans, Mary Anne (George Eliot) 194, *194*, 199n
Everyday Sexism Project (website) 36
evolutionary biology 42–7, 48, 131

F

Fabian Society 95, 126
Fairbairns, Zoe, *Benefits* 221
Fairbanks, Douglas 80
Faithfull, Emily 203, *203*, 205, 206
family allowances (welfare payments) 126
Family Planning Act (1967) 67
Fanon, Frantz 27
Fausto-Sterling, Anne 44
Fawcett, Dame Millicent 144, 151; *Josephine Butler 182*, 183; statue 15, 188, *190*, 221
Fawcett Society 121, 150, 151
female genital mutilation (FGM) 48
Feminist Archive 187
Feminist Library (London) 187, *187*, 188
FGM (female genital mutilation) 48
Field, Michael (Katharine Bradley and Edith Cooper) 197, *197*
film and cinema 21, 23, 29, 46, 80
Firestone, Shulamith, *The Dialectic of Sex* 223
Fisher, Lettice 66
Fitzgerald, Luchia 206
Fleming, Jacky, cartoon *180*
folk music 184–7, 221
Ford sewing machinists' protest (1968) 120, *120*
Fothergill, Tessa 67
Freer, Jean 187
Freewoman, The (periodical) 174, 175
French Revolution (1789) 93, 141
fundamentalism, religious 72

G

Galton, Sir Francis 46–7, 52, 66
gal-dem (magazine) 39, *39*, 210
Gaskell, Elizabeth 197
gay people 11, 38, 55–6, 61, 77, 81, 150, 178; *see also* lesbianism; same-sex marriage
gender-fluid and non-binary identities 11, 39, 41, 55–61, 179, 216, 223
gentrification 184
George Padmore Institute 109
Gilbert, Sandra M. 197
Gilroy, Beryl 103–4, *104*, 199; *In Praise of Love and Children* 197
Gingerbread (charity) 67, 75n
Glasgow Women's Library 188, 189, 221
Godwin, William, *Memories of the Author of A Vindication of the Rights of Woman* 140
González, Emma 11
Good Housekeeping (magazine) 35
Grant, Duncan 113
Grant, Henry, photograph 97
graphic novels 217
Greenham Common Women's Peace Camp 12, 159, 162–7, *163*, 164–5, *167*, 223
Gregory, Joy 30, *32*–3
Grenfell Tower fire (2017) 12, 30
Griffin, Gabriele 9, 155, 202–210
Grizelda, cartoon *128*
Grunwick industrial dispute (1976–8) 121, *122*–3
Guardianship of Infants Act (1925) 149
Gubar, Susan 197
Guy, Rosa 199
gynaecology and obstetrics 48, 65; *see also* pregnancy and childbirth

H

Haire, Norman 66
Hale, Brenda, Baroness 223
Hall, Radclyffe 56, *56*, 59; *The Well of Loneliness* 56, 59, 81
Hall, Stuart 30, *176*, 177
Hamilton, Cicely 160
Handmaid's Tale, The (television series) 221
Hansberry, Lorraine 214
Haraway, Donna 71
Hardie, Keir 172
Harvey, Anne 117
Harvey, Benjamin 117
Harvey Nichols (department store) 117
Haward, Elfrida Emma 56

Hawes, Keeley *82*, 83
Hawkins, Alice 188
Heape, Walter, *Sex Antagonism* 43
Hemmings, Susan (ed.), *Girls are Powerful* 11
Higgins, Grace 113, *113*
Hillcroft College (Surrey) 95
Hirschfeld, Magnus 55
Hobhouse, Arthur, 1st Baron 135
Hobhouse, Mary, Lady 135
Hogarth Press (publishers) *192*, 199
Holmes, Lucy-Anne 37
Holmes, Marion 183
homosexuality *see* gay people; lesbianism
hooks, bell 157, 203
Hope, Bob 23
Horwood, Rachel 209
Hossain, Rokeya Sakhawat, *Sultana's Dream* 222
housework 125–6, 141, 221
Hrdy, Sarah Blaffer 46
Hulanicki, Barbara 117
Hull, Augustine 56, *56*
Hussein, Leyla 48

I

Ifekoya, Evan 61
Illustrated London News 145
Imoke, Birdy 48
imperialism 26–7, 30, 89, 103, 107, 114, 131–4, 136–8
in vitro fertilisation (IVF) 59, 71
Indian Women's Education Association 134–5
infant mortality rates 71–2, 103
International Women's Day 14, *15*, 68, *168*, 177, 188
International Women's Peace Congress 149
intersex people 55, 56
IVF *see* in vitro fertilisation

J

Jacques, Juliet 8, 18, 54–61
James, C. L. R. 199
Jamil, Jameela 36, *37*
Jex-Blake, Sophia 94, *94*, 95
Joel, Daphna, *Gender Mosaic* 52
Johnson, Rebecca 223
Jolly, Alison 46, *46*
Jolly, Margaretta 6, 8, 220–23
Jones, Claudia 23, 24, 183, *183*, 199
Jones, Gwyneth, *Divine Endurance* 221

Jorgensen, Christine 59, *59*
Joshi, Kripa, cartoon *200*
Jus Suffragii (journal) 137

K

Kaur, Harnaam 36
Kay, Jackie 199
Kennard, Caroline 43, 44, *44*–5
Kenney, Annie 188
Kerr, Sandra 187
Keys, The (journal) 205
Khoikhoi people 46
King, Hetty 35
King, Sir Truby 103
Koubek, Zdeněk 55

L

La Rose, John 103
Ladder, The (magazine) 214
Ladies National Association for the Repeal of the Contagious Diseases Act 65, 141
Ladybird (children's book series) 97, *97*, *102*, 103
Lamara, Heiba 210
Lanchester, Edith 77–8, *78*
Langham Place group 203
Lau, Grace 35
Lawlor, Andrea, *Paul Takes the Form of a Mortal Girl* 59
LD Comics (comics forum) 217, *217*
League of Coloured Peoples 205
Lee, Alice 44
Leeds, Abbey House Museum 15
legal training 135–6
lemurs 46
lesbianism 35, 56, 61, *73*, 81, 150, 178, 203, 214;
    see also gay people
Level Up (feminist organisation) 84
Levy, Andrea, *A Small Island* 197
Lewes, George Henry 194
Lewis, Reina 27, 35
Libman, Angie 206
libraries, circulating 80
libraries, feminist *see* archives and libraries, feminist
Lightman, Sarah 217
Little, Dorothy 133, *133*
London School of Medicine *134*, 135
London University 94, 99, 100*n*
Lorde, Audre 199, 201, 203, 221
Lucas, Caroline 36, *36*

M

Maan, Shakila Taranum, banner 74
Macarthur, Mary 117, 118
McCall, Annie 65, 67
McKenley, Jan 109
McKenzie, Victoria 105
Mackie, Liz, cartoon *90*
McLaren, Dame Anne 59
Madagascar (film; 2005) 46
Made in Dagenham (film; 2010) 120
magazines and newspapers, women's 29, 35, 36, 39, 80, 84, 118, 131, 175, 205, 206;
    see also zines
Malcolm, Morgan Lloyd, *Emilia* 184, *184*
male impersonators 34, 35, *35*, 55
Malthusian League 66
Mambéty, Djibril Diop 29
Manchester: Abasindi Black Women's Co-operative 105, *106*, 107, 108;
    Owens College 94;
    People's History Museum 15
Manzoor-Khan, Suhaiymah 11
Markham, Violet 144
Markievicz, Constance 149, *149*
Marson, Una *204*, 205, 206
Martineau, Harriet 63
masturbation 78, 81, 83
Match Girls strike (1888) 117
maternity benefits and leave 65–6, 121
Maternity and Child Welfare Act (1918) 65–6
Matriarchy Study Group 187
Matrimonial Causes Act (1923) 149
May, Theresa 34–5, *34*
medical training 65, 94, 95, 108, 134–5;
    see also nursing
men's involvement in women's movements 12, 154, 170–79
Men's League for Women's Suffrage 172, *172*
Men's Political Union 172
menstruation 53
#MeToo movement 11, 84, 221
Michener, Diana 59
midwifery 7, 66, 116, 117
Mill, John Stuart *170*, 171–2, *212*, 213;
    The Subjection of Women 12, 133, 171
Miller, Gina *222*, 223
Mills & Boon (publishers) 80
minimum wage 118–20
Mirza, Heidi 91
Miss World (beauty contest) 22, 23
Mitchell, Juliet 11

Mohanty, Chandra 27, 29
Moody, Harold 205
Morejón, Nancy 199
Morris, Olive 183–4, *185*
Mother's Money (magazine) *127*, 128
Mothers' Union (charitable organisation) 144, 149
Mother's Union (magazine) 80, *81*
Mukherjee, Sumita 9, 14, 89, 114, 130–38, 145, 221
Mullan, John 193
Mulvey, Laura 21, 23–6, 29
music 160, 167, 184–7, 206–210, 221
music hall 34, 35, *35*
My Home (magazine) 35
Myriad Editions (publishers) 199

N

National Abortion Campaign 71
National Anti-Sweating League 117–18
National Council for the Unmarried Mother and her Child (NCUMC) 66, 75*n*
National Federation of Women Workers 118
National Health Service *see* NHS
National Indian Association (NIA) 134, 135
National Society for Women's Suffrage 203
National Union of Women's Suffrage Societies (NUWSS) 144, 145, 172
Nesbitt, Jo, cartoon *40*
New Beacon Books (publisher) 103
New Illustrated, The (magazine) *148*
News Chronicle (newspaper) 56
NHS (National Health Service) 67, 116, 117;
    provision of contraception 29, 67, 68, 221
Niazi, Sofia 210
Nichols, James 117
Nightingale, Florence 114
Nippers (children's book series) 103–4, *104*
Nixon, Richard 83
No Sweat (campaign group) 118
non-binary and gender-fluid identities 11, 39, 41, 55–61, 179, 216, 223
Nordin, Rose 210
Northern Women's Liberation Rock Band (NWLRB) 206, *207*
Norton, Caroline 72
Notting Hill Carnival 23, *24*–5
Now for Northern Ireland (activist

Index

229

campaign) 12, 70, *70*
nuclear weapons *see* anti-nuclear protests
nude women, depictions of 23, 35–6
nursing 114–17, *116*
see also midwifery
NUWSS (National Union of Women's Suffrage Societies) 144, 145, 172
NWLRB (Northern Women's Liberation Rock Band) 206, *207*

O

Oakley, Ann 65, *124*, 125
obstetrics and gynaecology 48, 65; see also pregnancy and childbirth
Oliveros, Pauline 209
Olympic Games (1928) 55
Omenala Press (publishers) 199
Onlywomen Press (publishers) 197, 206
Onwordi, Sylvester 199
OOMK ('One of My Kind'; zine) 209–210, *210*
Open University (OU) 99; Art and Environment Course 98, *98*
Organisation of Women of African and Asian Descent (OWAAD) 105, *105*, 109, 183
orgasm 48, 77, 83
Orientalism 27, 35
Osborn, Emily Mary, *Nameless and Friendless* 72, *73*
Our Bodies Ourselves (book; OBOS) 83, *83*
Outwrite (newspaper) 206
OWAAD *see* Organisation of Women of African and Asian Descent
Owanabae, Dorothy 117
Owen, Nicholas 9, 12, 154, 170–79
Owen, Ursula 184
Owenite communities 213
Oxford University 93, 99, 100*n*, 135

P

Pandora Press (publishers) 197, 206
Pankhurst, Christabel 131, 144, 149, 172
Pankhurst, Emmeline 133, 144, 149, 158, 160; statue 15, 188
Pankhurst, Richard 69
Pankhurst, Rita 188
Pankhurst, Sylvia 66, 69, 118, 149, 160, *161*, 172; *The Chainmaker* 118, *118*; *Save the Mothers* 66–7
Park, Frederick 'Fanny' 55, 56

parliament, women's representation 149–50
paternity leave 221
Paterson, Emma 203
peace campaigns 12, 149, 159, 162–7, 223
Peg's Paper (magazine) 80, *80*
Persephone Books (publishers) 206
Peter and Jane (children's book series) 103
Peter Jones (department store) 117
Pethick-Lawrence, Emmeline, Lady 172
Pethick-Lawrence, Frederick, 1st Baron 172, *173*
Phillips, Angela 83
Phillips, Stephanie 209
Phoenix, Ann 8, 88, 102–9
Physical Culture (magazine) 55
Piercy, Marge, *Woman on the Edge of Time* 222
pill, contraceptive 67, *68*, 177
Pizzey, Erin 72
Plan for Peace (Labour Party 1945 election manifesto) 149–50, *150*
Plunket Society 103
pornography 36, 177
Posener, Jill 29, *29*
Power, Jane 206
power dressing 34
Powles, Matilda Alice (Vesta Tilley) 34, *35*
pregnancy and childbirth 43, 64–72, 121; in vitro fertilisation (IVF) 59, 71
Primrose League (Conservative political organisation) 144
Prince, Mary 133
prostitution 65, 77, 118, 126, 127, *127*, 175
publishing and printing 187, 197–9, 203–6, 210–11, 221
Punch (magazine) *212*
punk 206–9

Q

Quant, Dame Mary 117

R

race and racism 24, 26–7, 30, 47, 66, 71, 91, 104–5, 130–38, 168*n*, 179, 183–4, 199, 201, 205; Race Equality Charter 108–9
Radcliffe College (Massachusetts) 44
Rage, Raju 61
Raha, Nat 61
Rai, Lala Lajpat 136
Raincoats, The (band) *208*, 209

Rakusen, Jill 83
rape 84; and abortion 71; convictions and sentencing 11, 177; marital 75
Rasamimanana, Hanta 46, *46*
Rathbone, Eleanor 126
Ravindran, T. K. Sundari 72
Reagan, Ronald 221
Reclaim the Night (activist movement) 74, 75, 159, 162, 171, 209
Reform Act (1832) 141
Reform Act (1867) 213
refugees and asylum-seekers 53, 169, 221
refuges, women's 11, 12, 72, *168*, 177
Remembering Olive Collective (ROC) 183, 184
Representation of the People Act (1918) 15*n*, 149, 190, 193; centenary 7, 11, 15, 188–91, *190*
Reproductive Health Matters (journal) 72, *72*
Reynold's News (newspaper) 56
Rich, Adrienne 181
Riddell, Carol 206
'riot grrrl' bands 209
Rippon, Gina, *The Gendered Brain* 52
Robinson, Jo 83
rock music 206–10
Roddick, Samantha 78
Roe, Emma 78–80
Rogers, E. W., *Three Young Ladies* 34, *35*
romantic fiction 80, 194
Roseneil, Sasha 9, 13, 154, 158–68, 221
Rough Trade (record company) 209
Roughgarden, Joan 44
Rowbotham, Sheila 9, 155, 212–16
Rowe, Marsha 29
Rowling, J. K. 197
Royal British Nurses' Association 114
Royal Free Hospital (London) 135
Rukhmabai 134–5, *134*
Russ, Joanna, *The Female Man* 222
Russell, Dora, Countess 162
Russell, Polly 6, 8, 10–15, 18–19, 88–9, 154–5

S

Said, Edward 27
Saini, Angela 8, 18, 42–52, 221
same-sex marriage 221
Saye, Khadija 11–12, *13*, 30, 216
SBS *see* Southall Black Sisters
Scafe, Suzanne, *The Heart of the Race* 107, *107*, 109

schools and schooling 88, 93, 94–9, 103–9
Schreiner, Olive 213; *Dreams* 213, *215*
science fiction 221–3
Scientific Women's Academic Network charter *see* Athena SWAN
Scott, Tara 48
Seacole, Mary 114, *116*
Second Reform Act (1867) 213
Seeger, Peggy 187
Selassie, Haile 205
self-examination, of genitals 83
self-portraiture 11, *13*, 30, *31–3*
self-publishing 209–210;
   see also zines
separatism 178, 187
servants, domestic 113–14, *113*, 125;
   ayahs 114, *114*, 131, 132, *132*
Sex Disqualification (Removal) Act (1919) 136, 149
Sex Pistols (band) 209
Sex Worker Advocacy and Rights Movement (SWARM) 126, *127*
sex workers *see* prostitution
sexology 55–6, 61, 77
sexual harassment and violence 11, 36, 84, 175, 177, 221;
   see also rape
sexual pleasure 48, 77–84
Shah, Bina, *Before She Sleeps* 222
Shakespeare, William 184, 193
Sharma, Krishna 72
Shaw, George Bernard, *Mrs Warren's Profession* 175, *175*
Sheba Feminist Publishers 197, 206
Sheffield Female Anti-Slavery Society 133, *133*
Sheik, The (film; 1921) 80
Shelley, Mary 193
SHINE leadership programme 109
Short, Clare 35–6
Singh, Sophia Duleep *130*, 131, 136–7, *136*, *137*, 145
single mothers *see* unmarried mothers
Sisterhood and After: The Women's Liberation Oral History Project 7, 15
Sisters Uncut (campaign group) 12, *12*, 159, 166, 167–8, *168*
Sjöö, Monica, *God Giving Birth* 187
slavery 26, 107, 126, 131–3;
   abolition 133;
   see also anti-slavery movement
Slawson, Eva 80
Smyth, Dame Ethel 172;
   'The March of the Women' 160, *161*

social media 11, 21, 36–8, 209
Society for Promoting the Employment of Women 203
Soofiya, *Vaginal Discharge* 48, *50–51*
Sorabji, Cornelia 134, 135–6, *135*
Southall Black Sisters (SBS) 72–5, *74*
Spare Rib (magazine) 28, 29, *29*, 67, 83, *98*, 206, 218;
   digitisation project 8, 15;
   Girls are Powerful: Young Women's Writings from Spare Rib 11
Spence, Jo 30, *31*
sport 55, 221
Stanton, Elizabeth Cody 133
statues, of women 15, 188, 221
STEM academic disciplines 12, 95, 99, 101, 108
Stemettes (social enterprise) 12, 101, *101*
sterilisation, forced 66
Stirling, Rachael *82*, 83
Stopes, Marie 66, *66*, 67, 71, 80–81
Streeten, Nicola 217
Stri Dharma (journal) 137
Strife (magazine) 206
strikes and industrial protest 117, 118, 120–21
Strimpel, Zoe 8, 19, 76–84, *218–19*
Sturgeon, Nicola 34–5, *34*
suffrage movement 12, 14, *14*, 43, 89, 125, 144–9, 158–61;
   commemoration 15, 188–91, 221;
   and imperialism 131–3, 136–8;
   media portrayals 26–7, *27*, 144, 145, *145*, *147*, 213;
   men's involvement 171–3, 179
Suffragette (film; 2015) 166, *167*
Suffragette, The (WSPU journal; later *Britannia*) 131, *131*, 145
sugar production 133
Sullivan, James 77–8
Sun, The (newspaper), 'Page 3' models 35–6, *36*
Supplementary Education movement 104, *105*, 107, 109
SWAN (Scientific Women's Academic Network) *see* Athena SWAN
SWARM (Sex Worker Advocacy and Rights Movement) 126, *127*
sweated labour 117–18
Symons, Donald 48

T
Tata, Herabai 137
Tata, Mithan 136, 137

Taylor, Harriet 171
Taylor-Stone, Chardine 209
temperance movement 141
'test tube babies' *see* in vitro fertilisation
Thatcher, Margaret, Baroness 150
thesauri 187
Thief of Bagdad, The (film; 1924) 80
300 Group (campaign for parliamentary representation) 150
Thunberg, Greta 11
Tilley, Vesta (Matilda Alice Powles) 34, *35*
Tipping the Velvet (television series) *82*, 83
Touki Bouki (film; 1973) 29
Towards a Pro-Consent Revolution (magazine) 84, *85*
Townswomen's Guilds 149
Trade Boards Act (1909) 118
trade unions 115, 117–18, 121–5
transgenderism and transexualism 11, 55–61, 71
transvestism *see* cross-dressing
Trash Kit (band) 209
Trivers, Robert 48
Trowbridge, Una, Lady 57
Trump, Donald, anti-Trump protests 48, 74

U
United Voices of the World (trade union) 115
universities and higher education 44, 93–4, 98–9, 108–9, 134–6, 193;
   Black Studies courses 108;
   legal training 135–6;
   medical training 65, 94, 95, 108, 134–5;
   teacher training 93, 103, 109;
   Women's Studies courses 98, 99, 108
unmarried mothers 66–7, *68*, 77
Urania (journal) 54, 55

V
Vagenda, The (online magazine) 36
Vaginal Discharge (zine) 48, *50–51*
Valentino, Rudolph 80
Varma, Shyam 104
veiling 48, 134
venereal disease 65;
   see also Contagious Diseases Acts
Victoria, Queen 203;
   as Empress of India 134;
   statues 188
Victoria Magazine 203
Victoria Press (printers and publishers) *202*, 203, 210

Victory, Grace 36
Vine, Sarah 35
Virago (publishers) 117, 184, 206;
    archives 7, 15;
    Modern Classics 187, 197–9, *198*
voting rights 141–4, 149;
    Representation of the People Act (1918) 15n, 66, 149, 190, 193;
    Equal Franchise Act (1928) 15n, 149, 193;
    see also suffrage movement
Vulva Quilt (artwork) 48, *49*, 216

W

Wallace, Liz 23
Wandor, Michelene 98
Warner, Sylvia Townsend 197;
    Lolly Willowes 214, *214*
Waters, Sarah, *Tipping the Velvet* 81, *82*, 83
Wearing, Gillian, statue of Millicent Fawcett 15, 188, *190*
Wells, H. G., *The New Machiavelli* 80
WEP (Women's Equality Party) 125
Weston, Mark 55, 56
Wharry, Olive 145, 146–7
White, Antonia, *Frost in May* 197
Wickets, Donald Furthman 55
Wife and Home (magazine) 35
Wigley, Mrs W. H., *Domestic Economy* 96, 97
Wilde, Oscar 55
Wilkinson, Ellen 95, 149–50
Withers, D-M 9, 15, 154, 182–91
Wittig, Monique 203
Wollstonecraft, Mary 11, 44, 93, 131, *140*, 213;
    A Vindication of the Rights of Woman 93, 131–3, 141, 149, 213
Woman and Home (magazine) 35
Woman Worker, The (newspaper) 118, *119*
'Womanopoly' (board game) 205, *205*
Women Against Fundamentalism (activist group) 72
Women for Life on Earth (activist group) 162
Women for Refugee Women (charity) 12, 169, *169*
Women's Aid networks 72–5, *74*
Women's Equality Party (WEP) 125
Women's Freedom League 160, *160*, 183
Women's Indian Association 137
Women's Institutes 149
Women's Labour League 144
Women's League for the Spread of Co-operation *see* Co-operative Women's Guild
Women's Liberal Federation 144
Women's Library (London) 187–8
Women's National Anti-Suffrage League 144–5
Women's Party (1917–19) 131, 149
Women's Press (publishers) 197, 206
Women's Printing Society 203
Women's Research and Resources Centres 108, 188
Women's Social and Political Union (WSPU) 27, 131, 144, 145, 149, 160, 172;
    Sunday March (June 1908) *158–9*, 159–60;
    see also Suffragette, The (journal)
Women's Studies 98, 99, 108; British Library guide to collections 7
Women's Tax Resistance League (WTRL) 131, 136
Women's World Games (1934) 55
Wood, Victoria 188, 221
Woolf, Virginia 59, 81, 113, 197, 199;
    Orlando 58, *59*;
    A Room of One's Own 23, *192*, 193, 197
Working Women's Charter (1974) 125
WSPU *see* Women's Social and Political Union
WTRL *see* Women's Tax Resistance League

X

X-Ray Spex (band) 209

Y

Yate-Lee, Albinia 144, 145
'Yorkshire Ripper' (murderer) 75, 127, 162
Young Women's Christian Association 144
Yousafzai, Malala 11

Z

zines (self-published magazines) 48, *50–51*, 84, *85*, 209–210, 221

ILLUSTRATION SOURCES

12. Sisters Uncut protesting against evictions in Stratford, September 2015. Photo Peter Marshall/Alamy Stock Photo.

13. Khadija Saye, *Peitaw*, 2017. Tintype from the series *Dwelling: in this space we breathe*. © Executor of the will of Khadija Saye.

14. Suffragettes making banners and pennants for a procession to Hyde Park, London, 23 July 1910. LSE Women's Library.

15. International Women's Day March Banner. DM2123//Box 17 from the Feminist Archive South held at the University of Bristol Library Special Collections.

20. *Body Shapes*, 2014. © Gemma Correll.

22. Miss World Protest leaflet, 1970. LSE Women's Library.

24–5. Caribbean Carnival Queen Contest souvenir programme, 1960. British Library, Andrew Salkey Archive Dep 10310 Box 33.

26 (left). *Daily Mirror*, 25 May 1914. British Library.

26 (right). Rosa May Billinghurst (1875–1953). LSE Women's Library.

28. First edition of *Spare Rib* magazine, July 1972. British Library, P.523/344, with permission Angela Philips.

29 (above). 'Tooth and Nail' from *Spare Rib* magazine, November 1977. British Library, P.523/344, with permission Angela Philips.

29 (below). Graffitied car advert, photographed by Jill Posener in 1979. © Jill Posener.

31. Jo Spence, *Remodelling Photo History: Colonization*, 1981–2. © Jo Spence Memorial Archive, Ryerson Image Centre.

32–3. Joy Gregory, *Autoportrait*, 1989. © Joy Gregory.

34. *Daily Mail*, 28 March 2017, British Library, NEWS.REg170. Daily Mail/Solo Syndication.

35. E. W. Rogers, *Three Young Ladies*, London, 1892. British Library, H.3981.p.(47).

36. MP Caroline Lucas wearing a T-shirt in support of Lucy-Anne Holmes' No More Page Three campaign, House of Commons, 2013. Parliamentary Recording Unit.

37 (above). The actor and activist Jameela Jamil standing triumphant by a smashed set of scales, from a 2019 edition of *Stylist* magazine. Photo Ramona Rosales/AUGUST.

37 (below). Beach Body Ready push-back by plus-size fashion label Navabi, 2018. © Navabi Fashion.

39. Front cover of *gal-dem* UNREST issue 2019/20. © gal-dem.

40. *It's a Lesbian*. © Jo Nesbitt.

42. William Cheselden, *Osteographia, or the Anatomy of the Bones*, London, 1733. British Library, 458.g.1.

44. Letter from Charles to Caroline Kennard, 9 January 1882. Reproduced by kind permission of the Syndics of Cambridge University Library.

45. Letter from Caroline Kennard to Charles Darwin, 28 January 1882. Reproduced by kind permission of the Syndics of Cambridge University Library.

46 (above). Field notebook of Alison Jolly, c.1962, documenting her discovery that ring-tailed lemurs were female dominant as a species. © M. Jolly.

46 (below). Alison Jolly's colleague Hanta Rasamimanana teaching in the Mandena Conservation Area, Madagascar. © M. Jolly.

47. The sextant used by eugenicist Sir Francis Galton in 1850 to measure, without permission or knowledge, a Khoikhoi woman's body in Namibia. Francis Galton collection, University College London.

48. Women taking inspiration from novelist Margaret Atwood's

The Handmaid's Tale to protest US President Donald Trump's visit to the UK, 4 June 2019. Photo © Richard Baker/In Pictures via Getty Images.

49. The Vulva Quilt, conceived by Tara Scott and made possible with the sisterhood of many contributors from far & wide including the Shoreditch Sisters of 2009/13, in sisterhood with Equality Now, Daughters Of Eve, Nimco Ali, Leyla Hussein & Birdy Imoke. Photo © Daniel Hambury/Stella Pictures Ltd.

50–1. Artist Soofiya's *Vaginal Discharge* zine. British Library, YD.2019.a.1532. © Soofiya.

53. Sequin tampon. Courtesy Bloody Good Period.

54. *Urania*, May 1936. LSE Women's Library.

56. Report about Augustine Hull from *Reynold's News*, October 1932. British Newspaper Archive.

57. The poet and author Radclyffe Hall with her lover and partner, the sculptor Una Trowbridge, photographed in 1927. Photo Fox Photos/Getty Images.

58 (above). Virginia Woolf, *Orlando*, Hogarth Press, London, 1928. British Library, 012614.i.3.

58 (below). Anne McLaren, Embryo Transfer notebook, 1955–9. British Library, Add Ms 83844, ff.130v–131r. © Anne McLaren.

59. Christine Jorgensen. Photo Everett Collection Inc./Alamy Stock Photo.

60. Travis Alabanza, *My Stubble Has No Gender*. © Travis Alabanza in collaboration with Denny Kaulbach.

62. *Get Me Off This Freaking Moor*. © Kate Beaton.

64. Poverty-stricken couple with five children, photographed in London's East End. Photo Hulton Deutsch Collection/Getty Images.

66. Prorace cervical cap, designed and promoted by Dr Marie Stopes. Wellcome Collection.

67. Photograph of Stopes' birth control clinic, 1920s. Wellcome Collection.

68 (above). Chris Gaine, *How to Run a Self-Help Group*, Single Parent Action Network, Bristol, 2006. British Library, yk.2009.b.4019.

68 (below). Norinyl-2, oral contraceptive pills. Science Museum 1986-248/30/1. Photo Science & Society Picture Library.

69. Sylvia Pankhurst with her son Richard, 1928. Sylvia Pankhurst Collection/International Institute of Social History (Amsterdam).

70. Marking the decriminalisation of abortion in Northern Ireland. Photo © Simon Graham/Amnesty International.

71. *Depo-Provera: A Report by the Campaign Against Depo-Provera*, London, 1983. British Library, X.329/18350.

72. *Reproductive Health Matters*, Blackwell Science, Oxford, November 2007. British Library, ZC.9.a.3563.

73 (above). The Lesbian Custody Charter, produced in the 1980s. LSE Women's Library.

73 (below). Emily Mary Osborn, *Nameless and Friendless*, 1857. Tate.

74 (above and below left). Banners for Southall Black Sisters. Courtesy Southall Black Sisters.

74 (below right). Women on a Reclaim the Night march, London, 2006. Photo © Molly Cooper/Photofusion.

76. Handbill distributed ahead of a talk about repealing the Contagious Diseases Act by campaigner Josephine Butler, during the 1872 Pontefract by-election. LSE Women's Library.

78. Edith Lanchester, from *The Bar Sinister and Licit Love: The First Biennial Proceedings of the Legitimation League*, London, 1895. British Library, 08416.ff.11.

79. Nineteenth-century ivory dildo. Private Collection.

80. *Peg's Paper*, London, November 1921. British Library, P.P.6004.sal.

81. The *Mother's Union* magazine for teenagers, 1979. British Library, 4107.eee.

82. *Tipping the Velvet*, BBC television series, 2002. BBC Photo Library.

83. Front covers of *Our Bodies Ourselves*, from editions published all over the world. Courtesy Our Bodies Ourselves (www.ourbodiesourselves.org).

85. *Towards a pro-consent revolution*, 2014. © Active Distribution.

90. *I really wanted to be a mechanic, but there were no apprenticeships for women*. © Liz Mackie.

92. Penny rocket firework thrown at women campaigning to be able to graduate from the University of Cambridge in 1897. Reproduced by kind permission of the Syndics of Cambridge University Library.

93. Photograph of crowds at Cambridge in 1897, protesting against women's petitions to get university degrees. Photo by Thomas Stearn, May 21, 1897.

94. Certificate presented to Sophia Jex-Blake in 1894 to honour her contribution to 'the cause of the Medical Education of Women [...and] the granting to Women the Medical Degree of the University of Edinburgh'. Edinburgh University Library.

96. *Murby's Special Readers for Girls: The Marshfield Maidens and the Fairy Ordina*, London, 1874. British Library, 012201.e.2.

97 (above). 'Mothercraft' lesson held in Archway, 1964. Photo © Henry Grant Collection/Museum of London.

97 (below). Ladybird Keyword series, *Things We Do*, 1966. The British Library, 12978.s.5. © Penguin.

98 (above). *The Great Divide: The Sexual Division of Labour, or 'Is it Art?'*, prepared for the Open University Art & Environment Course by The Collective, Michelene Wandor [...et al], Open University Press, Milton Keynes, 1976. British Library, x.512/5218.

98 (below left). *Spare Rib*, October 1987. British Library, P.523/344, with permission Angela Philips.

98 (below right). Jan Bradshaw, Wendy Davies, Patricia de Wolfe, *Women's Studies Courses in the UK*, Women's Research and Resources Centre, London, 1981. British Library, X.529/53408.

101. Outbox Incubator c.2015, group photo. Copyright @Stemettes.

102. Ladybird Keyword series, *Play with Us*, 1964. British Library, 12978.s.5. © Penguin.

104. Beryl Gilroy, *Nippers: A Visitor from Home* and *Nippers: New People at Twenty-Four*, London: Macmillan, 1973.

105. Handwritten notes from the OWAAD's third conference, at which education and the establishment of supplementary schools were a key focus. Black Cultural Archives © Stella Dadzie.

106. Newsletter published by the Abasindi Co-operative in 1985. Elouise Edwards Collection, Ahmed Iqbal Ullah Race Relations Centre, University of Manchester Archives.

107. Beverley Bryan, Stella Dadzie and Suzanne Scafe, *The Heart of the Race*, Virago, London, 1985. British Library, X.529/73423.

110. Riana Duncan, *That's an excellent suggestion, Miss Triggs...*, published in *Punch*, 8 January 1988. Punch Cartoon Library/TopFoto.

113. Grace Higgins' diary. British Library, Add Ms 83219, f.188v.

114. The Ayahs' Home in Hackney, London, around the start of the twentieth century. From George Robert Sims, *Living London: Its Work and Play, Its Humour and Its Pathos, Its Sights and Its Scenes*, Cassell & co., London, 1904–6. British Library 10349.h.12.

115. Strikers on the picket line. Courtesy United Voices of the World.

116. Photograph of the author's mother as a nurse. Courtesy Pam Cox.

117. Mary Seacole, *The Wonderful Adventures of Mrs Seacole in Many Lands*, London, 1846. British Library, 12601.h.20.

118 (left). Sylvia Pankhurst, *The Chainmaker*, oil on canvas, 1907. Private Collection/© The Estate of Sylvia Pankhurst.

118 (below right). Cradley Heath chainmaker's hammer, with indents made from a woman worker's hand. Reproduced with the Kind Permission of the Black Country Living Museum.

119. *The Woman Worker: Official Organ of the National Federation of Women Workers*, London, 1907. British Library, LOU.LON 795 [1907].

120. Commemorative plate from 1985 celebrating the success of the Ford Dagenham sewing machinist protests. LSE Women's Library.

121. Glasgow equal pay strike, October 2018. © Wattie Cheung Photography/CameraPress.

122–3. Grunwick workers strike and picket line, October 1977. © Sheila Gray/Photofusion.

124. Empirical research notes depicting the labour involved in managing a home, from Ann Oakley's landmark study in housework, 1974. British Library, DEP 11139. © Ann Oakley.

126. *Mother's Money*, a special Mother's Day publication for the International Wages for Housework Campaign, spring 1978. British Library, ZD.9.b.2777.

127 (above). Photograph from 1982 of members of the English Collective of Prostitutes with Labour MP Tony Benn and

Illustration sources

educationalist Caroline Benn. Courtesy The English Collective of Prostitutes.

127 (below). T-shirt fom the Sex Worker Advocacy and Resistance Movement (SWARM), https://www.swarmcollective.org/.

128. *Sexist Organisation*. © Grizelda/Private Eye.

130. Cutting from the surveillance records on Sophia Duleep Singh. British Library, IOR/L/PS/11/52, P.1608/1913, ff.270.

131. *Britannia*, 8 February 1918. British Newspaper Archives.

132. Examples of ayah's passports archived at the British Library's India Office Records archive. British Library, IOR/L/PJ/11/4/1486: 1935 and IOR/L/PJ/11/5/396: 1936.

133 (above). Handout produced by the Sheffield Female Anti-Slavery Society around 1825–33. © Religious Society of Friends (Quakers) in Britain.

133 (below). Dorothy Little's letter to the slavery compensation committee. The National Archives, T 71/1608.

134. Photograph of Rukhmabai (1864–1955) with other students at the London School of Medicine for Women. UCL Special Collections, Archives & Records. Photo: London Metropolitan Archives.

135. The Indian barrister Cornelia Sorabji (1866–1954) making a radio broadcast. Photo Hulton Archive/Getty Images.

136. Sophia Duleep Singh's diary entry for 17 February 1907. British Library, IOR Mss Eur E377/8, 17 Feb 1907.

137. Surveillance records for Sophia Duleep Singh. British Library, IOR/L/PS/11/52, P.1608/1913, ff.270.

138 & 139. The All India Women's Conference (AIWC), programme, 1973. British Library, Mss Eur F341/12.

140. Frontispiece portrait of Mary Wollstonecraft, from William Godwin, *Memories of the Author of A Vindication of the Rights of Woman*, London, 1798. British Library C.60.i.1.

142–3. George Cruikshank 'The Rights of Women, or, The Effects of Female Suffrage', published in *The Comic Almanack*, London, 1853. British Library, P.P.2496.aa.

144. Anti-suffrage postcard depicting a group of suffragists as sour-tempered and unattractive old maids, with the text 'Suffragettes who have never been kissed', 1900. Gado Images/Alamy Stock Photo.

145. 'Glass-Smashing for Votes! Suffragettes as Window-Breakers', *Illustrated London News*, 8 March 1912. British Library, P.P.7611.

146–7. Olive Wharry's scrapbook. British Library, Add Ms 499976.

148. *The New Illustrated*, November 1919. British Library, LOU. LON 597.

149. Constance Markievicz photographed in 1914 in the uniform of the Irish Citizen Army, published in Seán O' Faoláin, *Constance Markievicz; or, the Average Revolutionary*, London, 1934. British Library, 010825.ee.3.

150. Ellen Wilkinson, *Plan for Peace*, Labour Party, London, 1945. British Library, 08138.aa.34.

151. www.fawcettsociety.org.uk.

156. ...*wonderous web*... © Kate Evans.

158. Women's Sunday March, June 1908. LSE Women's Library.

160. The Women's Freedom League banner, 1908. LSE Women's Library.

161. Ethel Smyth, 'The March of the Women', 1911. Heritage Image Partnership/Alamy Stock Photo.

162. Sylvia Pankhurst poem written on prison toilet paper while serving a prison sentence in 1920. British Library Add Ms 88925/1/1. © The Estate of Sylvia Pankhurst.

163 (above). Dora Russell's Peace Caravan booklet. DM2123/7/Drawer 4 from the Feminist Archive South held at the University of Bristol Library Special Collections.

163 (below). Piece of souvenir Greenham Common fence wire. British Library, Add Ms 88899/6/13.

164–5. Greenham Common protest, 12 December 1982. Photo PA Images.

166. Sisters Uncut protesting at the 2015 opening night of *Suffragette* at the BFI London Film Festival in London. Photo © Tristan Fewings/Getty Images.

167. Greenham Common strike shawl consisting of dozens of individual spider web patterns crocheted by the women protestors and sewn together. DM2123/1/Box 23 from the Feminist Archive South held at the University of Bristol Library Special Collections.

168. Poem posted on the Underground by Sisters Uncut, International Women's Day 2019. Courtesy Sisters Uncut.

169. Women for Refugee Women protest. Photo Ana Norman Bemudez.

170. Spy (Leslie Ward), 'A Feminine Philosopher', *Vanity Fair*, 29 March 1873. British Library, P.P.5274.ha.

172. Men's League for Women's Suffrage badge, 1918. LSE Women's Library.

173. Letter from Frederick Pethick-Lawrence to Sylvia Pankhurst. British Library, Add Ms 88925/1/13.

174. *The Freewoman: A Weekly Feminist Review*, London, 1911. British Library, LOU.LON. 730 [1911].

175. Proof copy with amendments of George Bernard Shaw's play *Mrs Warren's Profession*, 1893. British Library, Add Ms 53654 H.

176. Activist and academic Stuart Hall and an unidentified man providing childcare at the Women's Liberation Movement Conference creche, Ruskin College, Oxford, 1970. Photo © Sally Fraser/Photofusion.

178. *Achilles Heel*, Autumn 1994. British Library, P.973/334.

180. *Dustbin of History*. © Jacky Fleming, from 'The Trouble with Women'.

182. Millicent Fawcett, *Josephine Butler: Her Work and Principals and Their Meaning for the Twentieth Century*, London, 1928. British Library, X.808/9022.

183. Celebration of the life and work of the Trinidadian-born feminist, activist, communist and community leader Claudia Jones (1936–1964), published by Camden Black Sisters Publications, 1988. British Library, LD.37.a.200.

184. *Emilia* poster. Courtesy Shakespeare's Globe.

185. Photograph of the activist Olive Morris. © Black Cultural Archives © Stella Dadzie.

186. Cover of *The Female Frolic* by the Critics Group, 1968. Decca Records.

187. Card catalogue from The Feminist Library, London. Feminist Library, London. Photo Eva Megias.

189. *Women in Profile*, issue no. 1, April 1989. Courtesy Glasgow Women's Library.

190. Bronze statue by the artist Gillian Wearing commemorating the life of the suffragist Millicent Fawcett, Parliament Square, London. Photo icona/Alamy Stock Photo.

192. Virginia Woolf, *A Room of One's Own*, Hogarth Press, London, 1929.

194. Draft manuscript for George Eliot's *Middlemarch*, 1871–2. British Library, Add. 34034, f.165.

195. Jane Austen, *Sense and Sensibility*, London, 1811. British Library, C.71.bb.14.

196. Buchi Emecheta, *In the Ditch*, Omenala Press, London, 1986. British Library, H.2019/6432.

197. 1890 manuscript journal of Michael Field. British Library, Add. 46778, f.94r.

198. Poster from 1985 depicting *Virago Modern Classics* titles. British Library, Add Ms 88904/5/3.

200. *Miss Moti*. © Kripa Joshi.

202. Women compositors at The Victoria Press Printing Office in London's Great Coram Street, published in the *Illustrated London News*, 16 June 1861. British Library, P.P.7611.

203. Emily Faithfull, 1891. Photo by W. & D. Downey, c.1890.

204. Una Marson broadcasting to British troops in the West Indies from a theatre in London, February 1942. Photo Fred Ramage/Keyston/Hulton Archive/Getty Images.

205. Stella Dadzie, *Womanopoly*. Black Cultural Archives © Stella Dadzie.

207. Northern Women's Liberation Rock Band Manifesto, 1974–6. Courtesy Angela Cooper.

208. Ana da Silva of The Raincoats performing at Alexandra Palace, London, June 1980. Photo © David Corio/Redferns/Getty Images.

209. Big Joanie outside the Salford Lad's Club, May 2017. © Estella Adeyeri/Big Joanie Archive.

211. OOMK zine, issue 5. Courtesy OOMK.

212. John Tenniel, 'Mill's Logic', published in *Punch*, 30 March 1867. British Library, P.P.5270.

214. Sylvia Townsend Warner (with wood engravings by Reynolds Stone), *Lolly Willowes, and Mr Fortune's Maggot*, London, 1967 (first published 1926). British Library, X.900/2367. © The Estate of Reynolds and Janet Stone.

215. Olive Schreiner, *Dreams*, London, 1891. British Library, 8610.i.27.

217. © LD Comics.

222. Gina Miller speaks to members of the media near the Supreme Court, London, 24 September 2019. Photo © Luke MacGregor/Bloomberg via Getty Images.